UNDERCURRENTS

UNDERCURRENTS

Episodes from a Life on the Edge

SHINTARO ISHIHARA

Translated by
Wayne P. Lammers

KODANSHA INTERNATIONAL
Tokyo · New York · London

Originally published in Japanese by Shinchosha, Tokyo
under the title: *Waga jinsei no toki no toki*.

This book has been selected by the Japanese Literature
Publishing Project (JLPP), which is run by the Japanese Literature
Publishing and Promotion Center (J-Lit Center) on behalf of
the Agency for Cultural Affairs of Japan.

First published in Japanese under the title
Waga jinsei no toki no toki in 1990.

Jacket photograph courtesy of
Shintaro Ishihara.

Distributed in the United States by Kodansha America, Inc., and in the
United Kingdom and continental Europe by Kodansha Europe Ltd.

Published by Kodansha International Ltd., 17–14 Otowa 1-chome,
Bunkyo-ku, Tokyo 112–8652, and Kodansha America, Inc.

First edition, 2005
05 06 07 08 09 10 11 12   10 9 8 7 6 5 4 3 2 1

C O N T E N T S

PREFACE

Many years ago now, a television network sent me to Germany to cover its active anti-nuclear movement, and I ran into Kenzaburo Oe, the Nobel Prize winner, who had come there for the same purpose. I hadn't seen him in quite some time.

As we waited for the cameramen to set up on the open-air observation platform in front of the Berlin Wall, we put aside our differing views on the nuclear issue and talked of other things.

I brought up my longtime hobby of scuba diving, and he listened with great interest when I told him about my experiences with the poisonous sea snake known as the Okinoerabu eel.

"Stories like that are more important to you than you realize yourself," he remarked after I finished. "You should write them down when you have a chance."

Sometime later, I decided to take his advice to heart. In whatever spare moments I could find, I began jotting down some of the more unforgettable things that had happened to me over the years. Once I got started, my interest grew: I realized these were the very moments when my life truly soared.

I owe a debt of gratitude to my old friend for prompting me to write down these stories at this stage of my life. I am grateful, too, to another old friend, my editor Tadao Sakamoto, for his patience and unstinting encouragement as I proceeded with this project entirely at my own pace, delivering a few short pieces at a time as the spirit moved me.

A point of note: in many of the stories included here, I write of hunting for game fish with spear guns, so I should mention that these events took place long ago, before the various prefectures passed laws restricting the free use of such devices. Today, the use of spear guns is no longer permitted anywhere in Japan other than Okinawa.

ADRIFT

He was one of Japan's pioneer scuba divers. You could even have called him something of a professional, but this was still long before anyone could make a living as a diving instructor, so we're talking about other ways of diving for pay. Once, for example—not that I entirely believe the story—a Chinese guy hired him to dive off the Yokohama North Pier in the dead of night to retrieve three foot-long packages wrapped in oilpaper, contents unspecified. Visibility was next to nothing on the bottom, and poking around blind in the silt merely turned up such treasures as dead cats and broken bicycles. Finally, after three nights at it, he managed to find two of the three mysterious packages. When his employer accused him of hiding the third, my friend turned the tables on him and suggested they take the matter to the authorities. He got paid the promised 300,000 yen per package, which was a lot of money in those days. Obviously, they must have contained drugs.

My diver friend's grandfather had been a peer, and his aristocratic family owned a summer villa in Hayama, where the locals used to embarrass him by calling him Master. Mostly he seemed to play cards for a living, though in better times he'd had a small nightclub in Shibuya. Occasionally, he would drop by and invite me to go hunting or deep-sea fishing. I always declined, thinking it best to keep my distance: I'd seen the types he hung out with—not gangsters, exactly, but real characters anyway—and I had my doubts whether the man was completely on the level himself. For the most part, though, he had a well-bred way of getting on the right side of people. Genial by nature, he seemed to be eager for company.

Now and then he would show up unannounced carrying some large game fish he'd speared. The hour, invariably, was late, which was in itself an imposition, and I wasn't particularly happy about having a load of dead fish thrust into my hands in the middle of the night, either. We'd exchange some small talk, then I'd send him away. He showed up bearing these gifts four or five times all told—less out of any particular fondness for me than as a show of machismo, probably. Back when scuba divers were few and far between, bringing someone the catch of the day was a splashy thing to do.

Later, after I myself took up diving and learned about spearfishing, I discovered that the amberjacks and such he'd brought me were in fact prize game fish.

The fellow eventually married a girl of mixed blood celebrated for her beauty in the Shonan area. One day I ran into him on the street with a cute little boy in his arms and asked him the child's name. He told me picking a name was such a hassle he'd decided simply to name him after the crown prince of the time. It was just the sort of thing he would do.

Sometime after I took up scuba diving myself, I recalled a story he once told me. I don't know the year, but the incident took place on a diving trip to Oshima in the Izu Islands with those dubious friends of his.

The owner of the boat was a Korean named Kaneda, a man with a record that included firing off his gun in a flap over a hotel takeover—not somebody you wanted to tangle with.

They went diving to the north off Motomachi. My friend stayed down by himself even after the others had surfaced, wanting to catch as many fish as he could with the air he had left. But when he finally ascended, no boat. A current had carried him nearly a kilometer away from the anchored vessel.

The seas had risen, and from the crest of a big wave he finally spotted the boat searching for him. He yelled at the top of his lungs, but the boat was too far upwind for his buddies to hear. Then, of all things, they moved even farther away and, after circling the area a while longer, gave up and headed back to port.

"I gave up too, and started swimming," my friend continued. "But as you probably know from sailing out that way, when the currents are strong, there's basically no way a swimmer can make it to shore. Knowing I had to lighten my load, the first thing I lose is my catch. I still remember those beauties—a grouper and four great big amberjacks—but I told myself I could always catch more fish. The shore still kept getting farther away, so next I dropped my weight belt. It's funny what you think about at times like that—wondering which is worth more, the fish or the weights. After that went my tank, then my spear gun. So there I was, drifting out to sea with just my regulator around my neck.

"I drifted past Chigasaki, then Kazahaya. The current around there flows toward Cape Nojima at the tip of the Chiba Peninsula, then veers out into the Pacific. The sky was still light, but beneath the waves it's already dark, and I'm getting pretty worried. I keep telling myself, once the current carries me to the mouth of Tokyo Bay, some large ship will see me and pick me up. But as the sun goes down and the light fades, I know I'm a goner.

"Once it gets dark, even if some ship comes along, who's gonna see a tiny head bobbing on the water? I'll probably get chewed up by the propellers instead, and spewed out into the Pacific as fish bait. But finally, after what seems like ages, a fishing boat comes along. It's my last chance, so I leap up out of the water and scream my head off. The boat still looks to be to heading right on by, no more than thirty or forty meters away, when suddenly I see their green running light change direction. Pretty soon I see a red light align with it, so I know it's coming toward me and I'm gonna be saved.

"After they pull me from the water, my rescuers say they spotted my head in the last glimmer of light in the sky—only they thought it was a stray float off a fishing net. They'd been debating whether to stop and pick it up when they heard me yelling. Their home port was Motomachi, but that night they were making for Okata on some family business, which is how they'd found me.

"They said I was a lucky man, and you better believe I knew it without them having to tell me. I sat there thinking not just how glad I was, but how incredible the odds were.

"I wanted to give them something by way of thanks, but I had absolutely nothing on me. So instead, I borrowed a thousand yen and had the Fisherman's Cooperative call me a taxi.

"I get back to Motomachi and the bastards aren't there, so I go on around to Habu. That's where I find them, all in the stern of the boat getting drunk. I walk up without a word, fling my regulator onto the table, and jump aboard. That jerk Kaneda gets to his feet and says, 'Hey, you're alive.'

"I don't say a word. I just punch him in the jaw, hard as I can, and he falls backwards onto the table. The others jump up to help him; one of them even pulls out his dive knife.

"'You think you're looking at a ghost?' I scream, at which point Kaneda motions everybody to calm down and says, 'Sorry, man. There wasn't anything we could do.'

"I had plenty more to say to him, but I just let it go."

"Why's that?" I asked. Even among his crowd, this was someone known for picking fights at the slightest provocation.

He shrugged. "That's just how things go at sea."

***

Years later, diving with my own boat, I'm reminded of his remark every so often. The last thing I'd ever want is to find myself alone in the water swimming after a boat that's left me behind. Nor would I want to be decked by a friend after leaving him adrift, no matter how much I deserved it.

THE SPECKLED BAND

Okinoerabu eel. The name sounds like just another kind of eel—maybe some grotesque species with a thick body. But this so-called eel is actually a sea snake with a lethal venom.

Encountering snakes at sea is a whole lot more disturbing than on land. Many years ago now, when I participated in the first South China Sea Yacht Race, we spent much of our second day out of Hong Kong in a dead calm surrounded by thick fog, unable to make way. When the fog finally lifted, we were startled to find the waters around us swarming with sea snakes of every imaginable size. The largest ones looked about the size of a boat hook, which would have made them over three meters long.

Okinoerabus don't reach nearly that size; they get to be a meter long at most. But despite their smaller proportions, these snakes are a disturbing sight—especially when you know that the venom of just one of the nasty little creatures is potent enough to bring down at least five cows. Although I've also heard that sea snakes are evolutionarily degenerate, with their fangs bent inward and too far back in the mouth to harm a human being, that doesn't change the toxicity of their venom.

I've never observed an Okinoerabu on the surface from a boat, only in the water when diving. The first time I caught sight of one, I didn't have to be told it was poisonous; I knew instantly. No reptile with such bright yellow and black bands could be anything but poisonous. As its name suggests, the Okinoerabu inhabits the waters around Okinoerabu Island and ranges southward from there, so you see them quite frequently when diving in Okinawan waters. In fact, my own first time was in the Yaeyama Islands.

Because they lack gills, sea snakes don't breathe underwater; they have to swim to the surface every so often for air, whatever the conditions. When you race yachts, you sometimes have to hold your course even in storms strong enough to send fishing boats scurrying back to harbor, and since most marine creatures probably take refuge deep below in weather like that, too, I remember talking with my crew once about how no one, not even fish, knew the full fury of the sea like we did when the weather turned really monstrous. But after I became a diver, I learned that air-breathing sea snakes have to keep shuttling back and forth between the depths and the surface even in a typhoon.

Oddly enough, I've never actually seen a sea snake return to the bottom after surfacing to breathe. Larger sea snakes will pause on their way up or down, approach a diver to check him out, even rub up against his scuba tanks and coil around his regulator hose. By contrast, Okinoerabus always make straight for the surface. Yet, as often as I've observed them going up for air, I have never seen them zipping back to the depths afterwards. Maybe they, too, like to pause on their way down—except that they do it somewhere out of our sight.

The first time I encountered an Okinoerabu during a dive, my immediate thought was that storytellers don't lie.

Shortly after the end of World War II, when radio still provided the only home entertainment, I often listened to voice actor Musei Tokugawa's grand readings of famous novels and short stories, among them some renditions of Sherlock Holmes. As a child, the story that terrified me most was one called "The Speckled Band."

The murderer sends a poisonous snake from one room to the next in an old English manor house—via a ventilation duct, if I recall—to have it sink its fangs into his intended victim. The victim dies shrieking and clawing at her throat, and the last words to emerge from her mouth are something about a "speckled band."

I can't claim any deep-seated interest in snakes, but when I've had occasion over the years to browse through things like animal encyclopedias, I've never come across any pictures that made me think, *This must be the speckled band of Conan Doyle's tale.* But the first time I saw an Okinoerabu in the water, my thoughts returned instantly to that story: those yellow and black bands stood out even in murky water, a vivid warning of toxicity, and this along with its small size suggested it might have made the perfect weapon for the murderer in the old manor house.

———————

Being underwater was already enough to put me on edge, and the sinister association with the Sherlock Holmes story made me even more nervous. So when I saw the Okinoerabu slithering up right past me—very likely just hurrying to the surface for air—my every instinct told me to give it more leeway than I would a shark. I moved aside as quickly as I could. Degenerated fangs or not, I knew the snake carried a deadly poison, and just to see that speckled yellow-and-black form slithering by was enough excitement for me. No doubt other sea creatures react like I did and steer clear of these snakes the same way. It's hardly a wonder their fangs have degenerated from disuse.

In a different way from the shark, which has protected and perpetuated itself by means of its prodigious strength, and thus evolved very little over the ages, the Okinoerabu is in a category by itself as a sea creature. If you doubt me, try visiting one underwater sometime. Watch the yellow-and-black thing making for the surface, and see if you can muster the nerve to reach out and touch it. Personally, it's all I can do to wave the tip of my spear gun at them and shoo them off.

Despite my aversion to sea snakes, another diver I know once showed me how to catch one. A seasoned old-timer from Okinawa named Kohashikawa, he and my dentist friend Shiroma taught me pretty much everything I know about spearfishing. To this day, I often still go fishing with Shiroma, but Kohashikawa couldn't keep away from the water and decided to turn pro. Now he occupies himself with commercial diving jobs, mostly in waters where he doesn't see much in the way of game fish.

I learned a lot from Kohashikawa, but one casual remark he made after waking from a shipboard snooze has stuck with me most: "If you want to be a deep-sea diver and spend time in the water, then any time some close call spooks you, you've got to go right back in the water and do it all over again. But do it right away, or you'll lose your nerve and drift away from diving. I know a bunch of guys like that."

He told me a story from when he'd only been diving a couple of years, about going on a night dive near the main island of Okinawa and getting tangled in a "hell net." As the name implies, it's a deadly contraption: lightweight net panels hang spaced apart in layers, so as to snag any fish larger than the space between them. Even big strong fish like sharks get all tangled up, and since sharks in particular can't breathe through gills, once they're immobilized they quickly suffocate.

Kohashikawa kicked and struggled to free himself, but when he realized he was running out of air, he cut himself out of his wet suit with his dive knife, jettisoned his tank and fins, and ascended bare-body from twenty meters down, slowly blowing air from his lungs like they teach the crews of disabled submarines to do.

"I was one step from the grave," he said, "or maybe more like half a step. But when I got to land, I knew if I went on home, I'd probably never want to go out there again. So I woke up a friend to borrow some gear and went back to where I'd got caught in the net. I have no idea who the net belonged to, but I cut it to shreds. I picked up the gear I'd left behind, and while I was at it I helped myself to the fish caught in the net. I sometimes think, if I'd just gone home and given up diving, I'd probably be making a much better living working at a proper job today."

The technique he taught me for catching Okinoerabus is remarkably simple, but still requires nerve: you wear a cotton work glove, and when you see an Okinoerabu heading for the surface nearby, you reach out and grab it; then you quickly pull the glove off, turning it inside out over the snake. The snake is now trapped inside the glove and can't get away. Just stuff it in your pocket and head for the surface.

"I don't think I want to catch one that bad," I said.

"But it's so easy. Works like magic."

"That may be true, but just thinking about it gives me the willies."

"Wear rubber gloves at first if it bothers you," he said, dismissing my objection.

On our last dive that day, an Okinoerabu swam up between us heading for the surface, and Kohashikawa deftly demonstrated the technique he'd described earlier. He didn't have any pockets, so he unzipped the top of his wet suit and stuffed the gloved snake inside.

Back in Naha, we loaded our gear into the back of Kohashikawa's station wagon and drove to my hotel to have the kitchen there prepare us some dinner from our day's catch.

"Oh, what about this?" said Kohashikawa, after we'd taken our dinner fish into the kitchen. He pulled the glove-bound Okinoerabu from inside his suit and held it out to me.

"No way I'm going to eat that," I said.

"Yeah, they don't really taste all that good anyway. Not like morays or other eels. So, what to do, then?"

As he pondered the question, he unrolled the glove back over his hand, keeping a good grip on the yellow-and-black snake the whole while. Evening had come, but even in the dwindling light, its colors appeared much brighter on land than in the water. Functional fangs or not, who could doubt it was venomous? The creature was decidedly out of place on a city street at the door of a large hotel, and it really did seem as if Kohashikawa had conjured it up by magic.

"What do you think I should do with it? I forgot I still had it."

"Well *I* don't want it."

"In that case . . . ," he said, taking a quick glance up and down the street. He dropped the snake onto a sewer grate by the rear wheel of the car and nudged it in with his toe.

Agape, I simply stood and watched.

"I suppose it's gonna die somewhere down there," I finally said.

"I doubt it," he said blithely. "They can breathe air. They're tough little critters."

We agreed on a time to meet back at the hotel restaurant for dinner, then Kohashikawa drove off to wash up and change into street clothes. After he'd gone, I peered down again at the sewer grate by my feet. A faint tinkling of water came from below. I raised my eyes toward the tall building I was about to enter.

The "speckled band" had been liberated from the glove. Would it now slither its way through the maze of underground passages into the hotel and crawl out of a ventilation duct or bathroom drain somewhere? Would some hotel guest come upon it coiled up in his sparkling white washbasin? The image was a bit unnerving, but also rather amusing—that is, so long as it wasn't my particular bathroom.

LIGHTNING STRIKE

We speak of something utterly unexpected as "a bolt from the blue." Yet even in a violent storm, if we happen to be close by when lightning strikes, it can give us the fright of our lives. Most of the time when we see lightning flashing, we simply assume it's too far away to actually hit us. So if a bolt does come crashing down nearby, it's a terrific shock—especially since we know it can kill.

Some time ago I was invited to a golf tournament sponsored by one of the major dailies. We had only one or two holes left to play, when suddenly the sky turned dark and lightning began flashing in the distance. We probably could have finished the round without incident, but a business executive in my foursome insisted it was too dangerous, saying we should return to the clubhouse immediately. Since none of us was going to win the tournament anyway, we quickly agreed and started back.

As we cut across the course toward the clubhouse, I noticed the man behaving rather strangely. He'd been the one to suggest we quit, so I could understand he might feel more anxious than the rest of us. But his whole face looked different somehow. He was covering his mouth every time he spoke.

"Is something the matter?" I asked.

"I took my dentures out and put them in my golf bag," he said. "I was afraid they might attract the lightning."

True enough, some denture bridges are metal. Still, how likely was it that a bolt of lightning would find its way into a person's mouth? Not impossible if the person were talking a blue streak, I suppose, but even so his caution seemed excessive.

"You don't take any chances, do you?" I blurted out.

"You may laugh," he said, "but I once got caught in an electrical storm out on a course in Kinugawa. We all thought we had plenty of time when *boom*, a thunderbolt struck the foursome in front of us and killed three of them—just like that. I couldn't believe my eyes. It was awful. When you see something like that, it really scares the shit out of you. After that, there's no way I'll ever wear golf shoes with metal spikes again."

He stopped to lift his shoe. It had a rubber sole.

Once I'd heard his story, I could understand his agitation. Who's to say the spikes on a golf shoe wouldn't attract lightning? As I gazed at his clunky rubber-soled shoes, an all-but-forgotten incident from years before came back to mind.

The summer of my sophomore year in college, I took a trip to the Tateyama mountains with the student alpine club. As we were hiking along a ridge from one peak to the next, thunderclouds rolled up from below, and thin purple streaks of light pulsed through them every so often. The air crackled with the threat of something a lot more menacing than rain.

The clouds were still below us when the climber behind me, the leader of our party, tapped me on the shoulder and pointed at the fellow ahead of us. The spikes on his boots were spitting tiny blue sparks each time they touched the ground.

Even though I was new to mountain climbing, I knew enough to feel alarmed.

Our leader called the column to a halt and told us all to remove our boots, backpacks, ice axes, watches—anything metallic. Stripped practically to our underwear, we put everything together in one place and hid behind some large boulders to wait for the thunderclouds to pass.

Fortunately, no lightning struck, but at the point when the clouds came closest, I could feel my hair stand on end from the electricity in the air.

I later learned that quite a few climbers have been killed by lightning in the Tateyama mountains over the years.

On land, even high up on a mountain, you can usually find refuge from lightning one way or another; at sea, you're utterly at the mercy of the storm.

Thunderclouds form over water just as they do over land, and of course lightning can and does strike—which is why larger seagoing vessels are equipped with lightning rods. But the boats my friends and I sail have no such devices.

Though I can find very few accounts of yachts being damaged or sunk by lightning, it does strike the flat open sea. I've seen it with my own eyes more than once.

———

The Enshu Sea off Hamamatsu, which I sail across each summer for the Toba Race, is well known for violent thunderstorms around that time of year. Back when I was first learning to sail, I often batted around with my crew the question of what might happen if we encountered lightning on the way. For the most part, everyone played it down: we all wore rubber-soled deck shoes; so long as we didn't touch a metal stay or something, we'd be safe even if the mast took a direct hit.

Then one summer, on our way to the annual race, we learned firsthand what it meant to run into lightning at sea—more graphically than we ever cared to find out.

The year was 1967, and we'd decided to turn the trip to Toba for the start of the race into a leisurely summer vacation cruise, putting in at Nishi Izu, Shikinejima island, and Omaezaki along the way. We changed crew at each port, with different friends joining us for different parts of the trip, so between waiting for people to show up and simply having a roaring good time, we kept falling behind schedule. By the time we left Omaezaki with our final crew aboard, we were cutting it close. Although it's not so very far from Omaezaki to Toba, we'd left ourselves no time to spare.

Dark clouds were already gathering overhead as we cast off, and once we reached open sea the sky over the Enshu coast looked positively sinister. Down the coast where we were headed, enormous thunderclouds lit up with periodic bursts of purple light, like a dark mantle over the glowing back of a fearsome monster. We watched uneasily as the clouds advanced.

To avoid them, we needed to head farther out to sea, but we had no time for that. Our only choice was to make straight for Toba and hope for the best. Unfortunately, about the time we came due south of the Tenryu River, we got caught.

Even with the clouds moving rapidly toward us, we were getting precious little wind at sea level, so we had to chug along on our auxiliary engine with its minimal horsepower. There simply was no escape. Before we knew it, we were right under the fierce, black, booming clouds.

I know very little about the physics of electrical storms, but even out there on the open sea, you could feel the air charged to the breaking point. The tiniest trigger invisible to the human eye could split the heavens apart at any instant. Jagged flashes of light loomed closer and closer. Thunder shook the air, not only with sound but with raw, jostling waves of energy. My body grew number by the moment, and there was no way to stop it.

Amidst this extraordinary display of nature's power, I had a strange foreboding that with no particular effort on the part of the cosmos, each and every one of us aboard was about to be turned into something no longer human.

Whether a nervous crewman had shut it down or it fainted from a mechanical fright of its own, the auxiliary engine was now silent. The boat lay at the mercy of the waves, helpless as an animal with paralyzed limbs.

Suddenly some vast, invisible hand stirred the air, skimming past our upturned cheeks. We waited in breathless silence for whatever might come next.

Every metal object around us began to emit a faint glow. The compass had long since gone berserk, the needle spinning in crazy circles, heedless of magnetic north. Every hair on my head stood up straight, each individual strand pointing skyward, a wire beckoning the next bolt of lightning.

Although it had no voice or form, we all sensed a palpable presence in the air—the presence of death itself. As perfect darkness alternated with blinding light, we saw for the first time how brilliant death could be. We simply stood there dumbfounded.

All was chaos, yet I remember being oddly impressed by one thing: the intense blackness of the shadows stamped onto the deck at our feet by the jagged prongs of lightning above. Never had I seen my shadow cast so vividly.

Moment by moment, inch by inch, the storm continued its inexorable advance. No longer even aware of where we were, we simply watched and waited. Then, with a frantic cry, one of the crew pointed toward the top of the mast. A blue flame danced on its tip, as if spurting from the very soul of the boat.

An instant later, that immense, unseen hand ripped something out of the sky before our eyes. We were a hair's breadth from being swept into its grip, as, less than a boat's length away, a dazzling purple flame erupted from the surface of the water, then slowly transformed into a column of radiant water, before finally vanishing like a shaft of light piercing the waves. A pale green halo lingered in the air after it had gone.

Had some unknown soul been taken in our stead?

Jagged forks of lightning continued to flash and explode all around us, but they were now dim sparks compared to the death-dealing display we'd just seen.

Unmistakably, a hand had brushed our cheeks, yet had not folded us into its palm. As this began to sink in, I found myself asking: why would it choose merely to touch us and move on by? But ponder as I might, the answer only grew more elusive. I knew I would never know why.

Slowly, ever so slowly, it came back to me that I was still alive.

THE SAME MAN

Years ago, if you went down the hill skirting the Akasaka Detached Palace from in front of the Gakushuin Primary School, a side street going off to the right about halfway to Gondawara would bring you to a small hotel called the Matsudaira.

I can't recall who chose that particular venue or why, but one December some sailing and poker buddies gathered there to ring out the waning year as well as to celebrate one fellow's birthday. Christmas was still quite a way off, but winter had come early that year, and an icy, bone-chilling rain was coming down outside.

The rain kept gaining force, and by ten or so it had turned into a blustering storm. Though most of us had come by car, the miserable weather discouraged us from adjourning elsewhere for a second round. A few of the guys decided to take a room, and they invited us up for all-night poker. One fellow, though, said he had to get back to Ningyocho by midnight, and since my friend Shimizu and I knew him best—we'd often gone bar hopping with him in that old merchant-quarter neighborhood of his—we offered to drive him home. We'd drop him off, then come back to the hotel to rejoin the two tables of poker the others had going.

Shimizu took the wheel, and I got in beside him; our homeward-bound companion sat in back. He'd had a good bit to drink, and fell asleep almost immediately, leaning up against the door.

The driving sleet was verging on snow, spattering so thickly on the glass that the wipers had trouble keeping up. There were no street lamps in the area then, and our headlights barely cut through the soggy darkness.

We reached the street skirting the Detached Palace and turned left, but hadn't gone a hundred meters before we saw something by the side of the road ahead. Only when we finally caught it square in our headlights did we recognize it as the figure of a man. We slowed down.

I suppose he was about our own age, in his mid-thirties. He simply stood there in the downpour, coat collar turned up, drenched to the bone. He made no attempt to flag us down—though obviously there weren't going to be any empty cabs cruising that stretch so late on a stormy December night.

The natural assumption, given the hour, was that the man had been drinking. While he did have on a raincoat, seeing him just standing there with no thought of protecting himself from the sleet was enough to send a shiver down my spine.

We'd had a few drinks ourselves, and perhaps encouraged by the warmth the car's heater had begun to throw out, Shimizu pulled to a stop and rolled his window halfway down before I even had a chance to suggest it. Now at close quarters, the man cast his eyes toward the car, but otherwise stood there unmoving and silent. In the dim light spilling from our headlights, I could see that his raincoat was soaked through and through.

"Why don't you let us give you a lift someplace you're more likely to find a cab," Shimizu said. "Or depending on where you're headed, maybe we can even take you there."

The man said he needed to go to Nihonbashi.

"That's right on our way. We're going to Ningyocho."

Even during this brief exchange, the sleet pelted through the half-open window, spraying all the way across to me in the passenger seat.

Shimizu reached around to open the rear door, and the man ducked into the back seat. Our Ningyocho passenger stayed sound asleep, oblivious to his new companion.

I only got a brief glimpse of the man's face when the ceiling light came on as the door opened. Whether from drink or simply from getting so chilled while waiting in the downpour, he just gave me a small nod of thanks, his eyes staring with a glazed intensity below a forehead plastered with dripping hair.

The window and door had been open for only a few seconds, but this frigid newcomer in our midst made the temperature inside the car plummet. Even in the front seat, I could feel the icy chill of the rain that soaked every stitch the man wore.

The back seat had to be a wet mess, but we couldn't very well ask the man to take his clothes off. Shimizu promptly pushed the heater to high. Even with the fan blowing full blast, the chill failed to dissipate.

———

Traffic was light. It didn't take long to reach Nihonbashi.

"This'll do fine right here," the man said as we approached the bridge on the main drag. He mumbled a simple thanks as he got out. The rain hadn't let up, and the streets were completely deserted. I wondered how many blocks of office buildings he still had to walk to get home.

As Shimizu pulled away from the curb, I turned around for another look, but the rear window was too fogged up to see.

The same question had apparently occurred to Shimizu. "You think he really knows where he's going?"

We woke our snoozing friend when we pulled up in front of his house in Ningyocho.

"What the hell? How'd I get so wet?" he groaned. "Man, it's like ice!"

"We found a guy standing in the rain along the way and gave him a lift," I said.

"I never noticed."

He hunched his shoulders against the downpour and made a dash for the eaves without looking back.

———

We retraced the same route back to the hotel. As we came to the bridge in Nihonbashi where we'd let the man out, I kept my eyes peeled, but I saw no sign of him.

The rain soon turned to sleet again. The wipers struggled valiantly, but visibility remained extremely poor.

"I'd rather have real snow than this miserable slop," Shimizu said. "For one thing, you can be out in snow as long as you want and never get soaked like that guy back there."

For some reason, the heater still hadn't restored warmth to the car.

We drove past the main gate of the Akasaka Detached Palace and turned left at the light in front of Gakushuin Primary School. On the way down the hill, I thought I saw something up ahead on the other side, just out of range of our headlights.

I wondered if I was imagining things, but it again proved to be the figure of a man. Almost exactly where we'd picked the fellow up on our way out.

And then I realized it was him.

The same man, in the same sodden raincoat, standing in exactly the same spot, soaked to the bone.

Shimizu had instinctively put his foot on the brake, but now he floored the gas and sped on by. We both looked away, yet our incredulous eyes couldn't help but see. There was no need to stop for a better look: without a shadow of a doubt, it was the same man as before.

Shimizu raced into the hotel garage and pulled to a halt. We looked at each other, then turned in unison to peer out the back window.

For some reason, the heater finally kicked in right at that moment.

"Do you believe it?" I asked.

"You kidding? That had to be a—"

Shimizu broke off in mid-sentence and turned back toward the steering wheel as if to shake something off, then jammed his hands down on the horn with all his might.

The guys looked up from their cards as we came in.

"Must've been hell out there," one of them said. "I tried to tell him he should stay. Anyway, pour yourselves a drink."

He motioned us with his eyes toward a bottle of whiskey on the table, then looked back at the cards in his hand.

A STARTING POSITION

I don't know how many epiphanies about the nature of life a person can have in a single lifetime, but in all my years I've experienced only one.

I wouldn't claim it was a life-altering event; I can't say that it changed everything that came afterwards. But it was a profound revelation for me about how a person should live his life and, more specifically, how he should conduct his relations with other people.

In the course of subsequent events, particularly in times of difficulty, I've often recalled that special moment, but I've never been able to bring back the sense of clarity I felt, nor to conduct myself in quite the same way. The difference, I can only suppose, is that I was young. In my adolescent mind, I'd convinced myself there was no other way out, and so I went for broke.

The event will no doubt seem trivial, but for me at the time it was do or die. They say a person can and will do anything if he gets desperate enough. Well, I guess I must have been pretty desperate at that particular moment.

Under the nationwide educational reforms carried out after World War II, my school was reorganized into middle and high school divisions of three years each. When I was in eighth grade at the new middle school, I joined the soccer team. Our high school team won the national championship that year, so to some extent I was simply jumping on the bandwagon, but I also thought it would be good for my health. Between my brother and me, I had the weaker constitution, and I was tired of always being the one to take to bed with a cold.

Those postwar years were a time of shortages all around, and our team had to share game jerseys with the high school team, position for position. For practice, I wore one of my dad's old shirts with the sleeves rolled up. As I recall, the tattered and unwashed look was still in; the ten matching game uniforms may have been treated with the utmost respect, but everybody on the team preferred to leave his sweat-soaked practice togs unlaundered for weeks at a time. And when we ripped our shirts, we just kept running about the field with the torn fabric flapping in the breeze rather than get them mended. I suppose it was a kind of fashion statement for my age group.

The reason our practice gear got so beat up, of course, was that the practice sessions themselves were rough. The upperclassmen who trained the team made us do things no one would ever stand for today. The drills went beyond being hard and relentless; they were downright mean. Still, no one complained.

I remember one day they lashed into us backfielders for sloppy heading. They had us line up for a rapid-fire heading drill. One by one, we had to stand in front of the goal while an upperclassman kicked balls at us from the penalty mark just a few meters away.

Like any goalkeeper, we had to dive for balls that veered to the sides—except we were expected to deflect them with our head instead of merely catching them in our hands. The drill could easily have given us all concussions. Anyone running that kind of drill today would be sent packing.

The kicker who took over when my turn came wasn't very good. His first ball came in low, at about knee height. I reflexively stuck out my foot to block it, only to have the drillmaster scream at me. This was heading practice; use of the feet was strictly forbidden. I was to return the ball with my head no matter where it came in.

The next kick was even lower, and I stuck out my foot again. More invective. Now I was to head the ball on my hands and knees.

I did as I was told, but the drillmaster didn't like my attitude. He told the kicker to send me a grounder. I was supposed to lie flat on my stomach and stop it with my head. Obviously, this kind of situation would never come up in a real game, but he made me do it anyway. And I for one wasn't about to give him the

29

satisfaction of breaking me, so I stubbornly kept at it.

Another time, the team leaders said our substitute goalkeeper needed to work on his saves. So they got us all in a circle with the goalie in the middle, and told us to throw the ball to one another at random. The goalie had to dive after each throw and try to block it, over and over and over. Each time he hit the ground, he'd turn his head sharply to one side to keep from smashing his face, which would cut off the flow of blood to his head momentarily. Eventually, he keeled over and fainted. As we gathered around, I figured I'd been lucky only to have to head grounders.

It's strange, but even these ordeals come back to me today as fond memories.

When practice was over at my school in Fujisawa, I'd get a drink of water and head straight home to Zushi by train. Since my house was a good hike from the station, and there wasn't much of a bus system at the time, I used to have another drink of water at a faucet just outside the ticket gate to sustain me for the walk. Oddly enough, I can still remember how good the tap water tasted back then—and I'm quite sure it's not just nostalgia playing tricks on me.

Even so, I would feel my energy starting to flag about halfway home. So when I got to the greengrocer along the way, I'd ask if I could get a drink from their well. I took a short break there before trudging onward.

Without a doubt, being on the soccer team improved my fitness. It also helped me shake off any timidity I had from my years of weaker health.

One event stands out as the emblematic high point of those years—their natural culmination even. It was my last chance to win a spot as a regular, thereby rectifying my failure to do so the year before.

I first joined the soccer team at the beginning of my eighth grade year, and I attended practices faithfully, virtually never missing a day. Because I was big for my age, I quickly became one of the team's long ball kickers—which was rare for an eighth-grader.

In those days, we played soccer in the old kick-and-run style and a 5-3-2 formation. Backs never crossed over into forward territory; they only moved the ball to the opponents' half of the field, and the forwards then took it in for the score. Now soccer is played more like basketball, so that may seem old-fashioned, but at the time I had every reason to believe my long kick would be a major asset to the team. I really thought I might have a chance at a regular position in my first year.

Unfortunately, I lost the spot and spent the year sitting on the bench. Back then, there were no substitutions during the game except for goalkeepers. Injured or not, the starting lineup went on battling it out, while the other players could only cheer from the bench. Once the regular starters were named, just about the only way a second-stringer got to play was if someone was hurt so badly he had to sit out the rest of the season.

Our official season was limited to the annual state-wide tournament. Practice matches were rare, and when we did have them, we played under the same rules, so second-stringers still had virtually no chance to see any action. It meant that a starting position was a much bigger deal in soccer than in, say, baseball or basketball.

The fellow eighth-grader who beat me out for the position had joined the team the year before, so he had seniority, but he hardly ever showed up for practices during the summer. He preferred to go to the beach rather than slog to school under the scorching sun to work out with his teammates. No one could deny, though, that he had a real gift for the game: he was especially good at faking out defenders as he dribbled down the field, and in two-on-one or three-on-two drills he would run right past his opponents or steal the ball from them with the greatest of ease.

Once vacation was over and we got into the autumn soccer season, he started showing up every day. Nobody was very happy about this, but his renewed presence had an obvious effect on our formations. As soon as he was sent in, the entire dynamic changed and the forwards quickly gained the upper hand. This was particularly true when he played inside right: the attacking forwards would twist even our best defenders in knots.

Ironically, in spite of all his absences during the summer, his moves just kept getting better and better the closer we got to our first game. And in the end, when the captain chose his regulars, he made room for him on the front line by moving another player to the backfield, where my hopes were pinned.

I still remember the moment well.

The day before our first game, after our end-of-practice stretches, the captain yelled for everybody to gather round. With his eyes closed as if still trying to decide the last few names, he ran down the lineup for the next day's game. When he named our summertime slacker at inside right, I felt a wave of surprise pass through the ranks. Some of my teammates glanced at the ninth-grader who ought to have had that position. I did, too.

But for some reason this older boy was smiling, as if he'd known it all along. It hit me like a flash: the captain had clued him in beforehand. I had a feeling I knew what was going to happen next.

And I was right. The captain named the ninth-grader to right halfback—the very position I'd been angling for. Now my teammates were all looking at *me*.

I knew I had a better kick than the ninth-grader, but the other kid was several cuts above us both. Recognizing this, the captain had decided to bump the older boy from the front line, but to save face for him he had slotted him in at halfback instead of me. I'd received my first lesson in the unsavory political juggling that can lie behind many a personnel decision.

For the rest of that season, I sat on the bench grinding my teeth in frustration.

The following autumn, the day before the state-wide tournament was to begin, I stood by with the events of a year earlier very much on my mind. Two positions were up for grabs: one as forward and one in the backfield. The formations we were about to try out would decide who filled them. My own prospects had actually gotten worse since the year before: I was still looking at right halfback, but because of new underclassmen and transfer students, I now had to compete against three other players for the spot.

If I let this opportunity get away, I told myself, then everything I'd done in the last year and a half would be meaningless. When I thought of it that way, there was a whole lot more riding on this than soccer: my entire life was on the line.

In all the contests I've participated in, sporting and otherwise, I don't believe I've ever staked my entire being with such complete abandon, or driven myself to perform with such complete disregard for possible injury, as I did that day.

Of the four players competing for the same defensive spot, the captain called me up second. The forwards started moving the ball toward us, until it came to the player I was marking. I feinted toward another forward, then proceeded to pull a stunt I'd never tried before—and almost never since. Slide tackling wasn't normally my thing, but now I flew feet-first at my mark, determined to block his kick with my stomach or chest or whatever part of my body I could get in the way—except I actually aimed for his shins rather than the ball. At that instant, I was betting it all—my place on the team, my entire place in life—and my decision to go for broke made me more than just bold; it made me fearsome.

Caught off guard by my do-or-die attack, my mark failed to dispose of the ball quickly enough. His legs flew out from under him, and he crashed to the ground. Still on my back, I swept my leg around and cleared the ball to one of the other backs, who promptly kicked it out of bounds.

Normally if backs played rough, the forwards returned the favor in kind, but my first hit had been so vicious the other forwards seemed scared they might be in for the same.

A new ball was thrown in, the whistle sounded, and I charged straight at the man in possession, who of course quickly passed the ball to someone else. I dropped back at full speed, chose my next mark, and charged him. Every one of the forwards passed almost right away, not wanting to fall victim to another of my sliding tackles, and their play became sloppy. They grew flustered whenever I moved in their direction; even if I didn't reach them in time to tackle them, they'd make a bad pass in their hurry to get rid of the ball.

Pressing my advantage, I played more and more aggressively, driving at my opponents, letting out screams and yelps as I feinted and tackled and stole the ball time after time. It was only a practice drill, but I doubt I ever played better defense or made so many spectacular stops as I did that day.

One time, after stealing the ball in a tackle, I dribbled it all the way down the field, right through the baseball players practicing at the other end, and shot it into the far goal before returning to formation.

Then I did it twice more.

As I dribbled the ball through baseball territory for the third time, the pitcher on the mound turned toward our end of the field and shouted something. Several others got up off the bench to complain. While one of the baseballers was fetching the ball I'd kicked into the unguarded goal, my captain blew his whistle and waved me back. The forwards had obviously had their fill of my antics, and when I reached our end of the field, the captain sent in the next contender. I'd done what I had to do, and done it better than I'd ever dared hope. More than satisfied, I felt a deep sense of liberation.

The contender who went in after me ought to have been my most formidable rival, but he too seemed intimidated by the show I'd put on. The forwards regrouped and attacked the new defense squad with a vengeance. Once his first attempt at a tackle failed, my rival seemed to tighten up; he didn't play half as well as usual.

We finished our formations, ran some laps, did the usual stretches, then everyone trooped up to hear the captain announce the next day's starters. I had no doubt about what to expect.

When the captain said, "Right halfback, Ishihara," it registered simply as a foregone conclusion.

I experienced neither the elation of victory nor the excitement that attends some achievement. But as I walked back to our locker room afterwards, each step I took felt both lighter and more firmly grounded than ever before. This is what life is all about, I told myself. If I want to live my own life, this is what I have to do.

I suppose what I went through that day was something akin to a conversion experience.

The longer I live, the more I realize that I have never felt so completely on my own as I did at that decisive moment. It was also the moment when I truly knew for the first time, deep down, that I had a regular starting position in life as well.

WILL-O'-THE-WISP

I can't recall how many summers ago this would have been, but one year a group of my golfing buddies and I got together for a weekend at Lake Yamanaka, where one of them had a vacation home. Since our only scheduled activity was the next day's round of golf, the drinking started early and the party lasted late into the night.

It being the season when spine-chilling stories are in favor, our conversation inevitably turned to the topic of ghosts and spirits.

One story led to another. Someone said he'd heard that Soichiro Honda, founder of the Honda Motor Company, had recently become an avid student of will-o'-the-wisps. The claim piqued my interest—especially since I knew Mr. Honda personally. It intrigued me that one of our country's great creative minds had chosen to take up this topic that has so long been the subject of physical and metaphysical speculation.

Although no one in the room could claim any specialized knowledge, a lively debate ensued: What exactly were will-o'-the-wisps? Were they an ectoplasm that oozed from human bodies? Were they puffs of phosphorus released by decaying corpses?

Predictably, members of the group soon started offering anecdotes about will-o'-the-wisp sightings—either claiming to have seen one themselves, or relating stories others had told them.

Then, to my surprise, my friend Arai broke in, declaring quite matter-of-factly, "I used to see will-o'-the-wisps all the time when I was a kid. I even used to catch them."

However unusual the topic of conversation was, this revelation struck the rest of us as quite beyond belief, and we all burst out laughing. I'd known Arai to do some wild things in his time, but basically he was a levelheaded guy, certainly not the sort to concoct bizarre stories or make empty boasts. As the director of a large private preschool, entrusted with the care and education of impressionable young minds, it would not do for him to go around fabricating tall tales.

"I must say, I've never heard of anyone actually catching one before," I noted incredulously.

"So even you don't believe me?" he said with a frown.

"Well, how exactly do you go about catching something like that?"

"With one of those landing nets anglers use when they're reeling in a big one." He spoke with such earnestness, everyone burst out laughing again.

"With a landing net?" said one of them, rather struck by the notion. "I do remember using one for dragonflies, but I never thought of will-o'-the-wisps."

"But that's exactly it. I'd be out chasing dragonflies, and then on my way home I'd go after will-o'-the-wisps."

"In other words, this net of yours was for landing the big dragonfly, not the big fish," teased another.

Arai remained dead earnest. "That's right. But especially on days when I didn't catch any, I'd go looking for will-o'-the-wisps on my way home after sundown."

He said this so soberly, no one knew quite what to make of it. Suddenly I realized everybody's eyes were on me. I was the one who knew Arai best.

"Whenabouts was this?" I asked.

"I was still pretty small—in grade school. There were lots of will-o'-the-wisps around where we lived."

"And where exactly would that be?" someone else chided, as though he still thought it had to be a joke.

"By the Edogawa River. The water was clean back then, and the marshes along the banks had lots of carp and koi. There were plenty of dragonflies, too, but the only ones we really cared about were the emperors."

"And will-o'-the-wisps."

"Those just happened to be on the way."

"Hey, it's on my way, so maybe I'll just catch me a few will-o'-the-wisps while I'm at it," one of the guys cracked, and everybody laughed again.

"Are you sure we're talking about real will-o'-the-wisps?" asked our host, possibly starting to take Arai a little more seriously.

"Well, they don't come out till evening, you know."

"So when the dragonflies were gone, you switched to hunting will-o'-the-wisps. Is that what you're saying?"

"That's right. When dragonflies are still flying around, you don't see any will-o'-the-wisps."

"Oh, sure. It all makes perfect sense now."

"Just shut up and hear him out," our host scolded, beating me to the punch. If it was really true that Arai had managed to net one, I wanted to hear the whole story.

"You sure you're not talking about fireflies?"

"Fireflies don't come out till later in the evening. Plus they're a completely different size."

"So when you used the landing net, you mean you caught them on the fly? In midair?" our host pursued. He was keeping a straight face but looked like he might burst out laughing at any moment.

"Right. They don't fly all that high, actually. Just high enough for us kids to reach with our nets."

"Were there a lot of graves near where you lived?" someone else asked.

"Yeah, quite a few."

"All right. So assuming your story's true, weren't you scared? I mean, you were just a little kid, after all."

"Well, in those days, there wasn't a whole lot else for a kid to do besides chase dragonflies, you know. I think maybe it scares me more to think about it now. It's true, though, I remember thinking it was kind of scary the very first time. Or at least a little creepy."

"Those things would give anybody the creeps. My dad said he saw one once when he was little, and he was so creeped out his knees turned to jelly."

"Just seeing them is nothing," Arai said, brushing him off. "I'm talking about the way it felt when I actually put my hand on it in the net. It had this weird, slimy texture—really disgusting. That's what was creepy."

The master of the house folded his arms. "So you're saying you've actually had your bare hands on a will-o'-the-wisp?"

"Sure, lots of times. That's why I'm telling you how creepy they felt."

"How'd you do it, exactly?"

"Once I had it in my net, I just grabbed hold of it."

He said this as if it were the most natural thing in the world. The room fell silent.

"So, what was it like to touch?" our host continued.

"Pretty damn unpleasant, I'd have to say. Of course, first you have to dunk it in the water to cool it off."

"Dunk it?"

"Uh-huh. They're always by a pond or marsh."

"So you dunked the thing in the pond?"

"To cool it off?" someone else howled.

"That's right. I mean, the thing was burning, after all. As a kid, your first thought is you don't want to burn your hands. So I swept it straight into the water, net and all."

"And then you grabbed it with your hand?"

"Uh-huh. I wanted to find out what the hell it was."

"So what did it feel like?"

"Not nice. I groped it all over but still couldn't figure out what it was. It felt all slimy—kind of gooey and formless. I really don't know how to describe it. Guess it was a bit like holding a great big, thick glob of snot."

The room fell silent again. Everyone was contemplating the testimony of our voice of experience.

"A great big glob of snot, eh?" someone finally said, quite struck by the analogy. "Interesting."

Somehow, I felt I knew exactly what Arai was trying to describe—or rather, I felt the sensation actually come across to me.

"What color were they?" I asked.

"Color? Sort of an off-white, I guess. Kind of translucent."

"And just how many do you figure you landed with that net of yours?"

"Too many to count. Like I said, there really wasn't a whole lot else for us to do back then for fun."

"So do you think the spirits of the will-o'-the-wisps you netted and doused in the pond were able to rise again and rest in peace?"

"Couldn't say. I did always set them free again, though."

"What did that involve?"

"I just turned the net inside out in the water and let them go, like fish."

"Did they come right to the surface and float off into the sky?"

"I don't think so. I mean, they were all waterlogged by then. I figure they had to swim or wash ashore first, then maybe they could take off from there."

No one could respond. We all just sat there, our eyes fixed on Arai, too flabbergasted to speak.

"Thinking back on it now, it does seem kind of creepy. But you know, kids can be totally fearless sometimes."

"Do you get bad dreams about it?" someone asked.

"No, never. Which makes sense, since from my perspective as a kid, these are good memories—though it's true, I never really knew what I was dealing with."

"But you're positive they were will-o'-the-wisps, right?"

"Not a doubt in my mind," Arai answered flat out.

"Between the will-o'-the-wisps flying or wafting your way after sundown, and the emperor dragonflies during the daylight hours, which excited you more?" I asked. "Which gave you the bigger thrill when you saw them coming?"

"Oh, the dragonflies for sure," said Arai without the slightest hesitation.

Judging from the way the subject kept popping up on the golf course the next day, Arai's story left a deep impression on the entire group. One guy in my own foursome waded off to look for a ball he'd hit into the rough, and came back empty-handed, joking that what he thought was his ball turned out to be a will-o'-the-wisp, but since he hadn't brought his net with him, it got away.

To tell the truth, Arai's story had rather grabbed me, too—partly because I knew the storyteller better than anyone else. Arai headed up a large private preschool in Hino, west of Tokyo. Since he was the director, he didn't actually teach the children, but as one who called himself an educator, he was straight as an arrow in his conduct and not given to making things up.

At any rate, the account he'd given of scooping will-o'-the-wisps out of the air with a fisherman's net he used for chasing dragonflies was quite unforgettable, no matter what you made of it.

Some time afterwards, I heard a story that reminded me of Arai's tale.

An older friend of my wife's was driving home with a mutual acquaintance late one night, coming over Asahina Pass toward Kamakura shortly after 1:00 A.M. As they reached Kamakura Cemetery near the top, a glowing ball of light rose from the side of the road—a bit hazy, but still very bright. It flew straight at the car and splattered against the windshield. The driver turned her wipers on right away, but to no avail.

Forced to pull over, the two women hopped out and wiped the glass clean by hand. The substance that came off on the tissue paper had an unpleasant, gooey texture.

They got back into the car, but neither of them volunteered a word as they resumed their journey over the pass. When they came to a filling station on their way down the other side, they pulled in to take another look at the windshield. The residue of whatever it was they'd wiped off still streaked the glass, proof positive that it hadn't just been their imagination.

This got them both shaking. Neither could find the courage to look the other in the eye all the rest of the way. When the owner of the car reached home after dropping her friend off, she headed straight to bed, pulled the covers all the way up over her head, and went to sleep without waking her husband.

"What do you think?" she asked me. "Can you believe it?"

"Sure, I can believe it," I nodded, and immediately repeated Arai's story.

"So we're not the only ones," she said, her eyes wide in astonishment. "But what do you suppose really happened to the will-o'-the-wisps he freed in the water?"

"I imagine they just dissolved," I said. "The bigger question is, what happened to the one you and your friend wiped up with those tissues and threw away."

My wife's friend screwed her face into a frown of contemplation, then swallowed with an exaggerated nod.

"Maybe it got all dry and crusty," she offered. "Or maybe it just evaporated."

NITROGEN NARCOSIS

Most people know the air we breathe is made up largely of nitrogen, but few are aware that nitrogen can sometimes have an intoxicating effect very similar to alcohol. One reason is that nitrogen narcosis, as it's called, seems to occur only in the context of deep-sea diving. And yet relatively few divers, who at least in theory know about the dangers, have ever experienced it themselves. While diver certification classes always include a lesson on nitrogen narcosis, no one—neither instructors nor learners—seems to take the dangers very seriously.

I myself learned about nitrogen narcosis well before I began diving, from a long-time diver friend of mine—in fact it was he who first urged me to take up the sport. He told me nothing could compare to the euphoria you experienced when you got high on nitrogen.

Divers typically become susceptible to nitrogen narcosis at depths of forty meters or more. And the deeper they go the more intense the intoxication becomes. But just as with alcohol, once you get used to the effects, you can learn to control your intoxication.

Even in the clearest water, below forty meters the colors all fade and everything looks steeped in blue ink. It's a magical tone, like the color of the stratosphere at twenty thousand meters. "Gazing into the depths, you feel yourself being pulled in, dissolving into that incomparable blue," my friend explained. "That's when the euphoria starts to come, and you know full well you're getting high, but you stay there because it feels so incredibly good. Of course, it's dangerous as hell, too. You're underwater, so any mistake can kill you. But that's part of the thrill."

When this man subsequently married, his actress fiancée consented only on condition that he give up his dangerous hobby. He'd never been a drinker before, but he missed the nitrogen high so much he took to the bottle and turned into an alcoholic.

As any diving manual will tell you, a diver under the influence of nitrogen loses all sense of danger. There's no predicting what fool thing he might do. I've heard of divers who shake off all efforts to help them, spit out their regulators, and drown themselves trying to wrap their arms around the fish in front of them.

I sometimes think I ought to experience nitrogen narcosis once myself, just to know what it's really like. But whenever I realize a fish has lured me deeper than I intended, I always hurry back to shallow waters too quickly for narcosis to set in.

I had been diving for a good while before I witnessed nitrogen narcosis with my own eyes. It nearly killed a diving companion of mine.

We'd had an unusually hot summer that year, and the intense heat persisted well into the fall. The waters around Hachijojima usually teemed with fish, but with water temperatures staying higher than normal, the big game fish had all taken refuge in the depths beyond reach. Finally, as October neared its close, a friend who lived on the island sent word that the fish had started to come back, so a group of us went to try our luck.

On our first day out, we decided to dive off Kannagi, where we'd spearfished before with great success. But contrary to our expectations, we found nothing. The current was strong, over two knots, and the water had cooled substantially, but no big fish swam into view. We soon started to get desperate, and even abandoned our diving buddies as we turned every which way in search of something to catch.

I had circled a large reef and found a spot on a shelf about thirty meters down where I could rest out of the current, when I saw Yamada—someone else's diving partner—come floating along in a very odd posture. Like a skydiver in free fall, his arms and legs were spread limply in wide arcs, and he didn't seem to be headed toward anything, only sinking deeper and deeper as the current carried him along.

It's not unusual for a diver to hitch a ride on a current for the fun of it—but normally only at shallow depths when you're fully in control and you know for sure a boat is close behind. None of those conditions applied to Yamada at that moment. From the way he kept sinking toward the reefless deep, it hardly looked like a time for enjoying an underwater joyride.

On the other hand, if he was being swept along against his will, why didn't I see him fighting the current, trying to swim out of its grip? Something had to be wrong. Suddenly Ehara angled out from behind a rock below me, swimming at a hard kick after Yamada. He obviously thought he was in trouble.

I pushed off from my sheltered perch to follow, and could tell immediately that the current was swifter than before. By the time we caught up with Yamada, we'd been carried fifty meters away—in what seemed like the blink of an eye.

Ehara had judged the situation correctly. He quickly wrapped his arm around Yamada and pressed the regulator back into his mouth. Yamada could barely keep it in place. Ehara didn't need to point out what was wrong: Yamada's eyes were half-glazed, as if drunk, and his body was almost completely limp. I also noticed for the first time that his spear was dangling loose from his gun, with the shock cord wrapped around his body.

When we grabbed him from both sides and gave him several good shakes, he turned his head from side to side and seemed to be waking up. But the next moment he relaxed completely, as if he knew he'd been rescued.

Even with two of us to do it, hauling a big man of over eighty kilos out of the deep, spear gun and all, while trying to hang on to our own guns, was no easy task. In the few seconds it took us to get ready, we'd sunk to nearly fifty meters.

A person that far gone on alcohol would take a good while to sober up, but recovery from nitrogen narcosis is remarkably quick. We were about two hundred meters from the boat when we reached the surface, and in just the time it took for the skipper to notice us and bring the boat around, Yamada was well on his way back to normal.

We dragged him from the water and laid him out on the deck, but in no more than five or six minutes he was picking himself up, his eyes no longer glazed.

"Do you have any idea what just happened?" I asked.

"I nearly lost it, didn't I?" he said, blinking his eyes as if waking from a deep sleep.

"You were out cold. We really had to bust our asses hauling you up from fifty meters down."

"That deep, eh? I only remember down to about twenty-five. I started to think I was in trouble, and kept telling myself to check my depth gauge, but I simply couldn't do it. I'd been trying to set the band on my spear gun, when all of a sudden this sweet drowsiness came over me. I could tell I was beginning to sink, but I just felt so unbelievably good. Like when you're drinking and you feel real mellow and sleepy, and you could swear your whole body's going to melt away. I could hear another voice inside me calling out, 'Don't go to sleep! You'll die if you go to sleep!' But there wasn't anything I could do. You know in those stories about people getting lost in the snow, how there's always someone yelling, 'Don't fall asleep! Don't fall asleep!' Well, I was that person yelling at myself, two people in one."

His dopey look was gone. He now appeared completely sober and relaxed.

"After that it was all like a dream. I was lying in a hospital somewhere. I wanted to go home, but for some reason I couldn't get out of bed. I was telling myself, *If you don't get up, you're gonna die, you're gonna die,* but this drowsiness just kept coming on more and more. In the end, lying there looking up at the ceiling, I was thinking, *If I die now, what's going to happen with my work?* I don't remember a thing after that."

Ehara handed him a soft drink. He peered at the bottle in his hand, then raised it to his lips and slowly drank it down, savoring every drop as if tasting it for the very first time. Suddenly, something seemed to connect, and a broad smile spread across his face. "Down there, when you shook me, I knew I was saved."

"But then you passed right out again," I said.

"I knew I was going to be okay, so I just let myself fall asleep on that hospital bed."

"And the next scene in your dream, you were in an ambulance being rushed to a different hospital?"

"Yeah. Thanks to you guys, I enjoyed a real nice ride from fifty meters down."

We dived again that afternoon. Luckily, Yamada managed not to fall asleep on any underwater hospital beds. Unluckily, even with cooler water temperatures, our three-day weekend of diving turned out to be a complete bust. But then I suppose that's just the way it goes.

CLOSE ENCOUNTERS

Meeting others is one of life's finer experiences, and indeed, even when the other is an animal, the experience may leave an indelible impression. Strong emotions can arise between people and animals just as they do between people—though I suppose this happens only when the encounter takes place under very unusual circumstances, or when a relationship develops over a long period of time.

The quickest, most effective catalyst for rendering an encounter between humans and animals unforgettable, however, is fear. Whatever the time or place, even if experienced only one-sidedly in most cases, terror will always make the encounter more intensely memorable.

For the object of terror, some might picture a venomous snake, but I think most of us are more likely to think of a creature vastly bigger than ourselves. And we can't help feeling at odds with nature to know that creatures far below us in intelligence are often far greater than us in size.

I once had a close encounter with a whale at sea—surprisingly close to home, in fact, well inside the busy waters of Sagami Bay. Of course, this was back in the 1960s, when even the more enclosed Tokyo Bay treated us to frequent sightings of small, dolphin-sized cetaceans, and when giant marlins rode the current right up to the tip of the Miura Peninsula.

Late one spring, some friends and I sailed together to Inatori Hot Springs in

Izu. On the way back, a seasonal rain front had settled right over Sagami Bay, coloring both sky and water a dull gray. Rain fell off and on, but we couldn't seem to catch any wind and so were forced to putt-putt along under our limited auxiliary power. We'd made it to east of Manazuru, near Mitsuishi Island, when we chanced upon a whale foraging for food among the flotsam caught in a large current rip.

The whale's long, dark back and the bobbing debris stood out sharply against the monochromatic gray of everything else around. At first, the whale appeared to be nothing more than a particularly large piece of flotsam, but as we got closer we saw it was alive.

Paddling unseen flippers, the leviathan slowly pushed through the water, bits of drifting refuse flowing back along his large flank. The changing light on the objects as they nudged against the dark gray skin and slid on by revealed the enormous bulk hidden beneath the water. Measuring from the head that periodically broke the surface to the tail flukes appearing and disappearing far behind, the creature was easily longer than our eleven-meter yacht.

We decided to approach the whale from downwind in the barely stirring air. We soon came within hearing of his breathing as he fed, not to mention smelling distance of his briny, damp-rotted sea creature stink.

With the recklessness of youth and the overconfidence of sailors traveling in familiar waters, we made light of the potential danger and brought the boat to within a boathook's length of the enormous beast. The whale, for his part, seemed unimpressed. He went on with his solitary, cheerless foraging, totally ignoring the strange visitors now studying him up close.

Between the increasingly powerful stink and the utter indifference he showed us, as if we were merely another piece of flotsam, the whale loomed as a truly intimidating presence. His glistening black hulk fitted right into the shades-of-gray gloom of the surrounding world, and he seemed almost to be carrying that entire gray-toned world on his solitary back. His size dwarfed our boat, making us look like a flimsy, throwaway toy.

All at once, on some spontaneous impulse, several of the crew began shouting at the beast, but their shouts slid off his massive, wet back into the waves with no discernible effect.

I have no idea what made me do what I did next—pure impulse, I suppose, like the men shouting. I hurried to load a .22 I kept stowed in the cabin and promptly discharged it into the body of the beast from just a couple of meters away. The dry pop of the small caliber rifle sounded pathetically weak in the murky gloom.

The next instant, the whale was gone in a motion at once too slow and deliberate to have come from the gunshot, yet over in the blink of an eye. He disappeared with barely a splash, leaving behind only a wide blue-black swirl to attest to the immensity that had floated there only moments before.

A numbing fear shot through me. What if that creature so much larger than our boat came bucking up through our hull? We swallowed nervously and waited for what might come.

Our wooden boat was a mere eleven meters long; our Moby Dick was at least thirteen.

We watched in silence as the moments went by. The sea remained calm, with neither wind nor wave; we heard only the sound of our own breathing.

As we looked on, the swirling vortex where the whale had disappeared gradually leveled off. Without exaggeration, in those moments every one of us was looking his own death square in the eye.

After a while—just how long is hard to say—the lookout in the bow shouted that he'd seen the whale surface in the distance, heading away. I hurriedly focused my binoculars in the direction he pointed, but failed to catch a glimpse of it.

What I experienced then was the joy of deliverance. Not only had I escaped harm, I'd been given a fresh lease on life.

Several years after my encounter with the whale, I had a similar experience on land. In this case, the meeting was purely innocent, or at least not the product of wanton human provocation. It took place in Alaska, where several colleagues and I had gone to scout locations for a television drama.

The Alaska Pulp Corporation was kind enough to lend us one of their foresters, a man named Dick, to be our guide into an old-growth forest outside Sitka. After driving a good distance through roadless hills, we ditched our jeep and proceeded on foot into still deeper growth. We'd walked through virgin forest for a couple of kilometers, when we came to a river some forty meters wide and started across, hopping from stone to stone with Dick in the lead. At about the halfway point, he turned around with a hushing finger to his lips, then slowly led us forward two or three more steps before stopping again, spreading his broad, stiff back to block any further advance. He unslung his rifle and grasped it in front of him.

I strained to hear over the babbling of the water and thought I detected some rustling directly ahead of us, on the far bank. A toppled hemlock lay along the bank, its trunk a good two meters across, and something seemed to be moving around behind it.

"Think it's a deer?" I asked.

Dick cocked his head, then nodded, and took another step forward.

Following his example, I drew the .22 caliber long-barrel handgun I'd borrowed at his office—a pistol suited more to target competitions than hunting but better than nothing.

When Dick suddenly spread his arms wide to stop us again, I saw the massive head of a bear emerge from behind the hemlock. The bear then placed his equally massive paws on the trunk and heaved himself up, looking straight in our direction.

I could scarcely believe my eyes: the beast stood literally head and shoulders above the two-meter tree trunk. The towering animal seemed so out of proportion to the fallen tree that I thought my whole sense of perspective must be out of whack.

Across the short distance separating us, the bear appeared to be sizing up the figures frozen in midstream, slowly rocking his head from side to side, then arching his neck forward as if to get a closer look. Even with a massive tree trunk in the way, something in his manner suggested he had at least half a mind to come after us.

"Back up," Dick hissed. "Back up real slow." His voice remained low, but was taut with tension. Keeping his rifle at the ready, he took a step backward, pushing right into me with the broad of his back.

I tried to step back, too, but my legs were like jelly—and discovering this fact seemed to sap their strength even more. I could hardly tell if I was still on my feet. Somehow I managed finally to yank a leg free from the mire of fear and take a step backward. But since I didn't look to see where I was going, my foot failed to find my last stepping-stone, and icy water gushed into my boot.

Luckily, the chill of the water revived the feeling in my legs, and my quaking knees seemed capable of supporting me again. As I took a second step backward, I remembered my handgun and raised it toward the bear, grasping it firmly with both hands.

"Don't shoot!" Dick snapped.

Actually, I never intended to shoot. I just knew I had to do something to help my poor legs hold me upright, and raising the gun seemed the best I could do.

Someone behind me fell into the river with a splash and a shout, and the bear leaned over the tree trunk again to see what the commotion was. As the fellow in the river tried to continue backward on the seat of his pants, Dick swung around to hook an arm under his shoulder and pull him to his feet.

Clearly, these movements had attracted the bear's attention. Growling low and slowly shaking his head back and forth, the giant seemed to be pondering whether to come after us or simply let us go.

Our retreat back across those twenty or so meters of river seemed to take forever, but finally my heels struck firm ground. As I made sure of my footing, I raised my eyes again toward the bear on the far bank. Even at twice the distance, the beast still looked enormous.

Apparently the bear had made up his mind to come after us: he began trying to clamber over the tree. At that, someone shouted "Run!" and everyone else made tracks into the woods. But when I saw Dick standing beside me, not budging, I raised my gun again, trained it carefully on my target across the river, and pulled the trigger. I could discern no sound or indication that the bullet had struck home.

All of a sudden, Dick was shouting in my ear, and I realized the foolishness of what I'd done. He thumped me on the shoulder and took off into the woods. In a panic, I sprinted after him. Running like a madman, I soon overtook the others, even though they'd started well ahead of me.

Spurred by the sound of my gun as well as the ferocity of my pace, the others poured it on as well, shouting as they ran.

I kept imagining the bear, wounded and angry, bounding across the river after us. Or maybe he was circling around to cut us off up ahead.

We raced down a gentle slope through the forest without slackening our pace. When finally our jeep came into view, Dick yelled that we could stop running. He probably thought it punishment enough that he'd let us run this far, and held off making any other comments.

As we came to a halt at the jeep, we all burst out laughing. We laughed so hard tears came to our eyes—all except Dick.

Over the years, I've been on a great many hunting trips and fired my weapon any number of times, but the two shots I fired at the whale and the bear are the ones that return to mind time and again. The whale I know I hit for sure, and these days I'm convinced I hit the bear as well.

Of course, a .22 bullet would be like a pinprick to a bear, let alone a whale. Each of those bullets no doubt remains buried somewhere in its host's body without doing any real harm. But I imagine both animals must feel slight twinges now and then from the foreign bodies lodged in their flesh. Those twinges are a message from me to them—a message to those enormous beasts from a creature of a different kind.

Whether alone in my study late at night after a hard day's work, or on the road home at dawn after a night of idle drinking, or simply in a random moment of rest among the tedious minutiae of daily life, I sometimes recall my encounters with the enormous bear outside Sitka or the solitary whale in Sagami Bay. At times, in fact, the recollection goes beyond remembering, as I find myself yearning to actually *be* that whale, that bear. With my spirit quickening, I feel myself metamorphosing into one of them, and as I do so, I can feel a tiny twinge throb to life from a wound deep in my flesh. Savoring that twinge of pain, I picture myself coursing a moonlit sea gazing up at a volcanic island erupting, or racing toward a roiling sunset beneath a brisk westerly wind, or creeping up on my prey in a primeval forest through flashes of purple lightning and a driving rain. And by imagining myself as the whale and the bear in this way, I can somehow know their experience as my own.

MIRACLE

Last-minute business pushed my departure back a flight, so it was almost three o'clock by the time I reached Kumejima.

The anticipation of new waters will make any diver champ at the bit. I dumped my luggage unceremoniously at the hotel and headed straight for the dock to join Shiroma and his two friends, Oku and Bize, both of whom I was meeting for the first time. The three had brought with them two collapsible duralumin boats from U.S. Army surplus in Naha, on the main island of Okinawa, and had long since assembled them, outboards mounted and ready to go.

Holiday Reef to the east of Kumejima is unlike any other in Japanese waters. It extends nearly ten kilometers out to sea, with kilometer-long sandy cays a hundred meters wide and a lighthouse at the easternmost point. Along its north flank, low tide exposes rocky flats, which drop off almost straight down to sixty or seventy meters. To the south, the shallows abound in marine life and diverse tidal flows where shifts in the earth's crust have broken the reef into irregular formations.

According to Shiroma, the tourist area around my hotel known as Eef Beach brought in droves of young weekenders, few of whom ever took the trouble to charter boats and explore farther afield. As a result, the outer cays remain relatively unspoiled—a diver's paradise.

This was just before the rainy season, right around the summer solstice. Sunset was seven o'clock, so we could stay in the water until at least six-thirty—plenty of time, even after our late start. We dropped anchor about three kilometers short of the lighthouse, and split up in pairs for our first dive.

The tide turned just about the time we'd finished the dive, but with the wind blowing against the receding waters we figured we wouldn't drift too far. We moved to another spot and dropped anchor for a second dive. The undersea vistas were every bit as stunning as Shiroma had led me to expect, and high tide brought in schools of emperors and sweetlips from the sea beyond, making for fabulous fishing conditions. Our haul also included several painted spiny lobsters found only in warmer waters, each measuring over a meter long with the antennae. All told, we had ourselves a field day of a hunt while also enjoying spectacular underwater sights.

On the south side of the reef, the dazzling white sand of the ocean floor was dotted with myriad coral-covered rocks, large and small, in every color and form imaginable, each breathtakingly beautiful. Searching out prey from rock to rock had the ethereal feeling of space travel—of venturing from one unknown planet to the next.

Shiroma and I had paired off, and we returned to the boat together shortly after six. Oku followed a few minutes later. We sat in the boats waiting for Bize to show, but six-thirty came and went with no sign of him. As the smallest among us, maybe he could stretch his air supply a bit, but he had to be reaching his limit. Even if he'd dumped his tank on a rock somewhere and switched to free diving, the dwindling light in the sky had to tell him it was time to be getting back.

We raised anchor, yanked our motors to life, and started searching the immediate vicinity, but to no avail. We split up to widen our search, but still failed to find him. The outboard motor tanks were none too generous; we began to worry that if we wasted too much gas conducting a search we might run short on the way back to port.

By now the sun had dipped into the East China Sea. Even the afterglow was beginning to fade. We decided to take one last look around, but when we met near a large break in the reef ten minutes later the results were the same.

"Man, just our luck! Our first day out, and already we have to scare up a search party." I tried to make it sound like a joke, but we all looked pretty grim.

"Where are we in the lunar cycle?"

"I think we're at the eighth or ninth."

"So we'd be at neap tide."

"I suppose it's possible he got washed out to sea."

Beyond the break in the reef, the waves looked too choppy and treacherous for us to carry out a search in our tiny craft. Perhaps we could anchor one here as a marker and go back to port to get a larger boat. As we were discussing this option, I thought I heard a shout from upwind. It sounded like it came from outside the reef, to the right of the break.

"I heard a shout."

"Yeah, I think I might've heard something, too," said Shiroma.

We scanned the top of the reef, but none of us could see a thing. Just to be sure, we kept our eyes peeled for another ten minutes or so before finally conceding that we'd better call in a larger search boat, as we'd discussed before.

But then came a second shout—this time clear enough for all of us to hear.

"Over that way!" Oku and I yelled simultaneously, pointing to the far right.

And almost immediately, we saw Bize waving his spear gun atop a swell much farther away than any of us had imagined, some five or six hundred meters along the reef from the break. As suspected, he'd unloaded his tank and catch on a rock when his air ran out so he could continue free diving, and the current had swept him to where we found him.

To our surprise, Bize seemed completely unaware of anything being amiss.

"Why didn't you come back to the boat when your air ran out?" Shiroma demanded.

Bize looked confused. "But when we went in, you said we'd stay down until six-thirty." He'd obviously misunderstood the whole thrust of our earlier conversation.

"But that was just—"

"Oh, forget it. Let's just be glad we didn't have to call in a search party."

"Search party? Who for?"

"For you," Oku said. "We've been looking all over the place for you. For nearly an hour."

"Then we finally heard you shout. At first I was the only one, but the second time we all heard you."

"You heard me shout?"

"Uh-huh."

"But I never shouted."

"What're you talking about? We all heard you."

"No, really. It couldn't have been me. I saw you guys sitting here in the boats, but I waited and waited and you didn't come. I kept wondering what the hell was going on, and then you looked my way, so I waved my spear gun, and you saw me, right?"

The three of us stared at each other in silence. We could now barely make out each other's faces in the darkness. Shiroma lit a cigarette behind cupped hands, took a couple of puffs, and passed it to Bize.

"Well, then, shall we be heading on back?" he said.

The motors sputtered to life. Under the din I heard Shiroma comment, mostly to himself, "Yeah, this shit sometimes happens at sea."

KEELING OVER

For a yachtsman, the whims of the wind remain an eternal enigma. No matter how many times you've experienced it, when you're on a run and the wind suddenly swings around against you, you gasp in disbelief at the lack of rhyme or reason. Yet you have no choice but to do as the wind commands, for you are wholly dependent on its power. I understand the principles perfectly well in the abstract, of course, but I never cease to be dumbfounded by what can happen when I try to sail my small craft through a point where two winds collide.

When I entered the first Ogasawara Race in 1979, the fleet started out from Futami Harbor on Chichijima under flawlessly clear skies with a southwesterly wind at our backs. My boat galloped along under spinnaker for most of the day at exhilarating speeds. But with the approach of evening, a thin layer of clouds spreading across the horizon ahead signaled an impending change in conditions.

As the sun sank lower in the sky, we speculated as to how many more hours we had left with the wind on our tail, and which direction it might turn. Then the moment the sun dropped beneath the horizon, the wind fell away to nothing, and I noticed that a thick band of clouds had arrived overhead.

With the spinnaker collapsed, I looked aloft thinking we probably needed to change the sails. At that very instant, a wind of fifteen or sixteen knots abruptly reappeared on the bow with a powerful *whoosh*. The spinnaker and mainsail, filled only moments before with a chasing wind, now came aback as if to push the boat in reverse, bringing us to a halt. The dark of night descended rapidly, leaving us no time to enjoy the twilight glow. We spent the next twenty-four hours beating hard to windward.

During the Okinawa Race the following year, a changing wind nearly sank our boat near the Tokara Islands. There, too, we were running downwind at a good clip under spinnaker when the clouds started looking ominous just before the change of watch in the evening.

The Tokaras mark a treacherous zone for the sailor. For one thing, the islands of the chain remain poorly charted to this day. On a return visit one summer, a friend and I explored numerous dive sites around the islands by powerboat, and it was truly alarming to see how many uncharted reefs we discovered. But even worse, the islands are situated where the Japan Current crosses over from the East China Sea into the Pacific through relatively shallow waters, so any time the wind turns away from the flow, it can whip up rogue waves in an instant. I've sailed in various parts of the world, but aside from the notorious Cape Horn, I know of no other waters quite so quick to change their mood as those around the Tokaras.

Here, too, the wind stopped dead. We all held our breath, and waited to see which way it would reappear. During the brief calm, a large shark swam up alongside the boat and stopped with its dorsal fin standing erect on the surface. Eerily, the shark remained motionless in that one spot—as if it, too, were waiting for something.

The wind that rose after the lull hadn't shifted enough for the spinnaker to come down; we adjusted our bearing slightly and sailed on with only a slight loss of speed. Which was an unfortunate move, as it turned out: we were still rejoicing over our luck when the first gust hit. The boat broached and heeled sharply, then quickly righted. I was coming off duty, so I told the next watch to drop the spinnaker, and headed below. But they were so pumped up about the race they wanted to see how far they could push it.

I thought I'd take a brief nap before dinner and lay down on my bunk, but then a second powerful gust tilted the boat sharply to one side again. I asked Ishikawa, who'd just come off watch with me, to go back up and warn our replacements not to press their luck, especially since night was falling.

As he got up to go, the boat shuddered under the force of yet another blast. We heeled again, though not as severely as before. Even inside the cabin, we could feel every inflection in the wind's fitful breathing. Nagata in the galley had put some water on to boil for dinner, so I advised him to keep a hand on the pot in case we tipped again. I sat up in my bunk to be ready for whatever might come.

Exactly as I anticipated, barely five or six seconds later another blast shook our fourteen-meter boat, this time knocking us all the way over on our side. Nagata and several others came tumbling across the cabin. His pot crashed onto the chart table, soaking the charts and logbook. Fortunately, the water hadn't come to a boil, so no one got scalded.

I found myself sitting cross-legged on the wall of my bunk to port, calmly and comfortably gazing about at everything turned ninety degrees on its side. It reminded me of something I'd seen in *Life* magazine as a boy—one of those trick pictures of a house thrown completely out of perspective. Even when you knew it was only an optical illusion, you were convinced the room was askew.

But here, our boat really had rolled a full ninety degrees onto her side—so fast, my senses couldn't adjust. I found myself sitting firm and upright on the wall, but my surroundings—or perhaps I should say the entire world—had been transformed. As if by magic, things that normally don't fly were hurtling through the air one after the other. Everything stowed in the starboard shelves— toiletry bags, life jackets, eyeglasses, instant noodle cups, a spare sextant—came leaping across the cabin as if suddenly brought to life. Of course, since the starboard wall was now the ceiling, all those objects were simply yielding to the force of gravity. Yet their flight seemed so marvelous, so engaging, that for a few brief seconds I forgot our dire circumstances and just sat there laughing out loud.

Then I heard seawater pouring through the companionway hatch abaft, so I yelled to Ishikawa to get the washboards in place. This sealed off the cabin so that the boat wouldn't flood and sink even if she lay on her side.

"How's everyone doing out there?" I asked when he was finished.

"They looked pretty peeved when they saw me shutting off the cabin, but I'm sure they'll manage."

Several minutes went by, and the magical migration of objects had mostly come to an end, but our belowdecks funhouse showed no sign of righting itself. Still sitting on the wall of my berth, I pulled on my foul weather gear and prepared to go outside. The passageway on its side was too narrow for standing, and even on hands and knees I had to crawl over fallen objects to reach the companionway. Lifting clear the washboards with everything still in this sideways position proved tricky as well, but with help from the other side, I managed to climb out into the cockpit.

Very little time had elapsed since I'd gone below, but the world outside was utterly changed. The near-gale winds that had knocked the yacht down raged on, but having arrived so abruptly they had yet to whip up waves, and the surface of the water was clouded with foam, a spread of white crepe as far as the eye could see.

One man dangled from the lifeline, another from the stern pulpit, stunned and at a loss. Two others clung to a sidestay with their feet planted on the boom, which lay underwater.

"Skipper, look!" yelled one of the crew, pointing past the tip of the mast in the water where the black fin of that same shark stood out like a well-honed blade against the white, foamy face of the sea.

The last gleam of daylight allowed us not only to see that fin, but to keep our wits about us as we dealt with our predicament. I shudder to think how much more difficult it would have been if this had happened in the middle of the night.

We managed to right the boat in about thirty minutes by sacrificing a halyard and hauling in the spinnaker. When we raised the sails again, the wind was on our bow, a fresh breeze out of the northeast at a steady seventeen to eighteen knots.

There are far more harrowing stories of yachts keeling over, even just among the ones I've heard firsthand.

Many years ago, an aging but sturdy ketch named *Tzu Hang* sailed into my home port of Aburatsubo. Her owner was a retired brigadier from Canada named Miles Smeeton; his only crew, his lifelong companion and wife, Beryl. Both were septuagenarians, but if they had a problem with their mast, he would man a winch on deck while she rode up the mast in a bosun's chair.

Their boat measured over fifteen meters in length, the beam about four. I remember being amazed to find an old upright piano propped against one wall of the cabin.

It came as no surprise to me that the piano didn't play. I'd already heard the Smeetons' tale of capsizing not once but twice during fierce storms near Cape Horn. Conditions had been horrendous even for those infamous waters. By their account, the largest seas had to have been well over thirty meters high, their massive slopes interrupted by smaller peaks of ten meters or so, which were in turn punctuated by waves of more than two meters—all of which came crashing down at once from different directions, making it impossible for the helmsman to know what to do.

As they sailed through these unspeakable conditions, the Smeetons' yacht was twice thrown on her head—in the first case, not rolling over sideways, but somersaulting forward stern-over-bow. No doubt that's when the piano sounded its last notes, lost amidst the deafening roar of the wind and waves.

Mr. Smeeton later gave me a copy of the book he'd written about that journey. I immediately sympathized with the sentiment of the title—*Once Is Enough*.

I'm quite sure not even the most heart-stopping of today's popular roller coasters comes remotely close to having heaven and earth reverse themselves on you on the raging sea. Anyone who's gone through that is, in a sense, both chosen and cursed.

More recently, I heard another gripping account of a boat capsizing. The vessel in question was a yacht named *Marishiten* on her way home from Hawaii to Japan after the 1982 Pan Am Clipper Cup race.

About the time they passed 165° east longitude, they picked up reports of a typhoon to the south. Depending on how it tracked, they'd have to be careful to avoid either Marcus Island to the northwest or the Northern Marianas due west. With the storm's bearing uncertain, they initially set a course based on historical data for typhoons arising around that time of year, but then the typhoon suddenly gained strength and changed both track and speed. Afraid of being caught in the dead of night near Marcus, where there was no light at all, skipper Takagi plotted a more southerly course and decided he would heave to once the typhoon actually hit.

That night the *Marishiten* sailed into the heart of the storm.

"By the time the sun went down," Takagi recalled, "the wind was already howling at sixty knots. The forecast said to expect winds in excess of eighty, so we'd taken down even the storm jib and were sailing under bare poles. Since we were still being blown to the southwest at over ten knots, I figured we could at least ride out the night without washing up on the island. The color of the sky at twilight was absolutely unforgettable. Just incredibly beautiful, but also with this eerie cast that made you think tomorrow might never come. Probably everybody felt like that.

"We streamed a sea anchor from the stern as best we could, and of course nobody stayed on watch; we all went below, and sealed ourselves in tight, reinforcing the washboards from inside. Then we crawled into our bunks and waited with bated breath. Sleep was completely out of the question; none of us felt like even trying. The boat was heaving around like you wouldn't believe. We passed the time trying to guess how many knots the wind was up to. Then around eleven o'clock, I think it was, the wind picked up another notch, and we could feel it whipping the seas even higher.

"The boat started rocking more violently, so I wondered aloud if maybe our sea anchor had cut loose. At that very second, we heeled sharply to port and righted, then suddenly rolled a full 360°, upside down and right back up, just like that. So quick, we didn't even have time to get scared. In fact, most of us probably thought, *Hey, that wasn't so bad. We can handle this.*

"Then about two hours later—at exactly 1:05, I remember—I felt another change in the waves. I mentioned it to Hiramatsu, who was in the next berth, when suddenly the boat lurched—actually, it felt more like some giant creature grabbed the boat at both ends and twisted her in its hands—and the next thing we knew we were upside down. I figured we would roll on around and pop back up like before, but this time, that was it—we stayed like that.

"Bilge water cascaded down from above and pooled on the ceiling, which was now the floor. I remember feeling really reassured, somehow, when the ceiling light kept burning even after it was covered with water.

"But I knew the light couldn't stay on for long, and I knew we needed to right the boat. We couldn't go outside, of course, so I figured our best bet was to shift all our weight to one side. I yelled for everybody to get over to port and lean hard, but it didn't seem to do any good.

"Someone said, 'We won't sink if we stay like this, right?' so someone else quipped, 'But staying like this might not be too handy,' which cracked some of the guys up.

"My first worry was the bilge. Water could start flooding in from somewhere and quickly fill the cabin. I also figured we'd lost our mast, which was obviously a concern. But the water on the ceiling wasn't rising, at least not noticeably. After a while it seemed like the waves were hitting the hull differently, so I thought maybe we'd have better luck tipping the boat. I had everybody grab whatever was loose and shift more weight to port. I have no idea what finally made the difference, but ever so slowly the boat started to roll back upright.

"I must've been pretty shook up by the whole ordeal, because I didn't think to look at my watch when we finally got all the way back up. I'd guess it took us at least five minutes. I doubt it was ten.

"We seemed to be over the worst of it, so we picked up all the stuff strewn about the cabin and put things in order. I decided topside could wait till tomorrow, and told everybody to get some shut-eye. Not that I remember getting much sleep that night myself."

I can just picture it: the entire crew heaving hard against one side of the upended cabin, trying to coax the boat upright, all the while keeping their eyes on the glow of the ceiling light in the murky bilge water. Even when things are utterly beyond our control, human nature compels us to take action in whatever way we can—or else we lose ourselves. Some unknowable power righted the *Marishiten*, but so far as I'm concerned, the crew deserve to believe they did it themselves.

In the morning, when the wind and the waves were just beginning to subside, Takagi ordered all hands on deck to address the damage. The mast had snapped about fifty centimeters above the deck, so they cut loose the boom for a substitute mast and managed to rig up a small sail. The wind was still blowing better than fifty knots, and the seas were a good six meters high.

"You know, it's funny. No matter how big the wind or seas, so long as you've got blue sky overhead you feel like you've got no worries in the world," Takagi said. "We get that jury-rig in place and suddenly we're wondering, *How many knots'll this baby do now?* We should've been breathing a big sigh of relief just to be alive, but it felt more like when you're messing around and trying some new rigging out for the hell of it.

"It did kind of give me the creeps, though, when one of the guys pointed out these incredibly big dolphinfish, a whole bunch of them, circling the boat. The seas were still towering over our heads, like I said, and we could see them eyeing us from inside those transparent walls of blue on all sides.

"Dolphinfish like to congregate around driftwood or drowning victims. They sort of latch onto goners, which is exactly what we must've looked like to them—a big piece of driftwood carrying a bunch of dead meat in the making. Anyway, there they were, hovering above eye level in the walls of water all around us, ogling us with their big glassy eyes the whole time we worked. Really quite spectacular in a way, but also kind of eerie and unpleasant."

Still, when those same blue-green dolphinfish visit Takagi and his crew in their dreams someday, staring out at them from inside towering walls of water, I suspect they'll all look back on the experience as one of their happiest memories.

UNDERWATER BALCONY SEATS

The floating lighthouse rose out of the sea two nautical miles west-southwest of Senbazaki Point on Izu Oshima island. It was quite large, some twenty-five meters tall and more than five meters across, and the first time I saw it coming up during a yacht race, I mistook it for a workboat of some kind steaming in our direction.

Although a revolving beacon did come on at night, strictly speaking the structure was not a lighthouse, having only been placed there as a temporary marker by Nippon Telegraph and Telephone for the purpose of laying undersea cable. Whatever ultimately became of it—whether NTT dismantled it, or it sank when a typhoon tore it from its underwater moorings—the installation played a role in the ocean-floor communications network.

Needless to say, when something that big suddenly pops up in the channel between Oshima and the Izu Peninsula, where part of the Japan Current breaks off to flow northward, it causes quite a stir among recreational boaters in the area. One year, the gigantic buoy even served as the double-back point in a quarter-ton class boat race.

A short time after the floating lighthouse appeared, some friends and I decided to have a closer look at it on our way home from a diving trip to Shi-kinejima. I remember how peculiar the tower looked—like a massive wooden *kokeshi* doll bobbing its long torso and large round head on swells from a moderate southwesterly breeze.

Considering how the tower was tossed about on such gentle waves, I wondered what it might do in a typhoon. Would even a monster buoy like that get blown all the way over on its side? What would the submerged part look like? How would it creak and struggle to right itself?

In some ways the tall lighthouse tower also reminded me of a large ballistic missile. It had a distinctly apocalyptic aura about it.

I've forgotten who first suggested we go spearfishing under the floating lighthouse.

As I recall, my friend Nishizaki was the one who told me that migratory fish schooled in the waters below. If he arrived at this insight merely from contemplating what could be seen of the structure above sea level, then I'd have to call him a genius. More likely, though, his information came, either directly or indirectly, from one of the construction divers who had actually been in the water under the tower.

I have no way of knowing what the interior of the lighthouse may have been like, but on the outside there was a large door with a grab bar, and a wide step sticking out roughly a meter above the waterline. Workers carrying a passkey could presumably gain access through this door. A railed gallery circled the tower about ten meters up, with another door opening onto it from inside.

But these features were of little interest to us. Our objective was the underwater handrail we'd heard about, supposedly running all the way around the base of the floating structure at a depth of some twenty meters to aid workers in going about their tasks.

The sea was calm when we arrived at the floating tower, with only a very light breeze out of the northeast. The lighthouse stood almost completely motionless, making the force of the current flowing past its base all the more obvious.

A northward stream of at least one to two knots runs through this channel at all times. Several yacht races each year send their fleets around Oshima, and only a rank amateur would neglect to account for this constant flow. As I steadied the boat into the current so we could tie up, one of the guys tossed an empty beer can over the side. We could tell by how quickly it floated past the boat that the flow on the surface easily exceeded two knots, even with an opposing light breeze.

Two knots may not sound like much, but when you're talking about a current that swimmers have to contend with in the water, it can be quite daunting. Over three knots swimmers have a hard time even keeping their balance.

The floating lighthouse was firmly anchored in the middle of this powerful current, but even with its large, five-meter-diameter base, if we failed to keep a firm grip we'd instantly be swept away. With this in mind, the three of us making the dive decided we should enter the water one at a time, each person following only after the last had latched onto the base and begun scaling down.

I'd done all sorts of diving by this time, but never into so strong a current; its force pressed my entire body hard against the steel wall of the lighthouse. Descending feet first with my arms stretched wide, I felt as if I held the lighthouse in my embrace, but I suppose we looked more like bugs clinging to the side of a telephone pole.

The south side, which faced the sun as well as the current, was slimy with algae. One slip and I knew I'd be washed away, so I let the pressure of the water hold me against the wall and concentrated on keeping my balance as I inched slowly downward. At about fifteen meters, I felt the force of the current start to ease.

The first man down was waiting for me at twenty-three meters, hanging onto the handrail we'd been told about. When our third companion joined us, we did a once-around along the handrail. On the east side we found a locked door, presumably for maintenance workers to go in and out in full diving gear. Another long handrail extended downward from right next to the door, suggesting some other maintenance point farther below. For our purposes, though, the rail circling the base at twenty-three meters was perfect. We returned to the southwestern wall, where a tiny bit of sunlight filtered down from the surface, and there we settled in. Hooking our legs over the rail, we leaned back against the wall and peered out into the deep. It was a decidedly odd sensation, unlike anything I'd ever experienced before.

Nothing but water, water, and more water filled our field of vision—a massive wall of blue that left me with almost no depth perception. Not one tiny fish came into view.

Which should have been no surprise: the channel was 120 meters deep, after all, and the smooth underwater surface of the lighthouse offered no nooks and crannies for fish to take up residence. I was sure that legions of fish lived on the sea floor below, but to such bottom dwellers twenty-three meters was too shallow, or simply too far afield to venture on a whim.

Perching on the side of a huge manmade steel structure in the midst of a fishless sea, I felt as precarious as an astronaut on a spacewalk clinging to the side of his spaceship. I knew I had friends waiting for me in the boat above, of course, yet I couldn't help worrying that if I lost my grip on the handrail, I'd be sucked into the current and swept away in an instant, never to return.

We rested a couple of minutes, but still saw nothing. Nishizaki had said we might only see migratory fish three times out of five.

We all exchanged glances. If this were on shore, we'd probably light up cigarettes and just sit tight, but instead we reached for the sea knives strapped to our legs. I began tapping the handrail; one of my two companions tapped the steel wall behind him, the other his air tank.

We tapped a while and stopped, then tapped again. We didn't want to overdo it. Fish are curious creatures, but too much tapping might just annoy them. And besides, no one actually knows what sounds attract or repel fish.

The way migratory fish emerge out of the depths is essentially the way I imagine angels appearing. Or maybe spaceships. They're definitely not like airplanes, which start out as tiny specks in the distant sky and then gradually approach closer and closer. Instead, one moment you see nothing, the next you're looking at a group of fish point-blank, without the slightest clue which direction they came from.

I suppose the scientific explanation is that no matter how clear the water may be, there are limits to its transparency. At any rate, all of a sudden the fish are simply there, without any prior notice.

By comparison, the movements of resident species like sea bream and grouper seem to generate subtle disturbances in the water that let you know they're coming. Only migratory species emerge suddenly from the void like angels or spaceships, as if they'd arrived at supersonic speed and careened to a halt the very moment you caught sight of them.

They may not have wings like angels, but without a doubt there *is* something otherworldly about them. It reminds me of the movies, when a huge spaceship comes in for a landing and for some reason the thing doesn't make a sound as it touches down.

A school of yellowtail amberjacks passed soundlessly before us like a sudden meteor shower. Clearly, they'd come to investigate our noises. And finding three bizarre creatures clinging to the base of the floating lighthouse with sinister-looking devices in their hands—maybe they'd encountered the likes of us before—they exercised their customary wariness and powered right on by, throwing us only cursory glances out of the corners of their eyes.

They disappeared with the same bewildering abruptness as they had appeared—so vividly before us one instant, gone without a trace the next.

At such moments, as you gaze after the vanished fish, you experience a kind of cosmic realization about how unimaginably deep and vast this ocean must be. It hits far closer to home than any epiphany you might experience on land while contemplating the universe beneath a starry sky.

We soon learned that the school of yellowtail amberjacks had been merely a preview of coming attractions. Minutes later, when we finally turned our attention back to closer water after giving up on their reappearance, we found we had some new company hovering before us like a gentle flock of curious angels. Having spied something alien, something not normally present when they came there to graze on algae, the newcomers approached for a closer look.

The first school of yellowtail amberjacks had apparently left no cautionary messages for their cousins. Or perhaps they had, but the ever-inquisitive greater amberjacks still felt they had to check us out for themselves.

In the Ogasawara (Bonin) Islands once, my friends and I encountered some greater amberjacks only about thirty centimeters long—youngsters undoubtedly seeing humans for the first time in their lives. So enthralled were they by the bubbles emerging from our breathing apparatus that they kept nosing up to our regulators no matter how many times we waved them away. They flitted about the plumes of bubbles as if they were playing in a Jacuzzi.

One of the traits of this species is that they pair off like buddies, and any time one of the pair gets speared, the other always comes back to find out what happened. Which means you're almost guaranteed to bag two in one go, especially if you're with a spearfishing buddy yourself.

By prior agreement, we all held our fire. We sat motionless in our underwater balcony seats watching the improvisations of these headliners, who had appeared on stage after the opening act of yellowtails had ended like a meteor shower.

In silhouette, every one of the greater amberjacks looked identical except for differences in size, yet when examined up close like this, each one clearly had its own unique personality. Some were unguardedly curious; others seemed to share this curiosity but couldn't quite get up the nerve for a closer peek. Still others seemed to mock these timid ones, strutting boldly forward and daring them to follow suit. Deliberately stopping short, they'd give us sidelong fisheye stares, then move away with a shake of their heads: "Oh, is *that* all?" But soon their curiosity got the better of them, and they would double back as if looking for something they'd forgotten.

And every one of them was a prime game fish of ten kilos or more.

Like a show you never tire of watching, we gazed on and on at the two dozen fish milling about before us. I soon felt I knew them so well I could give each of them a nickname.

Glancing at my pressure gauge, I decided we'd waited long enough. On my signal, we raised our guns and aimed at our closest targets. Spears flew; we pulled in our catch.

With three fish in hand and the rest of the school scattered, we slid a third of the way around the handrail in the opposite direction to their flight.

Soon they were back. Finding us in a new spot, they must have thought we were different people. Once again their curiosity got the better of them, providing the three of us in the balcony seats with an exciting second act.

For the third act we devised a new strategy: just two of us made the first strike, with the second shooter standing by to nab the mate of the first hit; then the first man reset his gun and joined the third waiting a short distance away to take in another pair—for a total of four in one act.

With ten greater amberjacks dangling from the handrail, the last of the actors in this underwater drama made their appearance: four blue sharks. They clearly had not come in response to our tapping. Rather, the death throes of the stricken fish had told them of unexpected events taking place in an unexpected place, and they'd come to investigate a possible feeding opportunity.

The three-meter sharks began circling about with their pectoral fins held stiffly downward, obviously excited over the prospect of a meal. The angels vanished beyond the curtain of water, yielding the stage to the four devils.

When one of the sharks came within range, I jabbed him hard in the snout with the tip of my spear gun. Startled by the spurt of blood, he and his companions backed off just long enough for us to cut loose two of our fish and release them into the current. As the bait drifted toward the bottom, the sharks went tearing after it. Meanwhile, we hastily gathered up the rest of our catch and headed for the surface. My two companions wormed their way up the base of the lighthouse on their bellies, the fish in their hands, and I backed up after them, keeping an eye out for the sharks.

Back at the surface, the ocean remained calm and sunny.

Our friends in the boat were eager to hear our tale, but I felt at a loss. How could one do justice to the drama we'd watched unfold from our special balcony seats twenty-three meters below? I felt like I'd returned not from the water a mere twenty-three meters down, but from a distant galaxy twenty-three million light years away.

ON THE TENNIS COURT

The sun was bright, but a chill breeze blew across the court, betraying the season.

My friend and I played two sets. Our matches usually ended in my favor, but this time I lost 6–4, 6–3. Afterwards we sat on the terrace beside the courts drinking lemonade-beer shandies.

"You let me win today," he said.

"The fire just wasn't in me."

"Got something on your mind? Do tell," he teased in his trademark lilt.

Hardly in the mood, I just stared straight ahead.

"Oh, so *that's* it," he said. "You've got love troubles."

He wasn't far off the mark, which made it all the more annoying.

This fellow, who tended to ooh and ahh effeminately over almost anything, came from a wealthy family that was much in the news a number of years back for its involvement in a loan scandal with a major bank. Since he and his relations all made a very good living off their real estate holdings, he never needed to hold down a job, and he hung out at the club nearly every day.

When he spoke in that falsetto voice, he came across as a namby-pamby rich kid, but every so often he'd shift into a normal way of speaking to say something serious, and then he'd seem like a completely different person.

From his diminutive stature and his speech mannerisms you'd hardly expect him to be the athletic type, but in the locker room he displayed a remarkably muscular physique, highly conditioned from head to toe—a product of his fourth-*dan* karate training.

For some reason, his swishy behavior disappeared whenever he mentioned karate.

"Am I right? Am I right?" he pressed, as if beating me at tennis gave him the right to probe. "I'm right, aren't I?"

"Is it that obvious?" I finally admitted. Maybe talking it out would make me feel better.

"So you broke up with someone? Just recently?"

"It shows, does it?"

"Well, I could sure tell your heart wasn't in your game," he said. "You know, the best thing is to just forget and move on. Quick as you can."

"It's not that easy." Now *I* was the one who sounded like a pansy.

He peered into his glass. "I know what you mean," he said without looking up. "At our age, breaking up can hit a guy pretty hard."

"Sounds like the voice of experience."

"Yeah."

He started to go on, but then seemed to think better of it. He leaned back in his chair and squinted at the sky.

Suddenly I remembered seeing him on the court with a woman the year before—big-boned, no girl certainly, but younger than him and obviously new to the game. Still, he played patiently at her level the entire afternoon. Then, when she'd had enough and retreated to the clubhouse for tea, he came around like a man set free, looking for someone else to play with.

"Women are fast, but it takes men at least six months," he said, still squinting into the blue. "To get over it, I mean."

"Six months?"

"Absolutely. And it's a long six months, too."

"I wouldn't be surprised if you're right."

"But ultimately, you always do manage to forget. And once you've done that, then even if something reminds you of her again, it doesn't matter any more."

"I don't know if I could stand being reminded after finally forgetting."

"No, really, it's no big deal once you've put it behind you. Of course there are exceptions. One guy I know got dumped by his girlfriend but just couldn't get over her. So when she broke up with the other guy three years later, he went after her and married her. I had to wonder, did that really make him happy? Boy, did we tease him, though. You see, when it comes right down to it, guys get more emotionally attached—a whole lot more than girls."

"You think so?"

"Sure. When a girl breaks up with a guy, the very next day it's ancient history. Even if she still loves him, like if they broke up for some other reason, the minute the next guy comes along, the past is gone and forgotten."

"Just like that, huh?"

"Oh, absolutely. Just like that," he said, nodding emphatically as he turned to face me. For some reason he was speaking in his karate voice. "So us guys've got to learn to forget more easily. We'd be fools not to."

"Six months for guys, but the next day for girls?"

"That's right. No doubt about it. The lucky bitches."

"Six months, you say," I repeated, trying to get a handle on what I was in for.

"Yep. How many months you got left?"

I didn't answer, but I was thinking: *Four and a half to go . . .*

All of a sudden, the shandy seemed to permeate every corner of my body.

Four and a half to go . . .

I repeated it to myself, letting it sink in. Meanwhile, he sat there, just waiting. He seemed to know exactly what I was thinking.

It struck me what a remarkable friend I had sitting next to me.

So this is how it's going to be.

Just then a cheer of mixed voices rose from one of the tennis courts; apparently someone had taken a point after a long rally.

Four and a half to go . . .

I repeated it in my mind one last time, then took a sip from my glass and raised my eyes high into the sky. Perhaps after a month and a half something was finally changing. Now, thanks to this unexpected exchange, I felt myself beginning to let go—just a little.

The cool, refreshing breeze continued to blow across the tennis courts awash in bright sunshine.

AT THE HARBOR IN WINTER

One evening near the end of December, I reached a convenient break in the writing I'd started after lunch, and decided to take a walk before dinner. On my way home I stopped in at the harbor. The sun was dropping beyond the horizon; the sky would soon be dark. A cold wind blew out of the north.

I found Christiansen working on his yacht in the slipway, meticulously sanding the hull. No one else was around. Rocking his large frame back and forth as he rubbed, he remained completely absorbed in his work, oblivious to my approach. I called out to him, and he turned to look, but after a quick smile and a nod he went right back to his sanding.

The season was over. No races were coming up during the winter, nor was it time to be making spring preparations. I sensed that something more than a work ethic was keeping him at his task until such an hour in the deserted harbor.

He worked like a man possessed, one hand rubbing the sandpaper vigorously over the boat's rounded bottom, the other sweeping back and forth across the sanded sections to check for roughness. Having nothing better to do, I stood there and watched him work.

We all knew what an avid yachtsman Christiansen was. An engineer by trade, he truly knew his stuff when it came to sailboats—which probably also explained why he was so unbending about certain rules.

When he became safety officer for the Yachting Association, inspections became extremely rigorous. With the tragic loss of two yachts and eleven crew still fresh in memory from the 1962 Hatsushima Race, he didn't hesitate to disqualify boats for the slightest defect in safety equipment. He once even "tested" a plywood hatch in the bow of a poorly maintained boat by jumping up and down on it—all meter-eighty, ninety kilos of him. When his foot went through, he barred the boat from the race.

On the other hand, when he crossed the Yokohama finish line in the 1958 Toba Race and learned his boat was the first one home, he was so happy he turned red in the face and bawled out loud.

Christiansen ignored me in the gathering dusk, applying himself single-mindedly to the bottom of his boat, almost as if he were trying to avoid something else. Suddenly I recalled a rumor I'd heard from the harbormaster early that autumn: Christiansen's Japanese wife had been diagnosed with cancer. I decided to ask about her.

He seemed to have been expecting exactly that question, and turned to look at me with an intense, haunted look in his eyes. "She has been died," he said in the halting Japanese I'd grown accustomed to hearing from him. At long last bringing his hands to a rest and tossing the sandpaper aside, he added in English, "Man loses much as he loves much." Then wanting to be sure I understood, he translated it for me into his awkward Japanese. "People, very much love, then very much lose. Is sadness."

His large eyes blinked furiously as he spoke, and in spite of the dusk I caught the glint of a tear in his eyes.

Gazing back at him awkwardly, not quite sure what to say, I pictured the woman I'd met only once or twice. She hadn't been a particularly striking or beautiful woman, and she'd always looked a little peaked—no doubt from battling her hidden illness.

"I'm so sorry," I said.

But even before I'd finished saying it, almost as if to cut me off, the tall blond man turned away, toward the sea. Spreading his arms wide, he took a single deep breath and slowly let it out into the chill north wind.

"Hmm, smells good!" he said, once again in English.

I nodded in silence and followed suit, filling my lungs with the bracing twilight air. The winter wind had that subtle burnt smell I always associate with the coldest season of the year.

How much could I really understand of what Christiansen was going through in his time of grief? What more could I do, besides stand there with him before the darkening sea and join him in a long, deep breath of wintry air?

NAVIGATION

The first time I experienced the panic of being lost was the day I started grade school. After the welcoming ceremony in the auditorium, my mother and I proceeded to my assigned classroom, but while everybody was still waiting for the teacher to arrive, I decided I wanted to explore. I slipped out into the hallway when my mother wasn't looking, and followed my curiosity one way and another until all of a sudden I realized I had no idea how to find my way back.

It was only a grade school, but to the eyes of a small child seeing the place for the first time in his life, it was a sprawling complex, big enough to paralyze all sense of direction. I can still remember the dizzying panic that came over me; I *knew* I was in trouble—and terrified that I might be lost and forgotten for all eternity.

I pulled myself together and concentrated on remembering anything that had caught my eye along the way. In the end, the open door to a hospital-like room where I could see a woman wearing a white uniform served to point me in the right direction.

I don't know how long I'd been gone, but it was long enough for my mother to be looking very worried when she saw me and demanded, "Where've you been?"

I had just returned from the very brink of extinction, a miraculous survivor, but I replied with cocky nonchalance, "Oh, I just went on a little walk."

Ever since, even long after reaching adulthood, whenever I come upon a weeping child who's lost his way or become separated from his parent, I always experience a deep sense of empathy that goes well beyond merely feeling sorry for the youngster.

Once, on vacation, I went with my family to the lighthouse at Irozaki, a magnificent scenic cape on the southern tip of the Izu Peninsula, which I'd seen many times from sea level when sailing past it during yacht races. For some reason my third boy decided to throw a tantrum and refused to walk the kilometer or so we had to hike to reach the viewpoint, so afterwards, as punishment, I made him stand at the side of the parking lot as we pulled out—fully intending, of course, to circle back in a minute or two to pick him up. But as I watched out the rear window and saw him standing there on the verge of tears, I was suddenly overcome by an irrational fear that we might lose him forever. Though in retrospect it seems rather irresolute of me, I quickly told my wife to back the car up and let him in.

Having learned my lesson the first time I got lost, I took care after that not to get into such a frightening situation again. But in later years, on two separate occasions, I found myself in circumstances where I genuinely feared I might not come back alive.

The summer of my sophomore year in college, I visited the Myoko Kogen highlands, and stayed at the mountain lodge my school owned there. One day I set out to climb Mt. Myoko with a fellow visitor. Considering that my companion was a member of the swim team, he proved to have surprisingly little stamina; about a fifth of the way from the summit, he told me he'd had it, and headed back down the mountain.

Unfortunately, the summit was socked in with clouds when I arrived, and there was no view, so I immediately started back down, taking the path for Tsubame Hot Springs that descended at right angles to the trail I'd just come up. Climbing to the summit, descending to Tsubame, and hiking back to Myoko Kogen along the foot of the mountain would make a total distance of about forty kilometers, but I was on the soccer team and in good shape, so I felt confident.

Part of the way down I ran into dense fog, which soon gave way to drizzle. I trekked on, not letting the rain bother me, but after a while I came to a split in the trail where the signpost pointing to Tsubame was lying on the ground, and I apparently made the wrong guess. To make matters worse, when I finally realized my mistake and doubled back after a considerable distance, I made another wrong turn at a fork I hadn't noticed when I came. That path turned out to be a dead end, which I suppose was fortunate, but as I doubled back yet again, I was starting to become thoroughly confused. In desperation, I shouted for help a couple of times, hoping there might be someone within earshot, but that only made me feel even more anxious, so I quickly gave it up.

I remembered my parents warning me when I was little about people being spirited away by the gods or supernatural creatures, and I began to think this must be the sort of thing that gave rise to such stories. Getting lost badly enough to need a rescue team wasn't just a calamity that happened to somebody else; for the first time in my life, I realized it could happen to me.

The cold worried me more than fatigue. In my ignorance, I'd taken the mountain much too lightly and come hopelessly underdressed. A polo shirt and shorts had seemed fine when I set out that hot summer morning.

On the bright side, visibility had improved with the change from fog to light rain. Yet even for such a remote mountain area, it bothered me that I hadn't seen a single other person since leaving the summit, no matter how far I walked.

Checking my watch, I reminded myself that if all else failed, I still had time to climb back to the summit and descend the path I'd originally come up. I immediately felt much better. When I got back to the spot where I'd made my original mistake, I calmly reassessed my choices, and this time selected the correct trail to Tsubame. Thanks to the way I was dressed and the cool drizzle, I wasn't even sweating when I arrived—in spite of all the walking I'd done.

A row of inns greeted me as I entered the village, and off-season visitors who had come for the hot-spring cure were strolling about. After my previous state of agitation, the tranquil atmosphere seemed utterly surreal. I stood gazing at the peaceful scene, a secret joy surging through my body—the ecstatic relief of a miraculous survivor returned from the brink of extinction.

I went to an inn that caught my fancy and asked the price of a meal. Since I had enough money on me, I stepped inside and ordered an early supper. I'll never forget the flavor of the mountain trout I had there, a pleasure as keen as the starvation I would have endured on the road to death had I lost my way forever on that mountain trail. Nothing could be more commonplace, of course, than the notion that food sustains one's existence, yet each and every bite reminded me anew of this simple truth.

When I finished eating, I laced up the canvas mountain boots I'd borrowed that morning at the college lodge, and left the inn behind. My spirits were high; I pictured myself back at the lodge, splurging on some saké to go with a second supper.

But soon I found myself facing another unexpected test. The trail I'd been directed to follow led to a tunnel—a crude mineshaft of a hole framed with only rough-hewn timbers for support, obviously something local work gangs had cobbled together. I could see that it went all the way through the hill, but there wasn't a single light anywhere along the entire passage, and the ceiling hung low enough for me to hit my head at every step. To try the courage of anyone who had made it this far, a narrow path veered off right before the mouth of the tunnel, presumably circling the hill to the far side. The tunnel itself was maybe two hundred meters long, but this other path promised a hike of four or five times that distance around the mountainside.

The sun was tilting low in the sky, and the tunnel looked as though it might collapse under the weight of nightfall. If the shaft caved in on me, not a soul would ever know. Maybe the tunnel was a final test of my good fortune for the day?

I stood there at the entrance a few seconds more, peering into the blackness, listening for anything hidden in the depths. Then, crouching low for the dash, I took off like a scared rabbit and raced pell-mell over the bumpy tunnel floor. When I emerged into open air again, the far side of the hill was already deep in twilight.

Terror and anxiety can cause painful stomach cramps, as I know all too well from getting an entire boat and her crew lost in the middle of the Pacific.

When my brother Yujiro and I were preparing to enter his yacht in the 1965

TransPac race, I unwisely agreed to be navigator after the scheduled crewman dropped out at the last minute. "Not to worry," the fellow assured me. "Navigation's a breeze. Especially the kind fishermen use. Any fool can learn it in no time at all. So long as your sextant's in good working order, you can't go wrong."

As I recalled, though, when this same fellow served as my navigator in the 1962 South China Sea Yacht Race, he skipped the sextant and instead tuned his large transistor radio to a Manila station playing Latin guitar music, turning it this way and that until he found the strongest signal. Then he'd tell us to bear in that direction.

At a pre-race meeting, I told the others what the man had said, and the next thing I knew I'd been volunteered for the job. In exchange, I wouldn't have to stand regular watch; I could decide for myself when to take my sightings or man the wheel. Since I always hated disturbing my regular sleep, it seemed well worth considering.

And that's how I wound up as a hastily self-taught novice navigator for my second TransPac. While the rest of the crew was busy readying the boat after our arrival in California, I stayed by the hotel pool drinking daiquiris as I read and re-read the book on celestial navigation I'd brought from Japan. That afternoon on the pool terrace overlooking the Pacific, I practiced sighting the horizon by sextant to determine the coordinates of the hotel. And I knew I'd be taking many, many sightings during the course of our voyage, so I copied out the complicated formulas over and over onto separate sheets of paper. Then when the time came, all I had to do was fill in the blanks from my readings and do the calculations. What could go wrong?

This being our second TransPac, I expected smoother sailing than our first, but as things turned out, nothing seemed to go right at all.

When we were ready to cast off from San Pedro Harbor and head for the starting line, the auxiliary motor refused to turn over. Of course, once the race began, we'd be strictly under sails, but that wasn't going to get us to the line in time for the gun. Much to our embarrassment, we had to ask a spectator boat headed that way to give us a tow.

Our actual start was just as disappointing. We had aboard the harbormaster who looked after my brother's boat in Honolulu—a man of advancing years named Foster—and we'd agreed to let him do the honors at the wheel, but his repeated flubs put us dead last across the starting line.

The sun was peeking through the clouds as we sailed past Santa Catalina, so I decided this was a good chance for a warm-up. I brought out my sextant to take a sighting, but for some reason the numbers I plugged into my formulas failed to give our position. Of course, I could see Santa Catalina right there in front of me, so I knew our position perfectly well, but my calculations weren't even close to the island on the chart. I grabbed a fresh sheet and started over, but the results were the same.

A numbing sense of panic shot through me, but I made sure not to show my agitation. On the pretext of testing the radio, I called the navigator aboard the *Chita*, a fellow Japanese boat, and asked him whether a minute of latitude was equal to one land mile or one nautical mile. I thought that might be where I was going wrong.

The man burst out laughing. "Isn't it kind of late to be asking that?" he asked. "You sure you're not in over your head?"

He was absolutely right, of course, but I was starting to feel a bit desperate. I asked him to stay on the radio while I went through my calculations again, only to wind up with exactly the same answer as before.

I could hardly afford to worry about appearances any more. I begged him to tell me what I was doing wrong, but it turned out he was using the more involved Yonemura method so we were basically speaking different languages.

"To begin with," he said, not mincing his words, "that old fishermen's system is nothing but kid's stuff. You're really pushing your luck if you think you can find your way across the big, wide Pacific with something like that."

Oh, well, I told myself. I just need to stay calm and keep trying. I'll get it right eventually. But I was thankful when the clouds soon covered up the sun.

Two days later as we made way in an offshoot of the cold Humboldt Current, the sun finally showed its face again. I went to retrieve my sextant and prayed, but my results were just as useless as before.

I felt undone. If this kept up and I never found our boat's correct position, we could sail right past Hawaii. Even if we realized it and turned back, it would mean having to sail directly into the trade winds and the large swells they created. A cold shudder traveled up and down my back.

The skies remained overcast for the next two days. In their boredom, the crew began wondering out loud about our position. I cringed every time I heard someone say, "How far do you suppose we've come?" or "I wonder whereabouts this is."

We'd also streamed a log from the stern, but estimating our progress from those readings meant an increasing margin of error the farther we went. Veteran navigators on the other boats were no doubt taking advantage of even the briefest appearance of the sun to get sightings and report their accurate positions during the scheduled roll calls. Meanwhile, I was forced to report our position based on primitive dead reckoning, which made it look as though we were making a lot more progress than we really were.

"Even if we discount what the log gives us by twenty percent, we're still making great headway," someone said gleefully, though to me his words felt like a stab in the gut.

"Hey, navigator! We've got sunshine!"

How I dreaded those words! I'd pretend to be asleep in my bunk, or justify my inaction by dismissing the speaker as an ignoramus. "Look," I'd say. "Sighting the sun once doesn't do me any good. I have to get two readings within a set period of time."

And so it went until one afternoon, lo and behold, we caught sight of another boat in the fleet sailing not far away. It was a gift from heaven. I immediately ordered a crewman up the mast to see if he could make out the number on the sail. If we could identify this boat, I could compare the position she reported during the daily roll call with my own dead reckoning. It was only a stopgap, but for the moment it was all I had.

The gods, however, did not smile upon my scheme: despite his best efforts, the man on the mast couldn't make out the sail number through his binoculars. With no accurate fix on our position, our only other option was to continue sailing southwest until we reached the same latitude as Honolulu, then sail due west by jibing back and forth. Fortunately, my book on celestial navigation described how to determine latitude from just the altitude of the North Star.

Of course, sailing down the latitude might sound easy in theory, but there was no telling how well it would work in practice for us. Even if we started jibing to head due west at Honolulu's latitude, we still had no way of knowing how much farther we had to go in terms of longitude. Not only that, jibing in heavy weather could be extremely dangerous, and if caution made us overextend a leg, we could wind up bypassing our destination in the middle of a squall or the black of night.

Then a new crisis reared its head. To fill in for a seasick crewman, my brother Yujiro had gallantly agreed to extend his watch through the night, but he got so chilled that his chronic appendicitis flared up. Soon he was doubled over in pain, and nothing seemed to help. One of the crew had brought along some moxa, so he sat with my brother in the cabin for hours on end, applying the herb to the appropriate therapeutic points and burning it, but to no effect. Yujiro toughed it out for two full days without relief before we decided it was too risky to wait any longer. We radioed the committee boat accompanying the fleet for a medical evacuation.

But in order to transfer my brother to the Coast Guard ship, we would have to rendezvous somewhere on the high seas, and for that to happen I had to be able to give them our accurate position. A person's life—the life of my very own, only brother—had now come to rest on my dubious navigational skills. It had been a long time since I'd prayed as hard as I did then.

Perhaps thanks to those prayers, we quite miraculously met up with the Coast Guard vessel at daybreak the next morning. Since we did at least know our latitude, the rest was simply a matter of approaching from east and west; we weren't exactly attempting the impossible. Still, my confidence was completely shattered by then, and I truly believed that guardian deities or ancestral spirits must have intervened on my brother's behalf.

I breathed a genuine sigh of relief when I saw my brother safely aboard the emergency launch sent to make the transfer, but I also couldn't help wondering what troubles might still lie ahead. I was sorely tempted to ask the Coast Guard for our precise current coordinates, but I knew this would disqualify us from the race. Then it hit me as we moved away that they couldn't possibly imagine we were out there in the middle of the Pacific sailing blind, so I might have been able to broach the subject in passing somehow. As I fretted over this missed opportunity, I felt my stomach clenching into a painful knot.

Complications continued.

Aboard the Coast Guard ship, a warm room and medicine quickly cleared up my brother's abdominal pain. The doctor told him he'd be fine so long as he avoided getting chilled again. And since he'd traveled all the way from Japan for the TransPac, they offered to return him to our boat so he could complete the race. When word came over the radio, the rest of the crew gave a happy cheer, but my own spirits sank.

For the next two days, I tried everything I could think of to get a better fix on our position, but to no avail. Our two vessels never caught sight of each other. The Coast Guard finally gave up in exasperation, and steamed off for Honolulu with my brother aboard. Through it all, I had to endure a constant stream of ragging from Yujiro over the radiotelephone about my incompetence as a navigator.

I was beside myself. Under the abnormal weather conditions the Pacific was experiencing that year, the sun continued to hide its face even as we neared Hawaii. I pinned my hopes on the North Star at night, but sighting that tiny, dim star was far more difficult than sighting the sun. At least the winds remained strong and drove the boat at a brisk pace, but since I still couldn't get a fix on our longitude, I had no way of knowing how far west we had come. I began genuinely to fear that we might sail right past the islands.

For the first time in my life, I was experiencing stress cramps of the kind I'd heard others describe. Even though I hadn't touched a drop of alcohol for days, an unrelenting coil of pain remained lodged in the pit of my stomach.

By this time, of course, the entire crew realized that my quick-and-dirty attempt to learn how to navigate had been a bust, and when they saw me moping about without the consolation of booze they genuinely felt sorry for me. Those who had crewed with me on the South China Sea race told me not to worry. We'd soon be close enough to find Honolulu on the radio. We could figure out our course that way and make our turn. But I found small comfort in such reassurances. I'd had quite a bit more sailing experience than my easygoing companions, and I knew anything could happen at sea. The more I thought about the dire possibilities, the less I slept at night.

Not knowing our longitude meant we had no idea how far we still had to go before reaching the finish in Honolulu. I continued to estimate our position based on readings from the log, but the margin of error was far too great by this time for my calculations to be anything but stabs in the dark. I learned afterwards that my reckonings were off by an average of ten miles a day—which of course accounted for our failure to meet up with the Coast Guard ship when they offered to return my brother.

Out of consideration for me, the Japanese members of the crew refrained from showing their concern. But after I blew my second and third attempts to make landfall, the Americans aboard grew quite distraught. Too demoralized to help with anything, Foster and his nephew David sat themselves down on the deck near the bow and refused to budge. All they did was stare vacantly at the horizon and let out one long sigh of despair after another.

Each time I brought out the sextant, my own hopes also diminishing, they'd look at me with pleading eyes and ask, "Where are we? Where are we?" Eventually Foster grew so overwrought at the prospect of being lost at sea for good that he declared he was going to radio the Coast Guard for a rescue. This caused immediate outrage among the rest of the crew: it'd be a disaster if the old geezer called the Coast Guard behind our backs and got us disqualified after coming all this way. They talked seriously about locking Foster in the head, but since that was hardly practicable in the cramped quarters on board, someone secretly removed a wire from the radio when Foster wasn't looking.

By now the committee boat had reached Honolulu to await the arrival of the fleet. Since I had to tell them some position during daily roll calls, I continued to feed them my hopelessly inaccurate guesses based on the log, which were then reported in the local newspaper. When the reports suggested we might arrive as early as that afternoon, my brother and our friends in Honolulu all traipsed down to the harbor to welcome us, only to go home disappointed when we failed to show.

Needless to say, not knowing when we might arrive was an even greater frustration for those of us on the boat. When the coordinates I gave said we should be making landfall by evening at the latest, we fixed our eyes on the horizon searching for any sign of land. But every time somebody raised a cry, the "island" would turn out to be a cloud. Most of the crew laughed it off, but as navigator, my stomach twisted into a tighter and tighter knot with each false alarm.

This kind of psychosomatic stomach pain is all the more unpleasant because it makes you feel bloated and takes away your appetite. Feeling sorry for me, one of the guys poured me an aperitif, but a single sip was all I could stomach. I chided myself for being so thin-skinned and not bearing up to the stress of responsibility, but of course this did nothing to make me feel the least bit better.

———

Then crewman Okazaki discovered an invaluable piece of information in the radio manual: at certain hours on a certain frequency, Makapu'u Point at the eastern end of Oahu broadcasts a signal that reaches 150 miles out to sea. If we could capture that signal, I could get a fairly accurate fix on our position just by taking a new sighting to determine our latitude. Perhaps we were not destined to become the lost children of the Pacific after all.

I dialed in the frequency given in the manual. Sure enough, there was the signal. It was as if a bright light had lit up over my dim chart table. That night, with the boat rolling violently to and fro, I tethered myself to the doghouse and peered intently at the northern sky, sextant in hand, waiting for a glimpse of Polaris. Luckily, there were more breaks in the clouds than usual, and shortly after 10:00 P.M. I got my reading. At long last, I knew where we were; I calculated our exact coordinates.

However much my dead reckoning had overstated our progress, I knew we had to be getting pretty close, and I was right. We were east of Molokai—a bit farther south than we wanted to be, right above Maui. A squall came over, severely limiting visibility, but on our present course we'd soon be nearing the lighthouse on the island's northern coast.

Sadly, because of all my false alarms, no one took me seriously when I said we needed to change direction. My calculations were never right anyway, they said, so we might as well stay on our present heading a while longer. But I fretted. Having no detailed charts of the coastline, there was no telling where we might ride up onto a hidden reef if we got too close under these conditions.

We emerged from the squall a short while later and immediately saw the lighthouse beacon flash off our port bow. As visibility continued to improve, we realized how dangerously close we were to the waves crashing against the foot of the cliff beneath the lighthouse. We executed a frantic jibe; while others attended to some trouble with the mainsheet, I kept a sharp eye on the pounding surf and suffered through more stomach pains.

When I plotted our course from the foot of the lighthouse after we completed the turn, I discovered to my great delight that we would have almost straight sailing to Koko Head on the southeast corner of Oahu. I could now leave the rest of the passage to the others.

The boat sailed into the Molokai Channel at daybreak, and the sun climbing into the sky behind us soon brightened Koko Head off in the distance.

"All right! We're home free, now!" one of the guys exclaimed, then added half in jest, "I guess even our navigator gets it right once in a while."

Foster and his nephew had regained their color, and the cook now brought out the last of the beer so everyone could start celebrating our impending finish. But somehow, even as I watched Koko Head slowly grow nearer, I wasn't in the mood for drinking. We'd conquered the vast Pacific, our destination now lay right under our noses, yet for some reason that wrenching pain still held its grip on my stomach.

It's funny, though: once we'd actually crossed the finish line and tied up at the dock, the moment I leapt ashore and had a mai tai thrust into my hands, the pain was gone and forgotten.

The welcoming committee included my brother, who had been kept from completing the race by my ineptitude. Next to him stood my local girlfriend, her lips in a pout, sorely upset at being stood up so many times when she came to the harbor bearing celebratory drinks based on my erroneous reports. Feeling awkward, I avoided looking either of them in the eye and just sipped at my mai tai.

I later learned the embarrassingly simple reason why I could never calculate our position: I neglected to compensate for daylight-saving time, which was in effect at the start of the race; this meant my conversions to Greenwich Mean

Time were always one hour off. Be that as it may, I do not intend to take on the position of boat's navigator ever again.

When a Russian cosmonaut whose space capsule malfunctioned beyond recovery was told in a final transmission from the Secretary-General of the Communist Party that he was to be awarded a prestigious medal, the doomed man is said to have screamed, "Forget the damn medal! Just get me back alive!" Thanks to my second TransPac, I think I can identify a little more closely with that cosmonaut than most people can.

THE ANGEL OF DEATH

The Angel of Death is a concept common to people in all countries, but the specific image any given person has seems to vary a great deal. A number of my own acquaintances claim they've seen the Angel of Death, and every one of them has described the face and figure quite differently. Since no Angel of Death would put in an appearance without connection to an actual death, perhaps the shape assumed depends on the death and how it relates to the onlooker.

An important, in fact essential, distinction must be made between the Angel of Death and a ghost: a ghost is in effect a decedent's own alter ego, while the Angel of Death is a separate agent come to bring on and see out the dying process.

Meeting the Angel of Death may be frightening, but it can also be a blessing, for it allows people to experience the full texture of the death more distinctly. Of course, whether the experience changes their lives from that time onward depends entirely on the individual.

A friend I've hung out with a lot over the years told me he once saw the Angel of Death as a child.

His dog died when he was in the third grade. He had loved the dog dearly and couldn't bear to let it go, yet even as a child he understood that it wasn't something he could keep. After thinking carefully about how he wanted to bury it, he decided he would return it to the sea, where he'd originally found it as a puppy.

It was winter when the dog died, and the beach was a long way away, so he thought he'd drop it off a nearby bridge into the Edogawa River and let the current carry it back to the sea. He placed the dog's cold body in a sturdy cardboard box, closed the flaps, then loaded it onto the luggage rack of his bicycle and set out for the river.

That part of Tokyo wasn't so densely populated in those days, and by evening the streets were almost empty. My friend stopped at the foot of the bridge and waited for pedestrian traffic to clear before walking his bicycle to the middle of the span. Once there, he looked in both directions again to make sure he was still alone before unstrapping the box. It was almost too much of an armful for a boy his size, but he managed to lift it from the bicycle rack up onto the railing of the bridge. Then, just as he was about to push it over the side, he heard a voice behind him.

He spun around with a start to find a woman with long, thick hair falling over her shoulders standing right behind him. In spite of the season, she was wearing a light summer kimono.

"Did you lose a friend?" she said very gently.

He opened his mouth to answer, but suddenly a wave of terror came over him and, shoving the box over the rail, he grabbed his bicycle and took off running.

When he came to the end of the bridge, he screwed up his courage and turned back for another look. In the deepening winter twilight, he could just make out the pale, distant form of the woman's summer kimono midway across the deserted bridge.

"It couldn't have been an ordinary person," my friend insisted. "I mean, I closed that box up good and tight. Nobody could've known there was a dead dog inside. And her voice, it was the most unbelievably tender voice I've ever heard. No way could it have come from an ordinary person. No human alive has that kind of tenderness in them."

Assuming that the woman was indeed the Angel of Death, why would she speak with such extraordinary tenderness at moments like that?

THE MANTA IN THE KERAMAS

While the rest of us were filling our air tanks and getting the boat ready, Oi spent his time trying to straighten the shaft of his spear, alternately scrutinizing it and pounding on it from every angle. When he was finally satisfied with the shaft, he set about sharpening the tip with a whetstone.

Each time I paused to check on his progress, he repeated the same explanation. "M-m-my eyes are so bad," he'd stutter, "the slightest bend m-m-makes me m-m-miss my target."

Shiroma's boat was in pathetic shape, and neither he nor his seasoned diver friends in their scraped and torn wet suits were much for appearances either. But this fellow Oi, whom I'd met that day for the first time, wore the most tattered suit of them all. The nylon fishing line he'd used to mend the tears in it marked him as a genuine old hand at deep-sea diving.

Oi needed corrective lenses in his facemask for near-sighted astigmatism. But instead of getting a mask with built-in correction, as other divers who had poor eyesight did, he'd removed the earpieces from an old pair of glasses and wedged the lens frame into a large regular mask with scraps of cloth to hold it in place.

Between that and the single-minded, squinty-eyed attention he gave to his spear, I wondered if perhaps, unlike the others, his entire family's livelihood was at stake in the underwater hunt on which we were about to embark.

The compressor was giving us trouble and some parts required replacing, so the preliminaries dragged on longer than expected. I grew impatient. Without bothering to put on my wet suit, I dived into the water with just facemask, snorkel, and fins, and swam out a short distance from the end of the pier.

The main islands of Japan were still under a late spring chill, but here in the Kerama Islands of Okinawa, summer was in the air. The bright sky and sparkling sea, washed with a warm southwesterly breeze, brought back memories of previous trips, and I was raring to go. I couldn't bear to let another hour go by just sitting there listening to the din of the compressor.

The water proved to be warm as well, fresh as a new summer against my skin.

The tide happened to be high, inviting a school of sixty- to seventy-centimeter emperors into the quiet channel scarcely fifty meters from the pier. After hurrying back to retrieve my spear gun, I circled wide to seaward and approached the school from up-current, easily taking the biggest of the lot. The others quickly scattered, but then predictably regrouped, circling around the inner part of the inlet to the other side of the rock where I lay in wait—at which point I speared another. In less than ten minutes of free diving, I'd bagged two very considerable prizes.

"In full form already, I see," said Shiroma when I got back to the boat.

Oi looked at me, then at the fish lying on the deck. "Pretty impressive! That's about as big as these suckers get, you know," he said, nodding earnestly.

My good fortune continued when we got to Kubajima. It wasn't a spot where you normally expected to see migratory species, but a confluence of tides and currents brought a meter-long giant trevally into my sights, and I nabbed it. I also picked up a painted spiny lobster, and speared two coral red trout—considered the tastiest fish in Okinawan waters. Most of the others did reasonably well, too. Only poor Oi had nothing to show.

"I n-never expected to see a giant trevally around here. You're really q-q-quite the hunter," Oi congratulated me, still cocking a baffled head over his own bad luck.

After that I saw him fussing with his spear again, raising it to eye level to check for kinks in the shaft, clicking his tongue as he pounded on one spot or another to straighten it.

"Did your spear behave so badly?" I teased.

"Actually, it's not so much the spear as these glasses," he said with a crooked grin, head cocked to one side again.

I was about to suggest he get some proper prescription goggles, but not knowing anything about his work or personal circumstances on shore, I kept my mouth shut.

Once a spear gets bent, it can never truly be straightened again, even if you take it to a pro. Yet Oi seemed determined to make do with this one, hammering at it himself, trying to cut corners. More than likely, prescription goggles were beyond his means.

As we were making our way to Shimonoze for another dive, I spied them first: a pair of large dorsal fins cutting the surface thirty meters to starboard. My first thought was sharks, but when the two fins remained perfectly synchronized as they appeared and disappeared among the waves, I realized it had to be a manta. Judging from the size of the fins, the creature had to be at least two meters across.

I'd seen a manta once before, from the terrace of a bungalow on Bora Bora in Tahiti. Attracted by the light of the torches set along the water's edge, the manta spent the entire night doing back flip after back flip beneath the terrace. It would be a whole new experience to see a manta at close quarters in the water. I'd stripped off my wet suit and didn't want to lose time putting it back on, so again I dived in with just a facemask, snorkel, and fins.

The manta was bouncing up and down on seas of one to two meters, so it was hard to get a fix on exactly where it was. I suppose it had its reasons for surfing like that, but as it dipped in and out of the foaming crests I could barely keep it in sight, until suddenly I found it right in front of me, no more than four or five meters away. It had in fact just that moment turned in my direction, and I was gazing straight into its huge maw, open wide to gather plankton and small fish. At first it looked more like a precisely engineered plastic replica than a real live fish.

But then a chill went down my spine as I watched it close and open its mouth.

The object before me, the object with which I shared this small patch of water, was most definitely a living fish—a gigantic, mind-boggling monster of a living fish. The creature's mouth extended wider than my shoulders, big enough to swallow my head in a single gulp. I could see blue water beyond the open gills on either side of the massive mouth cavity, like peering through a coarse reed blind, and this made the creature even more frightening.

I knew that mantas had no stingers in their tails, and I could see no menacing teeth, even this close to its open mouth. Still, staring down that enormous creature without even the protection of a wet suit or gloves took all the courage I had in me.

I gazed at its gray back and bluish white belly. What would its skin feel like? I've never been particularly fond of touching fish with my bare hands; in fact, their typically slimy, squirmy texture makes my skin crawl. But the figure before me resembled no normal fish, nor any other living creature I'd ever seen. It did not seem real.

As I kept my distance and studied the manta, I had the distinct impression that it was sizing me up, too, trying to decide whether to just go on by.

It reminded me of one of my visits to Minamijima in the Ogasawaras. Some friends and I were swimming through a narrow channel into the cove known as the Shark Pond. Just as we got to the narrows, I saw something about the size of a blanket gliding toward me from the other direction, and I realized it was a stingray. For an instant, I wondered how we'd fend off such a large opponent with a lethal stinger in its tail, but then the stingray took a sudden dip, like an aircraft taking evasive action after a warning from the tower, and swept by right below us, almost touching our bellies as it went.

Suddenly a large black shadow shot past me in the direction of the manta.

For a split second I thought it might be a shark or some other big fish. But no, it was Oi in his wet suit, swimming straight for the manta at full speed. Obviously startled by this sudden intrusion, the manta performed a diagonal back flip and flew off in the opposite direction into the deep.

Oi had come from a strange angle. Was he actually after something else? I quickly scanned the vicinity but saw nothing. Without waiting for him, I swam on back to the boat.

"What was Oi after?" I asked.

"He wanted to see the manta," said Shiroma.

Soon Oi returned. "Darn," he said, still breathing hard. "I was too late. I sure would have liked to see the thing up close."

"To see *what* up close?" I asked, bewildered.

"The manta. That's what it was, right? I mean, I saw two identical fins side by side." He raised both hands and waved his fingers as he spoke.

"But you were right beside—"

I stopped myself. Once again I felt like telling him he should forget about fixing his spear and just get some proper goggles, but I decided to let it drop.

We headed on to Shimonoze for another dive, but there, too, Oi alone came up empty-handed.

If I ever go diving with Oi again, and he still fails to catch anything, even at the risk of offending him, I think I'll have to make him a gift of a brand new spear—or better yet, a pair of prescription goggles.

PERIL IN SUMMER

Before my first child was born, I decided if it was a boy I'd name him Umihiko—after Umisachihiko, "he who is blessed by the sea," from an ancient Japanese folktale. Then I'd have to name the next boy Yamahiko—after Yamasachihiko, "he who is blessed by the mountains," from the same legend. This was before I'd given much thought to how many children we wanted, or to the possibility that we might easily get girls instead, so it was not a very carefully considered plan. But in any event, that was my thinking at the time.

As things turned out, we ended up with four boys—though none of them are named after the legendary brothers.

When I mentioned my plan to my wife's flower-arranging teacher, she immediately wrote down the names to count out the strokes in the Japanese characters and declared it a terrible idea. I started to argue, but she cut me off, saying people pooh-poohed name divination only because they didn't know what a terrible burden a name could be. Once I understood how serious the choice of a name was, she said, I wouldn't dare inflict names upon my dear little children based on some passing flight of fancy. Then she told me about Keishu Nakajima, the man who had taught her how important names were.

I knew that my own father had consulted an older acquaintance well versed in such things to select my name before I was born, so I decided it might be worth going to see this Mr. Nakajima. He lived in a hilly section of nearby Shichiriga-hama.

He turned out to be a most interesting man. When I arrived, he invited me into the yard and proudly demonstrated his skill with a samurai sword before launching into a discourse on names and naming. His thesis was quite straightforward: name divination is essentially a form of statistics. Only after sizing up a person's life can we know whether his given name was good or bad. Compiling and analyzing the data supplied by cumulative experience ultimately teaches us the correct way to select names.

Nakajima originally learned the principles of name divination from a Buddhist priest in Kyoto, but he was young at the time and didn't really take them very seriously. Then, during the war, he was drafted into the army and sent as a company commander to a fiercely contested battlefront in North China. He started checking the names of the men he lost in combat, and they all came up bad. When reinforcements arrived, he'd look over their names and joke that so-and-so would get killed—and often he'd be right. Unnerved by his uncanny prescience, the men asked him what was going on. Pretty soon the ones with problem names started asking him to find new ones for them, and they officially changed their names right there at the front.

I didn't ask if that curtailed the combat deaths and everyone got home safely.

After the war, Nakajima taught at a private girls' school in Kyoto. He decided to analyze his students' names and follow up on how they did after graduation. Sure enough, the ones whose names spelled trouble had difficult lives. They got divorced, or they never got married, or they married into unfortunate families, or they became estranged from their children. In the end, he was utterly convinced that everything in a person's life occurs according to what his or her name predicts.

"Once I saw that," he said, "I knew I had to use my knowledge to help people."

The moral of the story was plain as day. I decided then and there to abandon all romantic notions of naming my sons after a legendary fisherman and hunter, and asked Nakajima to select names for them based on his methods. So it is that all four of my boys bear names he divined—as it happens, rather stiff ones, like the priestly titles of Buddhist monks.

And so it is, too, that I've come to hold considerable respect for name divination and other schemes for looking into the future, which remain mysteries to the layperson. Not that I buy into such methodologies completely. As someone who fancies himself an intellectual, I lend these systems only so much credence. It depends a good deal on personal convenience.

For example, when some system tells me I shouldn't travel in a certain direction at a certain time, I follow the advice if my schedule permits; but if I simply can't adjust my schedule, I proceed as originally planned—and try not to let the possibility of repercussions weigh too heavily on my mind.

Filipino opposition leader Benigno "Ninoy" Aquino was a close friend of mine. When he made plans to return to Manila from exile in Boston prior to his assassination, my wife consulted the charts to calculate his personal *ki* and his auspicious and inauspicious directions. She immediately came to me saying that with this and that and the other signs all coming up together, the timing could hardly be worse for him to travel to the Philippines. Rumors had been circulating for some time that President Marcos wanted Ninoy killed, and she was worried that if he flew home as planned, the worst possible fate would befall him.

She got me so concerned that when I called Ninoy in Boston on other business, I took the opportunity to explain the danger. I urged him to move his homecoming back, if possible, to the following month. Surely there was no hurry to rush home right this minute, I pointed out, after having spent eight years in prison and three in exile.

But convincing someone from another culture, and in my limited English, proved too difficult. I didn't have the slightest idea how to begin explaining about *ki* or auspicious directions—something that involved a whole lot more than naming points on a compass.

"At any rate, just take it from me," I finally said. "It's not a good idea for you to move in that direction on that day. It's extremely dangerous."

"Dangerous because of what?" he replied, which was of course a natural thing to ask.

I tried to explain that there were principles corrolating time and directions and human movements from a kind of statistical summation of human experience.

"If the system really works, then whoever figured it out deserves a Nobel Prize," Ninoy said.

"This is much too ancient for a Nobel," I said.

"Any chance the person who figured it out was a Zen priest?"

Ninoy had long held an interest in Zen Buddhism, so perhaps if I'd simply said yes at that point, he'd have given more credit to my warning and done as I urged. The vague answer I gave instead was hardly persuasive.

"So you're basically talking about superstition, right?" he said. "Like a gypsy looking into a crystal ball. I never knew your wife was into that sort of thing."

And that was the end of that. The entire world witnessed the subsequent result.

The very last time I spoke with Ninoy, he'd just gotten off the phone with a colleague in New York who had told him about a specific assassination plot against him.

"The chances I'll survive the trip home to Manila are probably less than thirty percent," he said. "But if I'm going to die, I want to die on Philippine soil."

When I remember those words, I find myself wondering if perhaps the convergence of inauspicious signs my wife saw spelled not only the very worst personal *ki* for Ninoy, but also the very best.

Two summers later, my wife told me I faced essentially the same decision Ninoy had faced.

Early that spring, an acquaintance of mine had brought me some aerial photographs of Maug, a group of three deserted islands at the north end of the Mariana chain. Formed by the upthrust of a huge underwater volcano, the three islands crested the rim of the otherwise submerged crater. Out of all the countless photos of islands I'd ever seen, I couldn't remember any that struck me as looking quite so mysterious.

My acquaintance and I decided to go on a diving expedition to these islands and make a documentary, filming them both above and below water. We got a TV station on board, picked our production staff, and set our dates, only to have my wife raise a red flag. My signs for those dates were exactly like Ninoy's signs had been two years before—the very worst combination of forces imaginable.

We'd already put the project team together, so I could hardly call the whole trip off. I asked her how the following month looked.

"At least August gets you past the worst period," she said. "It's definitely not favorable—in fact it's actually still pretty scary. But at least you won't die."

Her last words were the only ones I really heard. "All right," I said. "We'll wait a month." And since we already had a project team standing by, we'd spend July filming a separate documentary in the Tokara Islands, which I'd visited once before. Although these islands were also to the south, my wife assured me the compass direction was far enough away from the Marianas to make them perfectly safe.

Whether or not that really made any difference, we had a grand time on our cruise to the Tokaras and back. To my mind, this augured well for our plans in the Marianas, and as soon as I returned I busily went about preparing for the next trip.

"Now, I want to make sure you understand, dear," my wife stressed. "I didn't say the Marianas are safe for you even this month. That direction's still very dangerous, and there's no telling what terrible things might happen. So don't blame me if something goes wrong."

"Just so long as I'm not going to get killed."

"Well, I don't think that's too likely," my oracle pronounced.

Satisfied that my life was not at stake, and reassured too by the advent of a new month, I set sail in high spirits for the mystical isles.

We'd chartered ourselves a thousand-ton steamer named *Festa* that specialized in diving excursions. The owner even agreed to let me use his own luxurious suite, where I could spread out on a great big double bed and immerse myself in reading to my heart's content, and our passage got off to a delightful start. As we cruised past Aogashima island, a large school of dolphins came to cavort in front of the bow as if to show us the way—surely a good omen.

The one frustration, whether because the ship was simply so old, or because so many mollusks had attached themselves to her hull over the years, was our slow cruising speed. The steamer was supposed to be good for nine knots, but we were doing less than eight. I worried this might cut into our filming schedule. Even so, I felt better after we stopped to dive at Sofugan, the solitary "Widow's Rock" that rises almost a hundred meters straight up out of the sea—a must-see for every deep-sea diver.

Another full day and night from Sofugan, skirting the Ogasawara Islands beyond the horizon and continuing southward far behind schedule, the northernmost island of the Mariana chain finally came into view at 3:00 the next afternoon: the volcanic Farallon de Pajaros. For the first time since the 1965 TransPac, I was reminded how welcome the sight of land can feel to a long-distance traveler on the high seas.

At the same time, as we drew near, I quickly saw just how volatile this fiery island must be. Crews of long-haul fishing boats that passed this way had said the island could completely change its shape in the course of one short month between going out to the fishing grounds and returning home. Steam spewed forth from countless vents all over it, and smoke billowed from the top; the whole cone was bloated as though it could barely contain the forces pushing up from deep within. It would have surprised no one if it had burst open in a massive explosion right before our eyes.

Rachel Carson wrote in her award-winning *The Sea Around Us* that islands floating all alone in the middle of remote oceans are invariably the product of underwater volcanoes thrusting their cones up through the depths, and that someday they're destined to blow their tops and disappear again beneath the face of the sea. I could see just by looking at it that this volcanic cone was a candidate for such a fate.

Even so, on doing a once-around of the island, we discovered that the south side leveled out into a small tableland where vegetation had taken root and waterfowl made their nests. The sea was choppier here than directly under the volcano, and we were downwind, but the captain said it would be safer to drop anchor where volcanic activity was visibly lowest. Quite obviously, if the mountain were to blow while we rested at its base, the barrage of volcanic bombs could sink our little ship instantly.

The entire project team was eager to get a dive in before dark, so we started putting on our gear as soon as we anchored. We weren't likely to find much game fish around an island like this, but we might discover a spectacular thermal vent like the one we'd seen the previous month at Akusekijima in the Tokaras. After poking along at an average seven knots for days, everybody was impatient to get going.

The rubber dinghy was lowered into the water and filled with divers and equipment. My turn came to hop down, with the cameraman to follow, but just as I was about to jump, the cameraman decided he wanted to get a shot of me from below.

"Hold on a sec," he said, pushing around me and dropping into the boat first.

I was thrown a little off balance, but proceeded to jump anyway from the height of the deck into the one tiny space left in the dinghy. Unfortunately, thanks to my momentary loss of balance and the fins I had on, I failed to push off hard enough. The tip of one of my fins caught on something, flipping me over sideways, and I landed with my back squarely on the cameraman's knee, which he'd raised to brace himself while filming. My entire weight fell on that single point, his kneecap; I heard a sharp crack from my back even before I felt the impact.

My immediate first thought was, *Uh-oh, I've broken something.* Which was followed an instant later by a second thought, *How about that? She was right!* This was exactly what my wife had warned me about.

I felt no real pain, only a sensation of pressure, but I'd heard an unmistakable crack—not just with my ears but with every nerve in my body. Still, I managed to remove my fins and climb back up on deck under my own power, so when I put both hands to my back and said, "I think I broke something," I got only dubious stares.

"If you'd broken a rib, you wouldn't be standing here like that. Or moving your arms. See. You can move your arms just fine. And it doesn't hurt when you do that, right?"

"When I broke a rib once," someone else put in, "it hurt so bad I could hardly breathe."

In spite of these voices of experience, I wasn't so sure. But it was true that I could swing my arms around without significant pain, and the only thing unusual was the dull ache I felt around the point of impact.

"By tomorrow you're going to have a real sore bruise, though, so you better get a good massage and rub in some liniment right away."

Following this advice, I took a shower, got a liniment rub, and had a plaster applied.

At sundown the rest of the crew returned from their dive without any game fish, much as expected. But then someone cast a line over the side from on deck and was soon reeling in a sizable prize.

Except for the sensation of the plaster against the sore spot on my back, I still felt perfectly normal at dinnertime, so I relaxed and had a few drinks with the others. When everybody went back to fishing over the side afterwards, I followed with glass in hand and stood near the line with the heaviest rig waiting to see what it might bring in.

I have no idea what may have triggered it, but all of a sudden I felt short of breath, and the next moment a shattering pain wrenched my back. The pain quickly escalated and soon became so intense I couldn't move. As sharp pangs radiated to my spine, it hit me that if I'd hurt my spinal cord, I could be in serious trouble indeed. It could even kill me—though my wife had assured me I wouldn't be in that kind of danger.

If this was a spinal injury, basic first-aid measures weren't going to cut it; I needed to get to the nearest full-service hospital. But the Ogasawara Islands we'd passed a day earlier had only limited medical facilities. We could turn back anyway and call in a seaplane for an emergency evacuation, or we could continue on south to Saipan or Guam and seek treatment there. The closest island where a plane might possibly land was Pagan, roughly in the middle of the Mariana chain. Uninhabited since a recent eruption, word had it that the island's airstrip was at least half buried by lava and ash.

We radioed the Coast Guard in Guam for advice, and they thought the airstrip on Pagan was probably usable. But no matter where we set our course, it was going to take forever to get there at the *Festa*'s seven-knot cruising speed. Fortunately, a friend of mine from Saipan named Mori was scheduled to meet us at Maug, our primary destination just one island to the south. I could ask Mori to take me to Pagan in his faster boat.

We left Farallon de Pajaros immediately, and I spent the night in bed, groaning in agony. We arrived at Maug early the next morning.

The islands were even more alluring than they'd appeared in the photographs, but of course I was in no shape to dive. Fortunately, Mori sailed into the lagoon right on schedule. No doubt he'd been itching to drop fishing lines as soon as he arrived, but when he learned what had happened, he generously agreed to take me to Pagan instead.

And so, only just barely arrived, we weighed anchor again. Sailing away from the islands I'd set my heart on for six months, I am not embarrassed to say I shed a few tears. *If only I could stay for just one dive*, I thought, but that was of course out of the question when I suspected damage to my spinal column. I consoled myself with the thought that there'd be other chances to visit—the world had grown smaller in recent years. But the Northern Mariana Islands were awfully out of the way. This could in fact be a once-in-a-lifetime opportunity.

For Mori, too, having to spend the next day and night doubling back to Pagan had to be a terrible letdown. But my old friend never showed the slightest hint of displeasure; he even gave up his own bed so I could rest more comfortably.

Unfortunately, though purchased in Saipan and scheduled for overhaul in Japan, Mori's boat had started her life ferrying passengers on inland waters in Louisiana. She had been designed as a riverboat and was ill suited to cruising the open sea, with a shallow draft and rounded hull that made her roll on the waves. Even lying flat on my back in bed, every motion of the boat sent lightning bolts of pain through my body. I had to endure a full day and night of this torture, gritting my teeth at each jolt.

Drifting in and out of fitful sleep, I hoped and prayed it was only a dream. But no, the pain was excruciatingly real—which told me my condition was serious; one false step and things could turn truly dire. At the end of André Malraux's *The Royal Way*, one of my favorite novels, the hero Perken gasps, "There is . . . no death. . . . There is only . . . myself . . . a lone man . . . who is dying. . . ." I could identify fully with that state of mind.

I have never felt so utterly alone as I did that night, and I don't mean lonely. It was a more primal sense of aloneness that seemed to pierce right through me.

When we finally arrived, Pagan proved to be another island of frightening aspect—though not quite as horrific as Farallon de Pajaros. An eruption to the north had buried half the island in lava and ash. There had been plumes of steam rising from Pajaros, but here billowing black smoke had given the entire island a dark, sooty veneer.

Before long an airplane appeared in the southern sky. The lone small aircraft banked into a large semicircular turn over the island and disappeared on the other side, evidently landing at the airstrip. Mori and crew quickly rigged a hoist to lower me in a rubber raft over the side—a procedure that proved to be a small ordeal in itself.

Although the island gave us some shelter, a stiff breeze was blowing, and the waves began tossing us briskly up and down as soon as we touched water. Once we started moving, the twisting and flexing of the inflatable boat exacerbated the sea's motions. I tried to support my back on the coaming, but since that too was rubber, sharp bolts of pain shot across my back with each wave we hit. All those stories of severely injured men drifting for days in rubber rafts had to be the product of novelists' imaginations, not true-life accounts. Half a day of this and they'd all be dead, no matter what their injuries. By the time we finally made the blackened beach, I was dismally assessing the damage to my system caused by our little jaunt.

More trials awaited me ashore. My feet felt like they were sinking halfway up my shins into the soft sand of the beach. It took an immense effort to keep my balance while walking with one arm in a sling. When we finally reached firmer ground with grass underfoot, I heaved a big sigh of relief, only to look up and see cattle and goats roaming all about, livestock returned to the wild when the residents fled the eruption.

"Damn, I left my knife on the boat," said one of the accompanying crew members.

"Don't worry," said another. "If they try to attack, we can just climb a tree."

Which was small comfort to me, since I was in no shape to scale any tree. Nor was it particularly reassuring to see dead goats and cows littering the ground here and there. Who knew how they'd met their end?

The animals eyed us with suspicion, no doubt recognizing us as cousins of their former masters who'd abandoned them to their own devices. For our part, we kept one eye cocked in their direction as we carefully made our way up to the tableland and the airstrip.

Our first glimpse of the small plateau made us all gasp. This sloped swath of grass two hundred meters long by some thirty or forty meters wide was presumably the airstrip we'd heard about, but right down the middle was an eight-meter-high wall of lava. Just to be sure, I asked one of the men to climb up onto it, whereupon he reported that the lava spread all the way across the island to the far shore. The small plane was nowhere to be seen; it had presumably sized up the situation from the air, completed its 180° turn, and headed on home.

In the raft on the way to the island, I'd had the hope of rescue to sustain me, but now on the return, that hope was dashed. The pain in my back brought me to new levels of agony, and I sank into deeper and deeper gloom.

Now we would have to reach Saipan by boat. I dreaded the pain this meant I'd have to endure, but I also felt sorry for Mori, who had been dragged willy-nilly into my own misadventure. Even if it was a mission of mercy, he was having to go all the way back to where he started—literally. What could I say to him? I was grateful that Mori seemed to view the situation with enlightened resignation, but the obvious disappointment that showed on the other crew members' faces made me feel very small indeed.

When we informed the others on the *Festa* that we'd be proceeding on south, they radioed back that the small plane we'd seen was only for reconnaissance. Now that they knew the state of the airstrip, the Coast Guard would be sending a different aircraft to handle the actual evacuation. But how could any plane land on such a short airstrip? Waiting was only a waste of time, I sulked, and went to lie down in the cabin, convinced that it just wasn't going to happen.

The better part of an hour later, I heard the drone of a plane approaching, and soon Mori poked his head in at the door to say a small aircraft had indeed touched down.

"All right, so maybe it landed safely, but are you sure the thing can get back up in the air from a place like that? I tell you, I don't have the energy for any more ordeals. Can't you just take me to Saipan on this boat?" I pleaded.

But Mori, who knew more about planes than I did, was full of reassurance. "Stop being so worried! These planes are designed for this. I fly the exact same plane in and out of all sorts of places when I go hunting in Alaska. I personally guarantee your safety."

Now I was even starting to resent Mori.

"Look," he went on. "I'll be happy to take you by boat if you really want me to, but you know you're going to suffer every minute of the way. What you want right now is to get to a hospital the quickest way possible."

He was right, of course. So I dragged myself out to the rubber raft, and headed for the island a second time.

Sure enough, when we retraced our steps to the grassy field, we found a small plane parked on the ground just below the wall of lava. It had extra wide wings for the size of its body—obviously to help with short takeoffs and landings. But landing was one thing and taking off was another: perversely, I was still doubtful whether the thing could get off the ground on such a short airstrip.

Before long the pilot and copilot returned from wherever they'd wandered off to and said they could take off any time I was ready. The copilot was carrying a chunk of lava as a souvenir. To me with my frayed nerves, it looked like nothing but dead weight and I told him to leave it behind, but he just laughed me off: the plane could carry four full-grown men, he said. And besides, we were taking off into the wind so we'd get plenty of lift.

Once I was inside the plane, the airstrip looked even steeper than it had on the ground. The prospect of getting airborne seemed more hopeless than ever. Uninjured, I knew I could save myself no matter what happened, but as a helpless invalid I'd never be able to extricate myself from the fuselage if the plane failed to rise and fell off the end of the runway into the ocean. I'd been in scary situations in airplanes before, but never had I been quite so terrified of these heavier-than-air machines that claw their way up through thin air.

With Mori and crew standing by, the plane started to roll. I braced myself rigidly in my seat and prayed out loud. The plane raced down its barely two hundred meters of grassy runway and, wonder of wonders, rose gently into the sky with room to spare. My prayers had been answered.

The flight to Saipan took us from Pagan over Sarigan, Anatahan, and the other islands I was supposed to have visited with the project team on the *Festa*. Having regained my presence of mind after successfully cheating death in a suicidal takeoff, I gazed down from above, speculating about which islands offered good fishing and which probably had swift tidal currents.

When we arrived in Saipan, a television news crew had somehow got wind of my mishap and greeted me at the airport with cameras. The doctor at the hospital informed me, however, that Saipan was not equipped for the kind of surgery a worst-case scenario might require, and sent us on to Guam. Throughout the second flight I fretted over what kind of "worst-case" surgery the elderly physician could have meant. He'd offered to give me an injection for the pain, and when I said I didn't need it, he patted me on the shoulder and told me, "You're a brave boy." Which left me with absolutely no idea what to expect if, say, I'd actually broken one of my vertebrae.

The U.S. Naval Hospital on Guam was much larger than the one on Saipan and no doubt well equipped for spinal repair. Still, I didn't relish the idea of undergoing major surgery on a tiny island in the middle of nowhere. If it came to that, I'd ask them to fly me back to Tokyo. In any case, the first order of business was to get an x-ray.

A novelist's powers of observation aren't necessarily any better than anyone else's, but when I saw the technician's face as he emerged from developing the film, my first thought was that I'd worried myself silly for nothing.

"How does it look?" I asked.

He shrugged. "You'll have to talk to the specialist."

The specialist in question looked scarcely older than an intern. He placed the x-ray on the light box and gave it a once-over.

"Looks fine to me," he said. "I don't see any signs of a fracture. The pain you're experiencing must be solely from the soft tissue trauma."

Since this was a specialist speaking, I accepted the verdict and started to breathe a sigh of relief.

But then the technician was pointing at the picture. "What about here, Doc?" The older man's tone was deferential but emphatic.

"Hmm," the young fellow said, brushing the same spot with his finger and taking a closer look. "You're right. Looks like there's a tiny little crack here."

All of a sudden I was worried again. "How about my spine?" I asked. "Is my spine okay?"

The technician popped his eyes wide, and waved his hand to reassure me, no, that wasn't a concern.

I completed the paperwork so I could take the x-ray with me to Tokyo. After I got to the hotel room they'd arranged for me, I held the film up to the light for another look, and even my untrained eye could make out the slight shadow of a crack. This faintest of hairlines was the source of all the pain and apprehension I'd suffered over the last two days. The more I looked at it, the more annoyed I became at just how negligible a crack it was. But before long my annoyance gave way to laughter as I lay reflecting on how this minuscule fracture had put me in such a tizzy to get to a hospital, which had taken me not just once but twice to that grassy airstrip on Pagan, where I'd somehow managed to escape tumbling into the sea, plane and all.

Curiously enough, the pain in my back receded dramatically after I'd had a good laugh. Rising from bed, I called the dining room to reserve a table, then took a shower against doctor's orders and headed downstairs.

I'd been rather pleased by the stylishly gaunt look that came from not eating for two days straight, but I ordered a full-course dinner with no looking back. Afterwards, I could think of no objections to a glass of sherry; with this I drank a solitary but heartfelt toast to my wife and children back home. When that small dose seemed to drive the pain in my back even further away, I naturally concluded that alcohol was my friend, and ordered a second drink. A highball, this time a double.

As the familiar mellowness of intoxication spread through my body, I became aware that a strangely lucid but distinctly off-phase passage of time had come to an end. And perversely enough, I already missed it. How quickly the survivor grows smug.

In the elevator going back upstairs, as if to vindicate the young doctor and his warning, the alcohol unleashed a massive jolt of pain very much like that on the night of the accident. But by this time I'd grown quite used to that level of discomfort. In fact, as I lay groaning on the bed in my room, I was startled to realize how accepting and tolerant I'd become of absolutely everything, including the pain.

Even when I landed at Tokyo's Narita Airport the next day, I don't think I was feeling particularly disappointed about my ruined voyage. My wife must have been quite taken aback to find the defeated invalid she had come to meet arriving in such good spirits.

So then, did she find her faith in *ki* astrology reinforced as a result of my ill fortune? For the time being, this was a subject I preferred not to discuss. But whatever the case may be on that point, I will surely never forget what went through my mind the instant I came down on the broad of my back in that rubber boat. I can pretend that such things don't concern me, but the truth is I never again want to go rushing about such remote parts of the world in mortal fear that I've broken my spine.

For that reason, ever since that experience, I've always made it a point to consult my wife's oracle when planning a trip that could entail any element of danger. Some may laugh or call me a wimp, but I would ask those people just how much they themselves know about what the future holds.

There is a postscript to this story.

When I was almost fully recovered and went back for my final x-ray, I suggested to the technician that he take it from a different angle this time. After all, the topography of the back is tricky to capture whether shot from in front or behind. I took the x-ray to my doctor.

He put it up on his light box and studied it for a moment. "Well, well," he said. "I thought it was only number six, but look at this. You broke number seven, too. You can see it from this angle."

And there's a second postscript as well.

A little over a year later, I went for the comprehensive health scan I get every few years, which included chest x-rays taken from a variety of angles. In filling out the medical history form, I of course reported my injury of two years before, so the doctor already knew the basic details when he looked at the films.

"Good grief," he said, "this is even worse than you said. You're lucky you didn't wind up with hemothorax with all these broken ribs. It wasn't just two. You can see from this angle, there's another break here. You had three broken ribs."

When broken bones knit back together, calcium continues to be deposited at the site of the break to strengthen the bone, which makes it easier to see in later x-rays. The film showed the healed scars of three small but distinct cracks. *In that case,* I thought to myself, *I should have had three drinks that night in Guam instead of just two.*

Once again, that triumphant smugness of the survivor had reared its head.

THE SHARK CAGE

Sharks may be savage beasts, but they're by no means stupid. Otherwise they could hardly have survived the rigors of natural selection with so little evolutionary change from the time of their emergence as a species until the present day. Compared to other creatures of the sea, they always remain vigilantly on guard, are capable of snap judgments, and have very sharp reflexes.

On the other hand, their eyesight is not particularly good. The eyes are small for their bodies, and even with the same spherical lenses as other fish, their visual field is more limited; their vision simply does not measure up to their phenomenal mobility. When a shark becomes aware of vulnerable prey and comes racing to the scene, it's certainly not its eyesight that tipped it off.

Nor, as widely believed, is it the scent of blood. Smells are transmitted through the movement of microscopic particles, so in an environment of underwater currents that are slow at best, the scent of blood from a stricken fish could never reach a shark several hundred meters or even a kilometer away so quickly.

Once while diving off Ishigakijima in Okinawa, we saw four or five large sharks swimming about at the first place we stopped, so we gave that spot a pass and moved a kilometer down current. At the new location, I quickly speared four coral red trout, that tastiest of Okinawan fish. As I continued the hunt, my spear gun started jiggling about under my arm even though the current wasn't particularly strong. I tightened my grip on it, but it kept moving, and then suddenly I felt a distinct tug. I turned to see two sharks devouring my catch, which

I'd looped on a fish ring at the end of a ten-meter line attached to the butt of my gun. I recognized one of the sharks from a kilometer up current because of the large scar on the tip of its snout.

Although separated by a distance of ten meters, seeing sharks make a meal of the fish I'd tethered to my spear gun was not exactly comforting. In fact, this was before I'd grown used to being near sharks in the water, so my first reaction was distinctly jittery.

As quickly as I could, I reached for my dive knife and cut the line loose. But to my horror, the trout started drifting in my direction, and the increasingly excited sharks came right with them, sending me into a panic.

Since the sharks had been up current, the scent of blood couldn't possibly have traveled in their direction. Only the sounds made by the fish impaled on my spear could have attracted them so quickly.

Some people doubt that fish can scream, but they are mistaken; fish do indeed cry out in pain or fear. Our human eardrums may be unable to detect it, but as you gain experience hunting underwater you get so you can sense it with your body. Whether it's the agonized sound of a mortally wounded fish trailing blue-black blood in depths unpenetrated by ultraviolet light, or the panic-stricken cry of its cousin scrambling for cover in the rocks after a close call, the seasoned spearfisherman feels the distress signals very clearly.

In fact, in a curious way, the sensation is more distinct and real than when a hunter brings down his winged or four-footed quarry on land.

From an evolutionary perspective, we humans are descended from aquatic creatures that crawled up onto land. No doubt memories from living in the sea still lurk somewhere in our primal genetic makeup. That might also explain why we adapt with such surprising ease to being nearly weightless underwater—even if we do have to strap ungainly air tanks on our backs in order to breathe.

Some merely attribute this to the time we spend suspended in amniotic fluid in our mother's womb. But that in itself retraces the evolution of our aquatic ancestors. At any rate, even if fish cries are of a wavelength that does not register on the human ear, they are surely audible to their kin, including the most accomplished hunter of the seas. At the same time, although we humans cannot hear the fish, they certainly hear us. When a swimmer sees a shark and screams in terror, the shark has been known to head straight for the swimmer and attack.

On the other hand, one of the techniques divers use to drive away sharks is to remove their regulators and yell.

I once went to Mukojima in the Ogasawara Islands with a group of friends to film the behavior of sharks for a television program. We spent about a week in the water in close contact with sharks, and I learned a great deal about them as a result.

I saw, for example, that sharks are very quick to acquire conditioned responses. One of the crew remarked that if we kept using our spear guns to catch bait for the sharks, they'd soon start coming at the mere sound of the guns. So after a couple of days, I tested his claim by firing my gun into empty water. Sure enough, sharks quickly cruised into view.

This was also when I learned to appreciate just how acute a shark's hearing is. Not surprisingly, by the end of that trip, I'd had quite my fill of sharks.

We took with us a steel cage three meters wide by two meters deep and two meters high. Some of us caught bait and tied it to the outside of the cage, while a camera crew waited safely inside to film the sharks that came to feed.

We went into the water three or four times each day to fish or film. Before long the sharks would arrive and cruise about eyeing our activities at a distance as soon as we entered the water—no doubt in conditioned response to all the noise we made.

The tidal currents around the island brought huge schools of dogtooth tuna and amberjacks into the inlet where we were filming. They circled in tight formation, like mosquitoes swarming in a column. We certainly had no shortage of bait for luring the sharks to our cameras.

Watching up close as sharks took turns ripping at the fish tied outside the cage was a far from pleasant sight. On first approach, the sharks would cruise in gracefully, but once they'd torn their first flesh, the smell of blood spreading through the water whipped them into a frenzy of pushing and shoving that was downright diabolical. And they'd keep coming back for more even after the bait was gone, often chomping on the steel cage instead. The force of their jaws crushed and crimped the pipes as if they'd been hammered by a heavy wrench. It was a spine-chilling sight.

It was also easy to see how sharks tear their prey to shreds with such dispatch. Behind the first row of teeth immediately visible in front are three or four more rows of sharp, serrated spares, so once a shark sinks its teeth into its quarry virtually nothing can prize away the jaws. Then with its teeth firmly set, the shark shakes and jerks its thick tail to lever the bite off.

I once saw a picture of a diver who had survived a shark attack in spite of massive wounds. From the size of his scars—which is to say, from the size of his assailant's jaws—it was obviously a miracle that the shark hadn't torn him completely to pieces, bones and all.

The sea was flat calm on our last day of filming, so we ventured out beyond the inlet and found a convenient rock ledge on which to set the shark cage. I got in with the cameraman and his assistant, while some other team members brought four or five amberjacks and groupers they'd caught and tied them to the outside of our steel grid.

Several sharks had already followed the bait crew to the cage, and once they began to feed, the excitement attracted three smaller sharks from beneath the rock shelf to join in the frenzied feast.

Soon fed up with getting rudely shoved aside by the larger sharks, two of the juveniles decided they might have better luck muscling in on the meal if they built up some momentum first. They swam a short distance away, made a U-turn, and accelerated straight for the cage. The bars of our cage were quite widely spaced for a less obstructed view when filming, and the next thing we knew two 120- to 130-centimeter sharks had slipped inside. The sharks were as startled to find themselves among us as we were. The cage was already cramped enough, and now we suddenly had two additional living, squirming bodies occupying the same space, making our every move that much more difficult.

Small as they were, the sharks were in a tight spot, too. Unexpectedly and inescapably rubbing skin with three human creatures, they were panic-striken; we could sense their fear. But they'd ridden in from the outside on sheer momentum—a condition not easily duplicated inside, no matter how eager they might be to get out. They darted between our arms and legs, slapping us with their fins and tails, but succeeded only in bashing their heads against the bars.

Needless to say, we wanted to be rid of the sharks as well, and tried to boost them through the bars. But the mere touch of our hands was sheer terror to them, making them squirm and thrash all the more just to escape our efforts.

Meanwhile, on the other side of the bars the larger sharks continued to scuffle and tear at the bait. Watching this feeding frenzy conjured terrifying visions of what could happen if the baby sharks inside the cage were suddenly to turn on us. Luckily, they were in too much of a panic to think about feeding, but we were getting increasingly frantic ourselves. We yelled and screamed through regulators held with one hand, even as we fended off the sharks with the other.

In all the commotion, the cage was jostled off its unstable perch on the ledge and fell ten meters farther down onto another rock. The shock of the landing unlatched the door, and the young sharks fled through the opening with a quick flick of their tails.

The other divers who'd been watching the entire drama from afar now approached, trailing bubbles of laughter behind them. By the time I pulled myself from the cage, the tension and absurdity and exasperation of it all had drained every ounce of strength from my body.

Back aboard the boat, I was surprised to see how many scrapes and scratches I'd sustained on my arms and legs because of the short-sleeved summer wet suit I was wearing. The sharks in the cage may only have been babies, but they were still sharks, and their coarse hides were like rough sandpaper on my exposed skin; some of the abrasions were starting to ooze blood.

At first we just laughed, but then as I rubbed my superficial wounds, someone wondered out loud, "What do you suppose would've happened if you'd gotten cut or bit and blood had flowed?"

"We'd have gone for our dive knives," I said, "and that probably would've got the sharks on the outside worked up even more. They might have started to chomp at us right through the cage. And if a couple of bars had come loose when we fell off that ledge, well, there's no telling what could've happened. . . ."

No one said anything more after that.

OVERBOARD

I suppose only yachtsmen know firsthand what it's like to fall off an oceangoing vessel into the deep blue sea.

Yachts do not go particularly fast, but try falling overboard when cruising at a mere two knots, and you'll quickly discover just how fast two knots is. Competitive swimmers might be up to the challenge, but it's impossible for a fully outfitted yachtsman to swim back to a boat traveling at that pace.

Once when I was out sailing in a virtual dead calm, barely able to make even one knot under full sails, I decided to go for a swim wearing a life jacket tethered to the stern pulpit. On board, the boat seemed to be standing still, but from the water I could see right away that she was definitely moving. After a while, the wind picked up enough to nearly double her speed. Yet even at less than two knots, the line started dragging me through the water with such force I seriously thought I might drown.

All the more, then, when a yacht is moving along at a healthy clip: fall into the water without a safety harness, and you'll quickly stray far behind; take a dive in heavy weather, and your situation becomes hopeless in the blink of an eye.

During a yacht race, you may have to contend with both calms and gales, but seldom does anyone fall overboard on flat seas; it's almost always in rough weather that people get tossed. And who but the yachtsman can ever know what it's really like to be washed overboard in the middle of a storm?

During the Mikomotojima Yacht Race in 1983, a boat named *Mariana* lost a member of her crew overboard. That year, like every year, the race was plagued by heavy weather, with a powerful northeasterly wind blowing at over forty-five knots. One boat after another got knocked down; more than ten of them were dismasted.

In *Mariana*'s case, it wasn't very far into the race that an accidental jibe knocked her only female crew member over the side. When the report came in to the race committee by radiotelephone in the middle of the night, the organizers apparently argued over who should make the call to the woman's family. In the end, a close friend of mine named Shimizu, then executive director of the Nippon Ocean Racing Club, was given the job.

A motherly-sounding voice answered the phone at 2:00 A.M. When Shimizu told the woman about her daughter going overboard, she didn't seem to know what to make of the news. Shimizu wondered whether to explain what it meant for someone to fall overboard in such weather, especially in the dead of night.

"Just a moment, please," said the woman, sensing his hesitation, and turned the phone over to her husband.

The missing woman's father seemed to grasp the implications immediately. "What are the sea conditions?" he asked.

"Pretty heavy. We're not getting the same winds here on land, but they're probably better than forty knots offshore."

"Can the search start right away?"

"We've already notified the Coast Guard, but it'll probably be first light before they can actually get going."

"I see," he said. Then as if reconfirming it to himself, he mumbled, "So she fell overboard." He seemed to understand what falling into the ocean meant for his daughter, yet no doubt he wished he didn't. Even though he knew she could swim.

The search continued for five days after the accident, both from the air and on the water. No sign was ever found of the woman. Few yachtsmen want to believe it, but a drowned body sinks like a stone even when the person is wearing a life jacket. The living are usually found and rescued, but I have yet to hear of the body of anyone who drowned or succumbed to hypothermia being recovered afloat.

Anyone who sails has to expect to go overboard sometime, or at least knows there's a genuine risk of it. But how does it feel the moment you realize it's actually happened to you?

In the tragic Hatsushima Race of 1962, a man named Miyashita fell overboard from the sloop *Nobu-chan*. He didn't know how to swim, yet had chosen not to don a life jacket. Initially, he somehow managed to stay afloat. When crewmates leaning over the pulpit caught him in the beam of their flashlight, he responded to their calls with an energetic yell. But the next instant a great wave crashed down over him, and he was gone. I can't help wondering what was going through his mind when he gave that yell. No sign of him was ever seen again.

Once during a Big Boat Series race at Sumoto, a fellow named Urabe on my crew slipped and fell overboard as we were rounding the leeward mark. We were racing an Olympic-style course, so there were numerous organizer and spectator boats nearby, and being on the Inland Sea the waves weren't very high, either. We immediately turned back to pick him up, of course, but in the mere five minutes or so it took to reach him, he'd been struggling in his foul-weather gear just to keep his head above water. I suppose it was partly because he was in shock, but this otherwise tough guy was so completely exhausted by the ordeal he couldn't get out of his bunk for the rest of the day.

When I go diving, I wear a stabilizer jacket that also serves as a backpack for my air cylinder and as a life vest. The neoprene wet suit I wear already gives me some buoyancy, but I can also feed air into the stab jacket to inflate it around my neck. Even then, I doubt I could remain afloat for days on end; if the seas turned choppy, I'd surely drown. I can scarcely imagine how much harder it has to be for a man loaded down with the heavy rubber rain-slicker and sea boots that yachters wear; even a kapok-filled life jacket on top of all that gear couldn't do much to boost his buoyancy.

If you get tossed wearing full foul-weather gear, then your only hope of crawling back out of the drink alive is to ditch your heavy boots and rain gear as quickly as you possibly can. Which is no easy feat—even in calm waters.

The Quarter-Ton World Championship Regatta was held in Japan in 1978 under horrendous weather conditions. Every boat in the fleet was dismasted at least once. One boat had to drop out of the competition altogether after losing three masts and running out of replacements.

The final and longest race of the series, the offshore race from Hatsushima around Mikomotojima and back, took place in full storm conditions. Only three boats completed it; three-quarters of them were dismasted; two sank. A nearby craft came to the aid of one of the boats that went down. The other foundered out of sight of the rest of the fleet, and when the four crewmen scrambled into their life raft, the raft capsized as well and two of the men got swept away. Unfortunately their boat went down in just about the worst possible spot: the wind and currents conspired to push both the raft and the two separated men swiftly out of Sagami Bay toward the open sea, where the Japan Current soon carried them past the Boso Peninsula. Finally, just as they were being swept out into the Pacific, a British freighter bound for Nagoya spotted them and picked them up.

Sure enough, according to their accounts, the first thing they did after being dunked was to take off their heavy sea boots. Then, gauging the temperature of the water and debating whether they'd rather drown or die of hypothermia, they removed just the pants of their foul-weather gear.

In any case, they came back alive.

I've seen some pretty hairy situations in my years at sea, but fortunately never had anyone die as a result of being tossed from my boat. Unlike some skippers, I feel quite confident I could rescue any crewman who fell from my vessel during daylight, even under the worst weather conditions, so long as he manages to keep himself afloat. After dark, though, all bets are off; rescue efforts become virtually hopeless. Visibility from aboard a yacht at night is five meters at best. Even with a light, you're not likely to see much past twenty meters. And if you're in weather heavy enough to hurl someone over the side, you'd be doing at least seven or eight knots, no matter how slowly you felt like you were moving. Plus, if a wave swells up between the boat and the swimmer, it's going to push him even farther away. What goes through the minds of the crew at times like that, as they strain valiantly to keep their eyes on the swimmer? What goes through the mind of the person in the water, as he struggles desperately not to lose sight of the boat's tiny lights? It chokes me up just to think about it.

One winter, a yacht named *Yamayuri* sustained damage en route from Enoshima to Oshima when a severe gale erupted out of the west. While making repairs, one of the crew tumbled overboard and was lost. The man's wife of only one month happened to be on board, and the shock drove her mad with grief for ten days. As devastating as the shock must have been for the bereft new bride, it could have been no small blow to the others who witnessed the event, either.

Thankfully, I myself have been spared a face-to-face encounter with a tragedy of this kind, but on one occasion I did indirectly witness a similar event.

The Okinawa Yacht Race held in May 1978 was uncharacteristically damp and chilly due to a massive cold front that appeared off the southern coast of Japan's main island. During the second half of the race, a series of low pressure cells along the Pacific coast generated strong northeasterly winds, neutralizing the Japan Current that should have been helping us along. The entire fleet got pinned up against the Kii Peninsula, where we were forced to battle rogue waves for four days, making no headway.

What it's like to endure four long days of driving rain, ten-meter seas, and Force 10 winds defies description. The storm eased briefly on the third day, giving us a glimpse of what we at first thought must be one of the Izu Islands, but our hearts sank when we realized we were looking at the hills near Daiozaki Point on the Shima Promontory—still just the other side of the Kii Peninsula. No one felt like talking any more.

The accident occurred that night. As we switched on the radiotelephone to stand by for the daily roll call scheduled at 10:00 P.M., a boat named *Toshi* was calling the Coast Guard on the distress frequency. A man had been washed overboard.

Toshi was a new boat, relatively unaccustomed to racing, and I had a nodding acquaintance with her navigator, a marine architect named Takeichi. As he gave the Coast Guard a rundown of the situation, his voice betrayed a tremendous effort not to lose his composure.

Half an hour earlier, the boat had been knocked on her side by a rogue wave, hitting a crewman named Matsushita with such force that it snapped his safety harness and swept him overboard. With the boat slow to right herself and no flashlight at hand—the wave had taken that, too—the crew lost too much time before trying to locate Matsushita in the water. They hastily lowered the jib and searched the area but found no trace of him.

No doubt a veteran of countless distress calls, the Coast Guard radio operator responded in flat, almost mechanical tones. This seemed to have a calming effect on Takeichi; I could hear the tension in his voice ease as the exchange continued.

Unless *Toshi* had sustained other damage, the Coast Guard instructed, she should maintain her position and continue searching.

Takeichi gave the boat's position as twenty miles south-southeast of Daiozaki—not far from where we were at the time. Next, Takeichi stated the name, age, address and occupation of the missing man, speaking very deliberately so as not to have to repeat anything: Ryoji Matsushita, age twenty-seven, Setagaya, Tokyo. But when he came to the man's occupation—"stylist," a foreign job description still new to the Japanese ear at the time—the Coast Guard operator failed to catch it.

"Say again please, over."

"Sierra Tango Yankee Lima India Sierra Tango. Stylist. Over."

"Is that stylist? Over."

"That's affirmative. Stylist."

I turned to my own radioman, Imaoka. "What's a stylist?"

"It's the latest thing among models and actors and people like that. I guess you could call them image consultants. They tell celebrities how they should style their hair and what they should wear," he said, then added, "I've actually been on a number of jobs with Matsushita." Imaoka worked for an ad agency.

"So he's a friend of yours?" I asked.

He nodded without saying anything further.

By this time, the crewmen who had been trying to get some sleep since coming off watch had rolled out of their bunks, and gathered around the radio. One of them stuck his head out the hatch to let the guys standing watch in the sodden cockpit know what was going on. When he ducked back inside, another fellow opened the hatch and yelled, "How're things looking out there?"

A head appeared upside down at the opening and shouted back, "The wind's picked up again. The seas are worse, too. Doesn't look good for the guy who fell in."

"It's been an hour and nine minutes," reckoned Imaoka. "What's the water temperature?"

"With this cold front we're in, couldn't be over fifteen."

"Which means he's got ten hours, tops."

"So the question is, can he hold out until daybreak?" said Imaoka, studying his watch.

"Forget it. Even if the water's warm, the waves'll get him. You can't just float on your back in seas like this."

"So you think he's still alive right now?"

Oddly enough, there was a liveliness in their voices that had been missing in recent days.

"So what's the story?" asked another upside-down head at the hatch. "Any more news about the guy who got tossed?"

"In these conditions, we figure he doesn't have much of a chance."

"How're you guys doing up top? You better all be wearing your safety harnesses."

"Don't worry. We're still alive and kicking."

Disrespectful as it may sound, from the moment we got word about the missing man, a certain excitement, even cheer, began to displace the gloom that had been in the air. In fact, this change of mood came over not just those of us in the cozy cabin below, but even over those out in the elements, bearing the full brunt of the driving rain and spray on deck. I recall listening to the radio exchange about the sailor's misfortune, thinking it could only mean he was doomed, and all the time feeling an indescribable sense of youthful vitality kindled within me. Of course I was sad: a fellow yachtsman had met his end. But quite apart from the tragedy, or perhaps precisely because of it, I found myself savoring the fact of still being alive, here and now, on the same raging sea that had claimed another man's life. I think all of us, each in his own way, experienced much the same feeling.

Was it an insult to the dead to feel like this? Were we secretly rejoicing in this man's misfortune, in his ultimate extinction? Honestly, I don't believe so. At any rate, there was no denying that the news of his accidental death sparked a burst of new energy in us. Once the roll call was over, we devised a plan to break away from all the other boats stuck in the same stretch of sea and, boldly setting a new shoreward course, we managed to close in on the frontrunners by noon the next day.

In retrospect, under the circumstances, I don't think we had the capacity of heart or mind to mourn the loss of another man's life—not when we remained in the grip of death ourselves. News of the man washed overboard from another boat allowed us to confirm our own ongoing place among the living. If we felt our hearts leap at the grim news, it was no doubt because his death reminded us of the plain and simple joy of being alive.

And surely the fallen sailor would not hold that against us.

THE RIVER BETWEEN
LIFE AND DEATH

When my father died, he appeared at the home of some friends. I learned about the extraordinary event sometime later, and it's a story I like very much.

One hears from time to time about such visitations, but knowing it was my own father made it all the more fascinating. Above all, it seemed so like him.

The friend who saw him was the matron of a venerable family named Kono. She and her husband had been the go-betweens for my parents' marriage many years before. She was hanging a scroll in her tearoom that evening when my father abruptly walked up through the garden without anyone having come to announce him. He removed his hat and sat down on the edge of the veranda.

"My goodness, Kiyoshi, you needn't sit out there," Mrs. Kono said. "Please come inside."

She hurried to get a cushion for him, but when she came back he was gone. Puzzled, she asked others in the house whether they'd noticed anyone in the garden, but none had.

No one can know how a ghost—if that's what this should be called—chooses the people he appears before, but it seems perfectly in character for my father, always a stickler for decorum, to pay a final call on the couple who arranged his marriage and became lifelong confidants to him and his wife. I can just picture my large-framed father advancing through the garden in the twilight and sitting down on the edge of the veranda with his borsalino in one hand.

The elderly Mr. Kono immediately phoned our house in Tokyo, and learned that my father had passed away that very hour.

I have no way of knowing what path my father took as he picked up his hat and left the Konos' tearoom behind. Nor, to begin with, can I know what path led him all the way from Tokyo to the Konos' teahouse in Ashiya, west of Osaka.

While the origins of the River of Three Crossings in Buddhism are well beyond my ken, the notion that something like a river flows between the realms of the living and the dead strikes a certain chord of truth. Some who have undergone near-death experiences report actually seeing this river.

I imagine it was on the way to the river that my father stopped to say goodbye to the Konos.

A close colleague of mine, the late legislator Kazuo Tamaki, once told me that he, too, had seen this river. Although Tamaki ultimately died of cancer, he had flirted with death much earlier when he failed to take the symptoms of severe diabetes seriously. Lying in a coma in intensive care at the hospital, he saw a faintly glimmering white band reminiscent of the Milky Way. He also saw his dead brother, who had been so kind when he was alive, standing against the wall of the hospital room.

"Don't suffer, Kazuo, come with me to the other side," his brother said to him gently, beckoning. "Here, give me your hand."

A glowing band of white stretched behind him like a river. Tamaki reached for his brother's hand many times, but in the end he held back, unable to take it. He gave the excuse that he still had things to do on this side, and so he stayed in his hospital bed.

"I really don't know what made me pull back," he said, "but if I'd taken his hand and let him lead me across the river, that would've been the end of me. The river was this glowing band of white. I distinctly remember coming right up next to it."

My brother Yujiro was another to visit this river and return to tell about it. He suffered a rare but often fatal condition called a "dissecting aortic aneurysm," which quite literally took him to hell and back.

I was away in the Ogasawaras for a yacht race when I received the call. In those days, the islands didn't have proper telephone connections to the main islands of Japan, so I had to listen to the doctor explain my brother's condition over a static-riddled radio link. Surgery would be very risky, he said, and he needed a male member of the patient's family to make the decision. He pressed me to fly back to Tokyo with all possible haste, the palpable urgency in his voice suggesting how dire my brother's situation was.

As the doctor described it, a dissecting aorta occurs when the middle layer of the aortic wall hardens and begins to break up, separating from the inner lining and the outer covering and creating a space between the layers of the wall. Something then causes a tear in the inner lining, allowing blood to be forced into that space, and as more blood enters with each contraction of the heart, it progressively splits the layers apart.

It did not take any special knowledge of human anatomy to understand that an aortic wall splitting up inside itself represented an extreme health hazard. After all, once the blood gets into the aortic wall and begins forcing the layers of tissue apart, where can it ultimately go? If the outer covering succumbs to the mounting pressure and ruptures, then the thoracic and abdominal cavities become a sea of blood.

The doctor went on to liken an aneurysm to pouring liquid into a plastic bag: when blood gets trapped between the layers of a weakened artery wall, it balloons up and impinges on the artery's normal blood channel, making it nearly impossible for blood to flow through it.

In my brother's case, blood had entered the artery wall about three centimeters from the aortic valve, and from there had forced its way forward inside the arterial wall some thirty-five centimeters down into his lower abdomen, almost to the point where the two arteries that supply blood to the legs branch off. There it had created a large bulge in the artery, which exerted pressure on the surrounding tissue and caused the arteries branching off from the aorta to collapse. Blood was no longer reaching the internal organs.

The aneurysm at waist level brought excruciating pain to my brother's lower back, and at the same time the loss of kidney function sent him into uremic shock. Then, miraculously, just when the doctors thought he'd slip into a coma, the inner lining of the artery wall tore open at the site of the aneurysm and released the blood collected there back into the main channel where it belonged, as if it had merely taken a detour. Suddenly, the kidneys and other organs that had shut down for lack of blood leapt back to life.

With the inner lining now open at both ends, the balloon full of blood dispersed, but the original tear up near the aortic valve where the blood entered the detour had widened. As the heart continued pumping blood full force against the torn lining, like a swift river flowing hard into a sharp bend where the levee has started to give way, there was no predicting how long the artery would hold up.

If Yujiro could be kept stable through the next ten days, then surgical repair became a possibility, but the doctor also warned that the tear could give way at any time. In operations undertaken within the first three days after a dissecting aneurysm occurs, the success rate was less than ten percent. If the aneurysm recurred during his first night and forced immediate surgery, chances dropped to less than five percent. Then again, with no surgery at all, it was a one hundred percent certainty that the artery would eventually tear away from the heart, and my brother would die.

Stressing that the aneurysm could recur even that very night, the doctor was concerned that a very quick decision might have to be made regarding this risky surgery. Neither he nor the women of the family could make that call, he said, so it was imperative that I return to Tokyo at once.

My brother's condition remained stable for five days, but then ultrasound images showed a change in the tear. It seemed doubtful that the artery could hold out much longer, so I gave the doctor my consent to operate. When I asked about Yujiro's chances at that point, just five days after the original event, he simply said he'd do his best and refused to give any odds. Another specialist I asked later said his chances were probably less than twenty percent.

Yujiro himself was in the dark about his condition, and once the initial pain had subsided, he relaxed and even got bored with his extended hospital stay. Seeing him just before he was wheeled into pre-op for anesthesia, I felt helplessly awkward, as if I were facing a patient being kept from the knowledge that his disease is incurable.

What Yujiro himself went through during the nine hours of surgery, I can't begin to know, but for his waiting family it was a time of fervent prayers—and of asking every visitor who came to inquire after him to join us in those prayers. How I passed those nine hours is a blur to me now. I vaguely recall making a trip home with my wife, because I wanted to pray in front of our family altar undistracted.

The possibility that Yujiro might die from surgical complications weighed heavily on our minds, but at the end of the nine hours we received word that everything had gone very well and he'd been transferred to intensive care.

I went in to see my brother the next day. Representing the entire family, I went in alone at just about the time the anesthesia was due to wear off. The doctor seemed a little nervous. He told me before we entered the room that the moment a patient comes out of extended anesthesia following major surgery was very critical; it was important that he regain full consciousness right away in order to avoid lingering effects later on. To help my brother wake up, he urged me to speak in a strong voice and not hold back.

Yujiro had gone off to the operating room with no real sense of the danger he was in; he behaved so normally it made me wonder if my anxieties weren't completely misplaced. But the way he looked after being worked over for nine hours with his chest cracked open like two sides of beef hanging in a butcher shop was a decidedly different story. A frightening tangle of tubes and wires connected his arms and nose and mouth and the base of his neck to a battery of medical devices. He looked like some junkyard cyborg from science fiction.

His expression was indeed that of someone emerging from a deep sleep. The doctor poked at his shoulder and told him to wake up in a voice loud enough to make me jump. Between the insistent prodding and the booming voice in his ear, my brother soon stirred from his artificially induced slumber. I stood by with bated breath, aware that I was witnessing a kind of rebirth; it was a very emotional moment.

"Say something to him," the doctor urged. "He can't talk, so we'll have him write." He asked a nurse to bring some blank sheets of paper and a clipboard.

I wasn't sure what to say, so I simply mimicked the doctor and shouted, "Hey, Yujiro, how're you feeling?"

"Do you recognize this man?" the doctor added. "It's your brother."

Yujiro dipped his head in a very distinct nod.

"You can't talk yet because of the tubes and gauze in your mouth, so we have a clipboard for you to write on." The doctor took the ballpoint pen the nurse held out and handed it to my brother, who accepted it with another nod.

"That won't work," I said. "It won't write upside down. Anyone got a pencil?"

A second nurse quickly pulled a red pencil from her chest pocket and handed it to Yujiro. The first nurse and I held the clipboard for him. He grasped the pencil, gave a moment's thought, then started writing.

"When is the operation?" I read his message aloud. His handwriting looked almost completely normal, hardly affected by his condition at all.

The doctor nodded in my direction to reassure me, then turned back toward Yujiro. "The operation is all over," he said. "It was yesterday. Everything went very well. But we kept you under sedation, so you're just waking up now. It's already the day after surgery. Do you understand what I'm saying?" He enunciated each phrase very deliberately.

Yujiro showed no particular surprise. Apparently satisfied with the explanation, he closed his eyes and started to go back to sleep.

"No, you don't need any more sleep now," the doctor quickly shouted. "We want you to stay awake."

It was several more days before I spoke directly with my brother. The doctor kept him heavily medicated at first, then finally decided it was time to discontinue the drugs and rouse him from his stupor.

"For the last few days we've kept him pretty well knocked out," he explained, "but now we want to get him off the sedatives and move on to the next phase of recovery. He'll have to tolerate a certain amount of pain. In any case, I want you to talk to him like you did the other day."

I called his name out loud, but he was not as responsive as before. Soon the doctor raised his voice to join in as well. By now the tubes had been removed from his nose and mouth, but Yujiro just nodded irritably and made no effort to speak.

Impatient, the doctor jabbed his shoulder and slapped him on the cheek. "Do you recognize this person next to me? I'm sure you do. Tell me who it is."

"I know him," he mumbled.

"Then tell me who it is. Speak up. Who's this person standing next to me?"

As the doctor and I peered down at him, Yujiro slowly opened his eyes again and looked at me. "Of course I know who it is," he said. "It's my lamebrain brother."

The doctor and I exchanged glances.

"You better believe I know who it is," Yujiro went on, closing his eyes as if he'd had enough of this nonsense.

When I asked him about it later, my brother couldn't recall a single thing from the entire post-operative period. He didn't remember waking up from the anesthetic; he didn't remember this second meeting or any of my subsequent visits.

Not even the doctor could tell how soon my brother might fully recover his memory. He responded appropriately enough when the doctor and nurses came to check on him, but that was the most he could do; he apparently didn't have the strength to record these experiences in his long-term memory yet. By Yujiro's own account, it took an entire week after surgery before he finally regained full normal consciousness.

"So what was it like after they stopped giving you the sedatives and pain killers?"

"They say I was complaining about the pain the whole time, but I don't remember a thing. Basically, I was half asleep for so long, what I remember more than any pain is drifting in and out of one dream after another, until finally I realized at one point that I was wide awake again. One particular dream I kept coming back to over and over for what seemed like forever. A really weird dream."

"How do you mean?"

"I was at this river on location to shoot a samurai picture—mostly a dry riverbed, actually. At first I was riding on a horse, but then suddenly I was bouncing over the rocks in a jeep with some guys from the film crew."

It was autumn, and large stands of tall plume grass swayed in the wind on either bank, their white fronds shimmering in the sunlight. Yujiro raced about in his jeep, shouting instructions by bullhorn to the crew about the next scene.

A large crowd of extras had been brought in, and for some reason the crew was having trouble setting up the scene. The extras were initially supposed to remain out of sight beyond the tall grass on the far bank, but they kept appearing between the swaying plumes. The cameras would be ready to roll, then suddenly everything would fall apart again.

And just then, of all times, Kobayashi went missing. Kobayashi was Yujiro's right-hand man on the set; he always called the shots for him during actual filming. Irked by his absence, Yujiro raced up and down the riverbed screaming for Kobayashi and berating the other members of the crew, water splashing high as the jeep plowed through puddles. Yet through it all he was thinking how pretty the sunlight was, on the shimmering fronds of swaying grass, in the sparkling spray kicked up by the jeep.

Fed up with the repeated delays, Yujiro yelled at whoever was at the wheel to drive on over to the other side, but every time the jeep turned in that direction, someone yanked the wheel the other way and brought it careening back to this side.

———

Yujiro said this same dream kept looping over and over, endlessly. "It must have been the River of Three Crossings. And all those extras on the other side, they must have been angels of death come to meet me. I don't know who it was that forced the jeep back to this side, but if I'd actually made it across I doubt I'd ever have returned."

"So you went right to the very brink," I said.

"Guess so. And man, let me tell you, everything about this river—the rocks in the riverbed, the water, the swaying grass—absolutely everything seemed to shine with this dazzling white light. The purest, most flawlessly transparent light. It was definitely the most beautiful river I've ever seen."

THE LIGHT

The last typhoon of the year crashed ashore on the Izu Peninsula, bringing several days of rain. When the skies finally cleared, it felt as if autumn had passed and winter was suddenly upon us. The following Sunday turned into the first warm, sunny day in quite some time, but instead of heading out for open water, people were busy winterizing their boats in the marina.

In the lobby of the clubhouse I ran into a visitor I was very surprised to see, and I dragged him out into the sunshine on the terrace for a drink. He'd come up from Nagoya to attend to some boat business and would be going back that evening on the bullet train. As we sat talking, I could hardly believe this was the same man who'd survived a major ordeal only a few days before.

I had learned about the downing of his yacht in the newspaper. The small article focused mainly on my friend's companion aboard the boat, whose life the storm had claimed, but it concluded with the single sentence: "Quite miraculously, his shipmate managed to save himself by swimming to shore through the storm-tossed seas."

That sounded exactly like the man I knew—though his fellow traveler must also have been a seaman of considerable skill. I had difficulty imagining the horrendous conditions that could have gotten the better of such a man. As typhoons go, the storm they encountered was of only moderate strength, but a typhoon is still a typhoon, and it had passed very near the two men and their yacht on the water.

They were delivering a newly launched eight-meter vessel from the boat-yard my friend worked at in Nagoya to a destination in Kanagawa, when they

133

ran smack into the typhoon on the Enshu Sea.

According to the forecast at the time they cast off, the typhoon was expected to track farther to the east. They figured they could pick up strong chasing winds on the outskirts of the storm and make a quick run up the Enshu Sea, but the typhoon veered sharply west and gained speed, drawing them into the semicircle of its greatest fury. They tried to beat a path around Omaezaki Point into safe harbor on the other side, but a huge wave caught them while they were still on the open sea.

"It was a gigantic rogue wave," my friend said. "Just as the bow was plowing into the wave ahead, an even bigger one crashed down on us from astern. It tore off the doghouse, and instantly filled the cabin with water. I'm manning the tiller, so I yell for my shipmate to start bailing, but he's so weak from all the knocking around, he doesn't have it in him. Another big one breaks over us, and we start sinking fast. Once it gets like that, an eight-meter yacht isn't going to float any better than if I threw this glass of beer in the water." He raised his glass and laughed, squinting as if looking into a bright light.

Seeing his companion about to go down with the boat, my friend grabbed him by the collar and held his head above water as he groped for their life jackets with the other hand. He only managed to find one. They began paddling through the night-black Enshu Sea with a single life jacket between them.

Trying to ride the swells that came up behind them one after the other, they quickly realized the cresting waves were a trap: the white crests weren't water but vortices of foam and bubbles incapable of buoying up their bodies. Ironically, in order to catch the driving crests, they had to hold their breaths and dive under.

My friend's shipmate had already swallowed half a lungful of water when they abandoned ship, and now he was swallowing even more with each coming wave. Soon he no longer had the strength to swim, and was merely hanging on like a dead weight. My friend tried to hold him up and swim on, but eventually, as another in the endless march of swells lifted and pushed them forward, the man shook his arm loose from its tether and slipped into the ink-black deep.

"I search the water under me and shout his name, but all I get is seawater. I realize I could easily drown, too, so I give up. Now that I'm alone, the next time I dip into a trough I tread water and pull on the life jacket, but it doesn't do any good. Those damn things don't give you any decent buoyancy when you wear them like they tell you to."

He took the jacket off and spread it under his chest like a kickboard instead.

"That gave me much better flotation. This's going to make a big difference, I'm thinking, when all of a sudden it hits me: I have no idea how many kilometers I have to swim. I start giving myself a pep talk, telling myself not to panic, being real careful not to swallow any more water. 'Stay calm, keep swimming, that's your only chance.' That's what I tell myself. 'The sun'll be up in another five hours. If you swim real easy and don't knock yourself out, you just might be able to make it.'"

He paddled along for the better part of an hour, gradually acclimatizing to the rhythm of the waves. He got so he could tell when the next one was coming, even in the dark. He'd hold his breath and stroke at precisely the right moment to hitch a ride on its forward motion, surfing just below the foaming crest rather than at the crest itself.

"You know, it's amazing how cocky a guy can get. It didn't take long before I'm thinking I can easily keep this up till morning. Of course, even if I did, there was no telling where I'd wash up, or what would happen to me there. I tried not to think about that part."

Instead, he tried to focus his mind on other things—his life on land, his family—but it was a lost cause. As he slowly chugged his way through the stormy darkness, he felt as if he were swimming endlessly in a tiny, enclosed space. He wished he could at least see his own arms and legs.

After swimming blindly like that for who knows how long, he noticed the waves getting steeper and realized he must be approaching shore. Several minutes later, a wave tossed him mercilessly up, down, right, and left before slamming him rudely down on solid land.

"Glad at least that I didn't get thrown onto some rocks, I figure I'm home safe on the Enshu coast. Then the next instant another wave comes crashing over me and drags me back out into the surf, and I'm sure I'm going to drown."

Again and again the waves cast him up on shore, only to promptly peel him off the beach and drag him back out to sea. Each time he swallowed more water. Just when he thought he couldn't hold out any longer, he felt an immense surge welling up beneath him. Summoning his last reserves of strength, he swung his arms forward to catch this massive wave. And this time when he was thrown onto the beach he clung to it with all his might, digging both hands into the sand, desperately fighting the pull of the water back toward the surf. The water receded, his body remained. He was finally on solid ground, no longer engulfed by water. As soon as he realized this, he began clawing at the ground beneath him, inching his way up the beach. There his strength gave out.

He felt another wave break and roll up the beach toward him. If the water reached him now, when all his energy was spent, he'd drown for sure. But the water barely licked his heels. As the wave receded, a tiny ball of light floated up before his eyes and he drifted off.

After a while, the cold brought him to. Very cautiously, he drew his elbows back, planted his palms in the sand, and pushed. He was able to lift himself off the ground. Drawing his legs forward, he got up onto his hands and knees, then continued to brace himself as he rose to his feet. His knees felt like they might buckle at any moment as he took one step, then another, determined to distance himself from the sea. Three steps, four steps, no matter how furiously the sea behind him seethed and raged, it couldn't catch him now. He had no desire to turn and see for sure. He simply walked straight away from the roar of the sea at his back.

As he walked, the ground beneath his feet changed from sand to pebbles and then to scruffy grass. He looked up, and saw in the distance a tiny ball of light exactly like the one he'd seen before. He set out in the direction of the light.

"What was it?" my curiosity demanded. "What was the ball of light you saw? Did it have a color?"

"I don't really know," he said. "What I can say, though, is that it was the truest light I ever saw. The very essence of light."

My friend, the survivor of this ordeal at sea, was once again squinting into a bright, unseen light.

THE OLD MAN AND THE SHARK

I'd always heard that shark bites are gruesome, and indeed the gaping scar old man Tonaki showed me on his thigh was a ghastly sight. The flesh was gouged away roughly in the shape of a right triangle, not unlike a square-cornered rip in a snagged shirt. But this was no mere tear in the skin: a sizable chunk of flesh had been ripped out by the shark's razor-sharp teeth. With vital muscle tissue gone, the leg would no longer bend, and Tonaki had had to limp around stiffly ever since. I sometimes saw him holding his hand to the spot when he walked, as though still unaccustomed to his debility. Or perhaps pains flared up from time to time.

"For about two years there, I couldn't walk at all. I could only crawl around the house," Tonaki said. "And that's why I vowed to get my revenge, to kill the son of a bitch, no matter what it took. If it had only been a flesh wound, I might've just decided to give up spearfishing."

When finally he could walk again, he started planning in earnest how to settle the score with his assailant.

The great white was nearly four meters long, and several other people had sighted it since his attack. They could tell it was the same shark because the shaft of a broken harpoon remained embedded in the flesh behind its left eye, right where Tonaki had driven it.

"Every time I heard some news about that shark, it was like a shot in the arm," he said.

Sharks are often attracted by a spearfisherman's catch. Tonaki had had three large octopuses tied to his waist, and the shark had been determined to get them, coming at him again and again.

"I figure that shark must really have had a thing about octopus," Tonaki later remarked. "Seeing octopus made him go a little crazy."

Whether particular sharks really prefer particular foods I couldn't say, but certainly Tonaki believed so, and once he was on his feet again, he prepared for his revenge accordingly. He bought up the octopuses fellow spearfishermen brought back from their outings, and set them out as live bait near where he'd been attacked, attaching them to the end of wires dangling from floats at just the right depth to make it easy for a shark to find them. But when he went to check on the bait later, it would be gone. Though he had no real way of knowing which shark had taken it, Tonaki was convinced it was his assailant.

To be completely sure, he decided to stay in the water and monitor the bait after setting it out, to see with his own eyes who was taking it. He continued his stakeout day after day, to no avail. Yet he'd come back the next day and find the bait missing. There was not a doubt in his mind: *his* great white had taken it as soon as he'd gone home.

Tonaki continued his watch for nearly six months until he finally witnessed what he'd expected all along. He saw his great white devouring one bait, then moving on to the next.

"He calmly polished off the octopuses one by one as if he owned them, then swam away."

"So, why didn't you hammer him while you had the chance?"

"I just couldn't do it. I mean, when I actually saw the monster again in the water, I couldn't believe how big he was. I even had my harpoon with me, all ready to go, but I simply couldn't bring myself to use it. Afterwards, I was so disgusted with myself for letting him get away, I cried myself to sleep that night. My wife thanked the gods for making me call it off, and told me to just forget the damn thing. But what could a woman know about how I felt? After years of waiting, I'd finally seen my attacker again. Sure enough, just like my fishing buddies said, the broken shaft was still right there behind his left eye."

Tonaki reassessed the situation. He obviously had no hope of challenging the great white face to face. The sea was the shark's domain, not Tonaki's. He'd have to bring some human ingenuity to bear on the contest.

"I'd gotten it into my head that I wanted to drill him with a harpoon," Tonaki said, "but I realized that was stupid. The son of a bitch was just too incredibly big. To be honest, I was a whole lot more scared seeing the shark this second time than the time he took a bite out of me. But I wasn't about to give up because of that, no matter what my wife said. I didn't want to wind up like some hopeless landlubber. I figured I'd just have to outsmart him."

In the end, human intelligence emerged victorious over the great ocean predator. Tonaki baited a large fishhook and attached it to a wire anchored to a big rock, so the shark wouldn't be able to get away once it took the bait. When Tonaki went back the next day, he found the great white swimming about with the hook in its mouth, dragging the wire behind. Other sharks were circling about nearby—not in sympathy, but in anticipation of their larger cousin's impending transformation into a feeding opportunity.

His sworn enemy now in custody, Tonaki pondered a fitting execution. Now that he could observe the shark calmly, he was amazed all over again by the animal's immense size. The more he looked at it, with the stub of his harpoon still protruding from behind its left eye, the more he understood what a tiny pinprick it had been for the huge beast.

Back in his boat, Tonaki had a live "popgun" cartridge he'd been carrying around just for the moment when he came face to face with the great white again. A friend in Okinawa had obtained the ammo for him from an American GI, and Tonaki had fashioned a casing to attach it to the shaft of a rubber-band harpoon. On impact, a firing pin in the bottom of the casing would ignite the primer and propel the bullet deep into the shark. Plug the monster's head with this, and it had to do some serious damage, no matter how big it might be. The only question was: would he ever have a chance to use it?

Tonaki swam back to his boat to fetch the deadly weapon, then returned to the scene. He had only the single round, so he had to get it right the first time. Even in less than ten meters of water, his timing was off the first few dives. Finally, on his fifth attempt, everything went perfectly: he came down directly above the circling shark, and drove the deadly harpoon right into the middle of its head.

Even underwater, he could feel the shock of the exploding propellant—nothing like an ordinary harpoon. The shark promptly rolled over on its side and, in Tonaki's own words, gave him the evil eye; then, writhing in the throes of death, it sank to the bottom.

But the great white was not finished yet. After resting for a brief time on the seabed, it abruptly started trying to swim again, reeling about like a drunk who comes lurching back to life just when you think he's nodded off.

This is my only chance, Tonaki thought. He let go of the harpoon and reached for his dive knife, then swam down to the shark struggling on the seabed, jabbed the long blade into its belly, and ripped it open. Surfacing once for air, he swam back down through the cloud of blood spreading around the shark, and this time he jammed the long blade into its back.

He was starting down for a third time, wondering how many more trips it might take, when something unexpected happened: halfway to the bottom he was shouldered aside by one of the circling sharks. All at once, they'd judged the time to be right, and now came swarming down upon their much bigger but mortally wounded cousin.

The great white lay helpless, writhing and spewing blood with the hook still lodged in its gullet. The other sharks began tearing large chunks of flesh from its sides. Grateful for this unexpected assistance, Tonaki returned to the surface and watched from there as the sharks fed in full frenzy. Before he knew it, more and more sharks emerged from the deep, swelling their numbers to almost twenty, large and small, tearing so furiously at the carcass of the great white that billowing clouds of blood soon obscured all view of it. Five minutes after it all began, only the great white's head remained.

When Tonaki climbed back into the boat, he realized he was crying. "I have no idea where the tears came from. It wasn't like I was overwhelmed with joy, nor for that matter was I in any way sad, yet for some reason they just kept coming and coming.

"In the end, I almost started to feel sorry for the damn thing," he admitted. "But when it comes right down to it, their kind are all the same—they're the absolute worst kind of savages, plain and simple. If I hadn't seen those other sharks in action, I might still be spearfishing today. But I did, and after that the spell of the ocean was broken. I hardly even think about fishing any more."

I'd like to think I understand how old man Tonaki feels, but there's no way I can begin to know what he lost and regained in this saga of revenge. After all, it wasn't me who had a chunk of flesh taken out of my leg by a shark.

THE LIGHTER

It was in the days when my brother Yujiro boarded with Takiko Mizunoe, the producer who gave him his start in show business. One December, Mme. Mizunoe hosted a party at her magnificent home for my brother and his girlfriend, Mie Kitahara. They were head over heels in love and had secretly gotten engaged. Only those in the know were invited and, given the season, the occasion doubled as a Christmas party.

It proved to be a pleasant gathering. Yujiro, in particular, must have been in seventh heaven: thanks to his breakthrough as an actor, he'd not only been brought together with, but become engaged to, the actress he'd been crazy about ever since his student days. As his older brother, I felt glad that fortune was smiling on him.

About the time the party started to come alive, I remembered I needed to make a phone call, and went outside to retrieve some related notes from my car. On the way back, I noticed a woman standing on the narrow hedge-lined path leading to the house.

As best as I could tell in the shadows, she looked about thirty. Show business fans back then weren't as brazen as they are today, but my first thought was that some fan of Yujiro's had come to see what she could of our party. Still, there was something about her demeanor that suggested perhaps there was more to it than that.

"Can I help you?" I asked.

She seemed relieved that I spoke first. "Um, if I may, I was wondering if Yujiro

Ishihara is inside?" Her polite and diffident tone suggested that she wasn't just some starry-eyed groupie.

"Yes, but I'm afraid the gathering is for friends and family only. I don't think he'll be able to come outside."

"Oh, no, that's not why I asked. Could you perhaps take this lighter to him? It belongs to him. He left it. I know it's very special to him, and I wanted to get it back to him sooner, but . . ."

She handed me a fancy Zippo lighter, a very popular brand at the time. We stood in the dark, but once I had the lighter in hand I could see it was engraved on one side.

"You just want me to give this to Yujiro?" I said. "I'd be happy to."

I accepted the lighter and went back inside, grateful to the unassuming visitor for going to this trouble.

The party was in full swing. I went from room to room until I found my brother, and got his attention.

"You left this somewhere and a woman delivered it just now," I said, handing him the lighter.

A look of astonishment came across his face. "What the hell?" he said. He cocked his head and furrowed his brow as he moved to examine the Zippo under a lamp.

"It *is* yours, right? She said it belonged to you."

"Who did?"

"The woman out front. That's what she told me when she gave it to me."

"But who was she? What kind of woman?"

"How should I know? I barely even saw her."

"Hold on a second, okay?" he said, knocking the side of his head in puzzlement as he tried to get the attention of a friend of his across the room. "Hey, Koichi! Koichi!" he shouted. "Come here a minute!"

Koichi Saito, then a photographer, later a cinematographer and film director, was one of Yujiro's closest friends.

"Look what showed up," my brother said, handing the lighter to him.

Koichi took one glance at it and burst out, "Hey, it's that lighter you lost! But wait a minute." He gave Yujiro a baffled look. "How the hell—?"

"Some woman out front asked Shintaro to bring it to me," Yujiro said. "It's got to be some kind of a joke, right?"

"How's it possible?"

I stood there staring in incomprehension, but they ignored me and huddled under the light to reexamine the Zippo in detail.

"It's that lighter, all right. No doubt about it," said my brother.

"Right. I remember the engraving. And this mark here—that's from when you dropped it on deck and it bashed into the bollard. I told you that was no way to treat a special gift from your girlfriend, remember? I warned you she'd have a fit."

"Yeah, I remember."

Koichi finally turned back to look at me. "You say someone found it and came to return it?"

"She didn't say 'found.' She said Yujiro left it somewhere."

"I didn't leave it anywhere. I lost it. I dropped it in the *ocean*."

"Then maybe somebody found it and picked it up when the tide went out."

"No, no, I lost it out on the open sea. We sailed out of Nagoya, and by the time I dropped it we were way south of the Kii Peninsula. The ship was completely out of sight of land, in the middle of the ocean."

"I don't understand," I said.

"Neither do I," he replied. A distinct look of tension, even fright, showed on his face.

He explained that Mie had given him the lighter as a birthday present at the end of the previous year. She'd had it engraved with both their initials, intricately intertwined. He loved it, and always slipped it into his pocket wherever he went.

Then in the spring, during filming *of The Eagle and the Hawk*, the studio chartered a coastal freighter to sail from Tokyo to Moji with a stop in Nagoya, and put the entire cast and crew on board to shoot ship scenes throughout the voyage. Yujiro didn't have any scenes to do for a while after they left Nagoya, so he and Koichi hung out on the upper deck drinking beer and watching the others work.

Koichi noticed the intricately engraved lighter he was fingering and asked him about it, remarking on the excellent workmanship. Yujiro denied it was anything

144

special, and started tossing the lighter up in the air; even after it bounced off the bollard and got nicked a bit, he went on flinging it about as if he couldn't care less about it. The more Koichi told him to be careful, the more reckless he became. Soon he was tossing it around out over the railing, and as you might expect, eventually his fingers slipped: the precious lighter fell into the water.

"We watched the silver Zippo trace a smooth arc from the upper deck all the way down into the drink."

"And I said, 'Told you so.'"

"Right away, I made Koichi promise, neither of us would tell Mie how I lost it. Then on second thought I said we shouldn't tell her I lost it at all."

"I see," I nodded—though the entire business was about as clear as mud.

None of us said anything for a few moments. I suppose we must have all looked as if we'd been tricked by a fox or something.

After a time my brother broke the silence. "So this woman, what was she like?"

"I don't know. Thirtyish, I suppose."

"Was she a looker?"

"No, I'd say she was pretty average."

"Was there anything strange about her?"

"Not that I noticed."

"She might still be around," Koichi broke in. "Shall I go see?"

"Maybe you should," I said.

"No, no, forget it," Yujiro said quickly. "Don't go. Don't bother."

"Why not?"

"Think about it. It's just not possible. I really did drop this lighter in the middle of the ocean. You were there. You saw it with your own eyes."

"Well, yeah, but . . . ," Koichi started to protest, then didn't know what to say next.

"You're sure it was this same lighter, right?" I said.

"Absolutely. That's why it doesn't make sense. I refuse to believe it," Yujiro protested.

"Believe it or don't, you said yourself it's the same one you lost. But wait, maybe you guys only *thought* you kept it a secret from Mie. Maybe she found out somehow. She could have had an exact duplicate made."

"You think?"

"There's only one way to find out," I said. "Go ask Mie herself."

We got Mie from the other room, but took care not to give anything away.

"Why should I want another lighter like that?" she said. "I don't even smoke."

While Yujiro stood there trying to find his tongue, I repeated to Mie what he'd already told me.

"Are you sure?" she said, turning to Yujiro. "You say you dropped it in the water, but maybe you just thought you did. Maybe you actually dropped it onto a lower deck."

"No, I'm positive. I actually saw it disappear into the waves."

Mie gingerly took the lighter in her hand.

"This is definitely it," she said as she put it back on the table. "I remember picking it out at Wako Jewelers." She eyed the object uneasily.

"Well, anyway," I said, "your precious gift found its way home. You should be glad."

"Are you kidding?" Yujiro said. "There's no way I'm using that thing after this. It's too spooky. Sorry, Mie, but somebody please just get rid of it for me."

"That hardly seems right," I said. "I mean, after all, whatever the real explanation, its recovery makes it pretty special. You can't just throw something like that away. I don't think that's a good idea at all."

"I agree," Mie said. "Think of how the woman who brought it back would feel."

"Who exactly was this woman, anyway?" my brother demanded, but of course that was a question no one could answer.

I replayed the brief encounter in my mind, trying to bring back a more detailed picture of the woman, but it was no use.

No one was about to let this throw cold water on the evening, however. We were all young, after all. Yujiro himself took the lead in describing the events to the others present, and everybody seemed to enjoy the strange, spooky story.

Except Takiko Mizunoe, our hostess, who was quite a bit older than the rest of us. She shook her shoulders in a shiver and said, "Oh, stop it. When I hear scary tales like that, I can't help taking them seriously."

To this day, I remember exactly how her comment sounded. But whatever anyone says, there can be no doubt about this: I personally accepted the lighter from an unidentified woman and delivered it to my brother with my own hands.

And in fact the Zippo still remains among the things my brother left behind when he died.

True to his word, Yujiro never used the lighter again, nor did he ever allow anyone else to touch it. What would really be spooky, though, is if someone tried to light it now and it actually produced a flame.

SPIRIT FIRES

My circle of friends included all kinds of people, but among them Takuji Sakai stood out as a particularly rough character. Always on edge, he seemed ready to explode at any second. We became friends through hunting, and I'd have to say there are probably few men whose temper was less suited to a sport that involves firearms.

Even in ordinary conversation, he'd turn on you with a quick tongue if he disagreed with something you said. And he was quick with a punch as well, which got him into frequent fights. He had a couple of scars on his forehead to prove it, souvenirs from altercations in his youth.

Not that he was universally unpopular, for he could in fact be a solicitous friend. Still, many kept their distance from him. If he were a horse, I suppose you'd call him skittish and ornery.

I've struck a man just once in my life, and that was when I was with Sakai. More precisely, I kicked the man in the side.

One winter, a fisherman acquaintance in Miura called to say that flocks of wild ducks had descended on a stretch of water nearby: maybe we'd like to come down for some shooting? Sakai and I immediately jumped into the car and raced down there. Come afternoon, winds would whip up waves and unsettle the ducks, so time was of the essence.

Sakai was at the wheel. Near Misaki we turned left off the prefectural highway onto a road leading to a tiny fishing port called Bishamon. It was a one-lane road, and we soon got caught behind a slow-moving dump truck that refused to pull over and let us pass no matter how hard Sakai honked.

Sakai was getting restless and irritated. Sitting next to him, I could tell he was ready to blow his top any second. Finally seeing his chance, he muscled around the truck by riding up on the roadside embankment. A short distance ahead, he screeched to a halt with the car blocking the road sideways. Sakai shot out of his seat to meet the truck, which of course had to stop then leapt onto the cabin step, and grabbed the driver by the collar to drag him out. Screaming abuse at the man, Sakai soon knocked him to the ground with a couple of hard blows, and was about to kick him in the head when I ran over to restrain him.

"You son of a bitch! You son of a bitch!" he was screaming, working himself into even more of a fury. Partly to defuse Sakai and partly because I had a mind to teach the jerk a lesson myself, I yelled at him too and gave him a couple of good kicks in the side for good measure—though I took care to keep clear of his head.

But before we left the man lying there and drove away, Sakai just had to get in one last lick. He bent over the fallen man and delivered a karate chop straight down the middle of his face, exactly the way you see karate masters delivering a chop to a stack of roof tiles.

The truck getting in our way had fouled our mood, and when early winds cut short our duck hunt, the day turned out to be a total bust. It was still mid-afternoon when we got off the boat and headed back to Tokyo.

The truck driver and an elderly police officer stood waiting for us on the one-lane road back to the prefectural highway. The driver pointed toward us as we approached, and the policeman waved us down.

"Officer, that man there's a real son of a bitch!" Sakai shouted as the policeman walked up to the car.

The cop raised his hand in a calming gesture. "I know, I know. He admits that he obstructed traffic. But he also says you two punched him and kicked him. Isn't that right? I must tell you that assault is a far more serious offense than blocking traffic."

Having sought out medical attention in the interim, the driver had some gauze taped across his nose as well as a place on his head.

With the officer acting as mediator, we agreed to settle things on the spot. He let us go after Sakai and I each paid the driver fifteen thousand yen.

Oddly enough, when I recall the incident now, it doesn't come back to me as a particularly unwelcome memory. Even though fifteen thousand yen was worth a good bit more then than it is today, it didn't feel like such a terrible loss. Perhaps a little bit of my friend Sakai's character had rubbed off on me.

Another of Sakai's not-so-endearing quirks was his overt skepticism toward any talk the slightest bit out of the ordinary. This made him a rather disagreeable listener. Invariably, his response to anything unusual was "Yeah, right," said in such a sarcastic tone it made everyone present feel awkward.

One time he and I and some other friends went deer hunting in Hokkaido. We split up into two groups of three as we headed into the mountains. When we joined up again, the other group had bagged a magnificent buck. As the lucky trio triumphantly recounted how they'd taken their trophy, Sakai's annoyance at not sharing their good fortune provoked a string of his trademark *Yeah, right*s, which began to get on everyone's nerves. The next thing I knew, the argument had escalated into a shouting match with the two sides pointing their hunting rifles at each other.

His skepticism may have been partly inborn, but no doubt some of it derived from his experiences as a used-car dealer—a business plagued with false claims.

Just once, I witnessed this inveterate skeptic defending himself so heatedly against his listeners' incredulity that his entire face started twitching.

Again we were on a hunting trip—this time with a group of men who were all older than we were. At our lodgings one night, the others were proudly regaling us with their wartime experiences, essentially to "separate the men from the boys," when Sakai chimed in with his own. As he launched into his story, I remembered him boasting to me once before that he'd been a cadet in the Junior Pilot Training Corps at the end of the war.

One day they were on their second round of solo flights, when two planes went down with their pilots one after the other. Cadets waiting their turn on the ground jumped into trucks and rushed to the crash sites to recover the victims' bodies.

"The last to go down was the guy in the bunk next to mine," Sakai said. "When his plane went into a tailspin, he obviously knew he was going to die and bailed out. His altitude was 150, maybe 160 meters, which should have been just barely enough for his chute to open. But it didn't. It didn't even come out of his pack. All we saw was this little black dot plummeting straight to the ground. When we found him, his body was like squashed tofu. Pretty horrible. To think that this was what a man could come to made me feel just sick at heart."

As a reward for training so hard, the cadets were scheduled to have a talent show that evening. In spite of the tragic accidents, the commandant decided the show should go on, hoping it would help bolster morale. After a moment of silence in memory of the dead, the singing and dancing began.

"I'm sure they hoped it would lift our spirits, but as you might expect under the circumstances, the mood stayed pretty grim. Those were the first guys from our class to die."

Still, the participants did their best as one act followed another, and then came a brief intermission to allow the next group to set up. Halfway through the break, almost as if someone had called for silence, a sudden hush fell over the audience. For some reason, everybody turned to look toward the runway behind them, in the opposite direction from the stage.

A gentle twilight glow still lingered in the sky over the stage, but the sky beyond the runway had fallen dark. Out of the deepening darkness at that end of the runway, two big balls of fire rose from the ground, burning bright red and trailing long tails of flame behind them as they ascended straight toward the heavens. They made no sound, yet somehow a silent roar seemed to reverberate through the air as they climbed.

The cadets watched breathlessly as the balls of fire soared higher and higher until finally they were gone. When the last traces disappeared, someone gave an order and everybody raised their hands in a salute to the empty sky. I don't recall Sakai saying anything about what happened to the variety show after that.

"The balls of fire were bigger than the planes that had gone down that afternoon, and they climbed into the sky with this silent roar that seemed to shake us to the bone."

By now, the other hunters and I were listening to Sakai's story in rapt silence.

"Were they pretty?" I asked. "The balls of fire."

"Not pretty so much as just spellbinding. I don't know that we really felt anything as we watched—we were just frozen numb. And I remember thinking, *So this is what it means to die.*"

I can picture in my mind what those fireballs must have looked like: burning souls appearing for one final farewell before flying up to heaven. And I think I know what went through Sakai's mind when he said he realized what it meant to die.

The night Sakai told that story, I felt I now understood him a little better, in a way I never could before.

A few years later, I heard another account of spirits appearing as balls of fire.

The events, as recounted to me by Tome Torihama, took place in the town of Chiran in southern Kyushu, home to a kamikaze base during the war. Mrs. Torihama, an elderly woman whose story is well known in Japan, ran an inn where young pilots often passed time waiting for their fateful orders. The kamikaze pilots were mere boys, still of an age when they missed their mothers, and they all called Mrs. Torihama "Mother."

I'd read about this woman in a book, and wanted to meet her in person, so when I went to nearby Miyakonojo for a speaking engagement, I made a little detour to Chiran to ask her to tell me about her wartime experiences.

The countrified old lady spoke haltingly. From the lips of some other narrator, the stories might have come across as more heroic or tragic, but her unadorned descriptions of those young pilots sent on suicide missions under deteriorating war conditions had a simple power and beauty. Each story went straight to the heart. I felt as if I'd rediscovered some ancient oral tradition before the advent of writing, when important events were recounted by those directly involved, in their own words.

The stories hit me like a sledgehammer—from the plight of pilots never ordered out on their final missions, to the tale of the boy who promised Mrs. Torihama the day before his mission that he would come back as a firefly. He'd always been fond of fireflies, and sure enough, at that very hour the next day, she saw a single firefly emerge from the well under the wisteria arbor in her back yard.

The story that left the deepest impression, though, was an anecdote from after the war—after the young pilots had long since gone home.

One evening Mrs. Torihama had to go to the neighboring village on an errand, which took her along the fence skirting what had once been the kamikaze air base. She'd gone there often during the war to say a little prayer each time another wave of young men took off to their deaths, but she hadn't been back in quite some time. Twilight descended over the entire area, the airfield now transformed into a field of canola blossoms.

Across the field, right about where the barracks used to stand, a single string of bobbing flames suddenly lit up as if to welcome her—a wavering line of lights dancing about vigorously in the air.

A maid from the inn was with her, and they both stopped in their tracks and began praying. Soon, as if their prayers had been heard, the countless spirit fires began to flicker and go out, one by one.

"It was a frightening sight, but also very pretty," she said, closing her eyes to picture the scene again in her mind.

Countless spirits of young men who died in vain during wartime, undulating in the dim twilight as flickering balls of karmic fire: does anyone have the words to really do justice to such a scene?

I suppose that's why my editor companion and I both found ourselves sitting stiffly upright when she finished.

BUDDHA ON THE HIGHWAY

I was an extremely reckless driver in my twenties. My friends and I would use the long hill in front of a certain inn in Izu for time trials, or we'd all set out from some point in Tokyo and race each other to a friend's villa in Karuizawa to see who could run the most lights on the way and get there in the fastest time.

This was back when no one said a thing about drinking and driving. I once spent an evening at a bar in Ginza, drinking late into the night, then bet myself that I could make it home to my front door in Zushi in so many minutes. I drove as fast as I could the entire way. Tokyo-Yokohama Highway No. 2 still had a green median strip at the time, and traffic lights had only recently been installed at main intersections.

When I think back on it now, clocking in at forty-two minutes from Ginza to Zushi is a pretty scary record, particularly considering it was a rainy night. My Dodge Royal Lancer had plenty of horsepower, and I remember how the power steering made cornering a real thrill.

I usually drove when I went into Tokyo, and I always drank until the wee hours before coming home. Which is how I learned both the seduction and dangers of dozing off at the wheel. Speeding along a midnight highway half asleep brings on an indescribable sense of unreality. You think you know exactly where you are and what you're doing, but you don't. Not really. On the one hand, you're verging on new euphoric highs; on the other, the last vestiges of your better judgment are calling out for attention. You don't know which to obey, but that very dilemma brings an edgy elation. Maybe it's a kind of masochism.

After a while, you sometimes begin to see shadowy wings, like a raven flitting back and forth before your eyes. One night when no amount of waving would chase the bird away, I tried to actually catch it, and for a moment my hands left the wheel. The car nearly plunged over the edge of the highway into the ocean at Sugita. One wheel had gone over the shoulder, but I managed to get the car back on the road. At that point I figured I'd better play it safe, so I had a brief snooze, and ten minutes later I felt so sober I could have sworn it had all been a dream.

Others who have fallen asleep at the wheel say they've seen the same flittering black bird. Perhaps it's the shadow of death—in which case, I can understand why they sometimes say that death, when she comes, is bewitching.

Besides the Dodge, I also drove an MG TF and, a little later, a Triumph TR3. In those days imported cars were objects of adulation; domestic models weren't up to international standards yet. When it came to sports cars—or more specifically roadsters—Japanese auto makers had yet to produce a single one; foreign makes were the only option, and even they were few and far between, so they had a definite snob appeal. When two such cars met about town, the drivers wouldn't wave but merely raise a forefinger atop the steering wheel and give the horn a light toot as they passed. I suppose it was something like a secret handshake between members of an exclusive club.

Once I was on my way home after a round of golf in Hakone, and nightfall brought rain. A car fell in behind me around Chigasaki and tailed me all along the coast. Finally, as we were coming up to Inamuragasaki, he recklessly forced his way around me, sped ahead to the bottom of the hill, and pulled over. He immediately put out his hand and signaled me to stop.

The car was another roadster—an Austin-Healey. A Westerner I'd never seen before emerged from the driver's seat. He had a young Japanese woman with him.

"Look," he said abruptly when I rolled down the window of my soft-top. "I've been following you for a good while, and your driving scares the life out of me. In just the time I've been behind you, you've already stepped on your brakes six times. You obviously have no idea how to drive a car like this." It was after dark, but I could see he had to be at least fifty. "Damn it, man, don't you know the only time you should have to use your brakes in a sports car is when you pull in and out of the garage?"

You've got to be kidding, I thought, but I could tell he was dead serious—he wasn't just trying to show off in front of his girlfriend. Did driving similar cars give him the right to correct my driving habits? In any case, I found it all quite amusing.

"You don't have to tell me that," I said. "I always used to downshift into curves, but all that action wore the car out. Unlike your girlfriend here, this baby's no spring chicken; she's more like a grande dame of fifty, well past her prime. If I downshifted into every curve, I'd break her back."

The fellow burst out laughing. "Can I buy you a drink?"

We drove up the road a short distance to a restaurant called Venus, the only such establishment along that stretch of highway. There he introduced his none-too-elegant-looking girlfriend and himself—his name was Goodman—and we each tossed back a shot of whiskey before going our separate ways. It was the sort of nighttime encounter on the road that would never happen today.

I continued to drive that TR3 hard and fast for quite some time, riding the brakes as usual, until finally one day something happened that changed me forever.

I was about to enter Kawasaki on my way to Tokyo when I got into a passing contest with an off-duty cab. I overtook him first, and then he quickly passed me back. A short time later I eased past him again, without really meaning to, but when the cab blew by me a second time, I realized that he saw it as a race.

I put him behind me again, and for quite some distance after that the cabbie continued tailing me and trying to pass. I easily held him off, sometimes even toying with him a bit, and eventually pulled well ahead. It was kid's play, really, just an amusing little episode on my trip into Tokyo.

Not too far after crossing the river that separates Kawasaki from Tokyo, I came to a section where one lane had been blocked off to facilitate repair work on a railway bridge overhead. As the two lanes squeezed into one, traffic backed up and came to a virtual standstill. I had just merged into the single file of cars, when suddenly the cab that I'd long since lost sight of in my rear view mirror pulled up beside me.

I suppose you're going to wedge your way in somewhere up ahead, you shameless bastard, I thought as I turned to glare at the driver. But to my surprise, I found a fortyish man in the prime of his life peering back at me with a look of keen interest.

"You're quite a driver," he called out with what sounded like genuine admiration. "I've been in this business a long time, but you're the best I've seen."

His words took me so by surprise I had no idea how to respond. He peered back at me for a few seconds more, as though he had something else to say, but then with a sudden tilt of his head that seemed to encompass a whole variety of feelings for which he could not find words, he made a quick U-turn and drove back the way he'd come.

I turned to watch him go, but like a defeated contestant who slinks away to hide his shame, he'd already disappeared. Just then the line of cars finally began to move, and I shifted into gear, feeling somehow as though I'd been blindsided.

It occurred to me that the man was just playing with me, though he'd looked dead serious. He was unmistakably the same guy I'd engaged in that impromptu race with earlier, and he said himself that he'd been a taxi driver for a long time; he looked old enough to have been at it a couple of decades or more. So why should someone like that go out of his way to come and offer kudos to an amateur like me? I cocked my head in puzzlement and drove on.

About two traffic lights later, the answer suddenly hit me: the man wasn't an ordinary person; he was some kind of messenger from beyond—perhaps one of my ancestors, maybe even my father—appearing before me in the guise of a cab driver to give me a warning. I understood then and there for the first time what it meant to have a revelation.

What am I doing? I thought. *I've been putting my life on the line for nothing but cheap thrills.* It was a realization that came from the very core of my being, and I gave a deep shudder when it hit home.

From that moment on, I started to drive more responsibly. To my mind, that experience was like a tap on the shoulder from the Buddha himself. And I was unmistakably changed as a result: I still went drinking that night and drove myself home to Zushi afterwards, but I took nearly twice as long as I had on my record night.

In the autumn of that same year, the first Japanese Grand Prix was held at the newly completed Suzuka Circuit. The various auto makers sought out people known for their gutsy driving, and asked them to man company-sponsored cars modified for the race. This was before there were professional race drivers in Japan.

The owner of a Toyota dealership I knew approached me and asked if I'd like to race in the 2000cc class at Suzuka. A year earlier I would have leapt at the chance, but now I dismissed the request out of hand.

My would-be sponsor seemed taken aback, and wanted to know why. When it started to sound like he was going to offer better terms, I cut him off.

"Look, I do still drive," I said. "But I've graduated from that kind of driving."

Because of meeting the Buddha on the highway.

Come to think of it, though, I have no idea what happened to the demon I met earlier—that fellow by the name of Goodman.

NEWLYWEDS

The occupants of the house changed frequently, no doubt because it was located near the navy base in Yokosuka and rented exclusively to navy men. The tenants were always men of officer rank, and the turnover was even more rapid as the war situation deteriorated and threatening clouds began to spread over the homeland itself. We would notice that someone else had moved in, and then the next thing we knew the place would be empty again.

The son of the landlord was one of my playmates. His family owned a number of properties in the neighborhood as well as a rental boat business nearby. Since the house in question was right next door to where they lived, the son would take his pals inside on rainy days if the place happened to be between tenants. The empty rooms became our indoor playground.

I remember one particular day when several of us started playing tag in the yard before noticing a young couple in the sitting room having tea. They didn't say anything, so we went on with our game. In fact, they smiled and seemed to enjoy watching us play, so we got even bolder and louder as we raced about the yard.

After a while the man came out to the veranda. He wanted to know what grade we were in at school. I was the leader of the local boys' association, so I acted as spokesman and told him each of our grades. Then I added that I myself would be taking the exam for the nearby Shonan Middle School the following spring.

"Well, well," he said, looking at me with new respect.

I knew he had to be an officer, and if he'd come up through the Naval Academy at Etajima, he also probably knew that Shonan Middle School sent more of its graduates to the Academy than any other school in Japan.

He invited us all in and gave us each a handful of sugar candies. It was a time of shortages, and even this simple sweet was a rare treat.

Knowing their stay would be brief, they hadn't bothered to furnish the place with anything but the barest of necessities. In the nearly empty sitting room, we sat in a circle around a rather forlorn-looking table sucking on the first candy we'd tasted in ages. I can still remember the sweetness in my mouth.

In that makeshift setting, the young couple seemed an almost dazzling presence. The man was a burly fellow with short-cropped hair; he wore a traditional kimono and gave the impression of enjoying his first relaxing day at home in quite some time. How long had it been for him since his last day off? The woman was slim and quite tall, and even to a child's eye she seemed very stylish and pretty. They were of course much older than we were, but somehow they had an air of innocence about them.

Young as I was, I sensed that they felt at a loss with each other—being alone together like this in the middle of the day. That, no doubt, was why they had invited us in.

We'd barged into their yard without asking, just to play, but now I started to think that maybe we'd been brought there for a purpose, to sit around that table and give the two of them someone to talk to. Which is to say, I must have intuitively sensed the precariousness of being young and married in that time of war.

At any rate, the young couple exuded an endearing quality that touched even a child's heart. Their present happiness couldn't possibly survive the times we lived in, yet all the more for it, I wished them well from the bottom of my heart.

Maybe I was experiencing my first taste of erotic feelings there in the midst of wartime.

"You're newlyweds, aren't you?" I asked at one point.

This prompted a light nudge on the head from the man, but he and his wife both beamed ear to ear as they exchanged glances. I was pretty pleased with myself, too, to see them smile so happily at my correct guess. I think what I felt went beyond the usual child's desire to please grown-ups; it was more of an empathy for something beautiful and desirable that was destined to perish. Or again, perhaps it was my first time to know the catharsis of viewing something tragic. This was before I came to know life's cruelties large and small, yet I was mourning for them from the bottom of my heart.

"When do you have to go back to the war?" I asked hesitantly. It seemed like a question one of us ought to ask.

The man turned to look at me and studied me for a moment, then forced a smile that seemed to withhold a storm of emotions.

"All too soon," he said.

Suddenly he spread his arms wide as he beckoned for us to come, and he pulled each of us tightly into his embrace, rubbing his cheek against ours.

It was a sudden, even startling, gesture. But precisely for that reason it hit me all the harder: this was how a person says goodbye. As I felt the sandpaper roughness of the man's beard rubbing against my face, I knew without a shadow of a doubt that this couple would never have children of their own.

"You grow up big and strong, now, you hear? Grow up big and strong," the man repeated, almost pleading. I wanted desperately to hug him back, but I was pinned too tightly in his arms, so I just nodded over and over with all the conviction I could muster.

Less than a week later, they were gone. The husband departed for the southern battlefront, leaving his new bride behind, and she presumably went back to live with her parents. No doubt, the young officer's ship had come back to the naval base in Yokosuka for supplies, and that house had served as the newlyweds' cozy little love nest for those precious few days he had in port.

And on one of those precious few evenings they'd been given, we boys gatecrashed their quiet retreat. What could we have possibly meant to them? Were we like those cherubs you see hovering in paintings like *The Union of Venus and Mars*? I've imagined us in that light sometimes since then.

About six months later, as winter gave way to spring, I was asked to represent the children of my school at a memorial observance for a fallen serviceman. This duty fell to me from time to time as captain of the school patrol, whenever the ashes of someone from our neighborhood were brought home.

I was taken to the house my friend's family owned. A curtain with broad black and white stripes had been draped all around the house for the service. I went inside to wait for the ceremony to start, and presently the young bride I'd seen the previous autumn came in the front door bearing a white box containing her husband's ashes. She wore a black kimono and appeared to have aged considerably. Behind her came an older man, obviously her father-in-law, holding a large picture of her husband in a black frame against his chest. In the picture, her husband looked much younger than when I had seen him; in fact, he looked like a mere boy.

A grave but calm sense of inevitability filled the room: what everyone knew would happen had happened. No tears were shed, no voices raised in lament. Even the emotionless blank of the widow's face seemed wholly as it should be.

Following the lead of my elders, I went forward and offered incense. As I passed on the way back to my seat, the widow bowed to me with that same placid blankness. We lived in a time when no one was spared such events; everyone's stock of life and death emotions had long since been depleted.

The next day, the young widow was gone. After holding a wake in Yokosuka for those who had known her husband, she'd returned to the country with his parents.

"The white box didn't really have any ashes in it, you know," the landlord's son remarked to me smugly.

"Then what?" I asked. "The man's things?"

"No, stupid. His ship's at the bottom of the sea, remember? They just put a little wooden tablet in there that says 'Spirit of Fallen Hero So-and-so.' That's what I heard."

I didn't doubt him. I pictured the young widow in a private moment after the funeral, quietly opening the box to see what was inside. However slightly, I thought that finding the box empty would actually be a greater comfort to her.

Quite recently, when I went to visit an acquaintance who lived near the old neighborhood, I decided to look in on where that house had been decades before.

Virtually all of the surrounding houses had been replaced with newer structures during the intervening years, but apart from having new coats of paint, that house and the landlord's next to it were the same as ever. When I was little, the yard had been open to the street, allowing us to enter from anywhere, but now a low bamboo fence enclosed the shrubbery that surrounded the house.

I looked over the fence into the yard. From the house came the sound of a television and children's voices. Soon afterwards, the front door swung open, and out came a young married couple and their two children, a boy and a girl near school age. They were apparently setting out on a family outing.

I stood there in a daze, unable to move. The small dead-end alley led nowhere but to the two houses—theirs and the landlord's. The young mother and father cast suspicious glances at this stranger who stood mutely staring at them.

Yet all I could do was stand there in a trance, enthralled.

THE CHILDREN WHO MISSED
GOING TO WAR

Awareness of death came to me literally out of the blue one day. A particular event suddenly awakened me not so much to a fear of death per se, but at least to the genuine possibility that it could intrude on my own sphere of activity.

In the spring of the year the war ended, I entered Shonan Middle School. Because this school effectively served as a prep school for the Naval Academy, long after students elsewhere had been mobilized in labor corps to help the war effort, we had a special dispensation to continue our studies. We even had English classes.

As the war situation continued to deteriorate and air raids became more frequent, school officials grew increasingly concerned about the safety of the promising young future officer candidates in their charge, so any time the alert sounded they would quickly cancel classes and send us home. Needless to say, these alerts were highly popular among us students.

I commuted between my home in Zushi and the school in Fujisawa by rail. The trains were always packed both coming and going. I sometimes even had to stand on the coupling between cars in my wooden clogs, hanging on for dear life. Compared to that thrill, the peril of making my way home as B29s flew overhead toward targets in Tokyo seemed rather anticlimactic.

One day, the by then familiar B29s arrived overhead shortly after my class-mates and I had come out of the schoolyard. We continued walking toward the station without giving them much thought, when somebody suddenly cried out and pointed to the sky. The planes were dropping propaganda leaflets urging surrender, which came fluttering down all over the sky. We'd heard about these leaflets, but we also knew that you could get into serious trouble if caught with one in your possession. So even though we were curious, we'd never actually laid eyes on one.

As the enemy leaflets fluttered across the bright spring sky like an enormous flock of birds, my classmates and I stood there in the middle of a wheat field and watched them descend, eager for this chance to see with our own eyes what the leaflets said while gathering them up on the pretext of assisting the authorities.

Suddenly a large, dark object skimmed past our heads and crashed into the field a short distance away—not in the blink of an eye, but at a speed that allowed us to become momentarily aware of its approach before it hit the ground.

Most of us remained focused on the handbills—all except for one boy named Murata, who apparently noticed the object when it was still a tiny black dot. As he watched it quickly grow bigger and crash to earth near where we stood, he was convinced it was a bomb. Thinking we'd all be blown to bits, he threw himself on the ground and shouted a warning at two of us standing close by. To this day, I can see the scene as if it were a slow-motion film.

"So long, Ishihara! Chiba!" he yelled as he dived between rows of spring wheat.

Perhaps because I was young at the time, the sequence of events seems rather silly and illogical to me now. Obviously, if the falling object had been a bomb, Murata would never have had time to call our names and bid us farewell, nor would we have been around to hear him shout. Yet both Chiba and I implicitly understood what Murata was doing and why, for we immediately followed suit and threw ourselves to the ground. That is, in the split second before it hit, both Chiba and I must have been aware, if not quite so clearly as Murata, that something like a bomb was coming down near us.

The three of us lay flat on the ground with our hands over our eyes and ears and nose as we'd been taught. Several other classmates rushed over to see what the commotion was about. Hearing their voices told me I was still alive. Yet at that very same instant, it truly struck me for the first time in my life that death applied as much to me as to anyone else.

When our classmates asked what was going on, Murata pointed behind us and said, "It's a bomb!"

165

Rising to my feet, I turned to look and saw a large black object lying on the ground about ten meters away.

"It could still go off!" someone shouted.

Those who'd already started running toward the object stopped dead in their tracks and peered at it from a distance. It looked nothing like the drawings and photographs of bombs we'd been shown. The entire middle section was an open skeleton; you could see right through it. As we nervously edged closer, and then a little closer still, even we adolescents deduced that the unidentified falling object must be the empty shell that disgorged the propaganda leaflets still dancing in the sky overhead.

Once this became clear, the rest of the group began poking fun at the three of us who'd thrown ourselves to the ground thinking it was a bomb. Murata quickly countered that if it had been a real bomb, we'd all be dead. Even before he said this, I knew the dark shape we'd seen out of the corner of our eyes had been the shadow of death.

The experience drove home to me, with keen immediacy, the true nature of war. As the outlook for Japan continued to worsen, a number of other experiences brought me face to face with the realities of war; in each case, I connected what I saw with my own mortality, doubtless as a lingering echo of the powerful blow I sustained to my psyche that day in the wheat field.

Soon the towns around where I lived started to be targeted by carrier-launched fighter planes. I learned that a boy in my own grade got hit in the leg during a strafing attack near his home, and the doctors had been forced to amputate. Even though we were in the same grade, it was early in the school year and I couldn't yet associate a face with the name, but all the same I felt almost as if what had happened to him had happened to me.

After all, that strange falling object had crashed to the ground barely ten meters from where I stood. That experience made it easy to see that the random-ness with which a stray bullet had shattered my schoolmate's leg was in fact the essential logic of war.

Not long after I heard about my schoolmate's misfortune, I personally experienced an attack similar to his.

Once again an air raid siren had sent us hurrying homeward, but a second alert sounded just as we were cutting through the wheat field on our way from the school to the station. Suddenly, even before the shriek of the siren had faded, the thunder of an engine came roaring up behind me. I turned to see an enemy plane skimming across the ground. I'd seen pictures of planes like that before, but this was the first time I'd ever seen one firsthand—and so close. Unlike the B29 bombers I'd grown used to squinting at high up in the sky, this was a fighter, streaking straight at us with the ferocity of a hunting dog.

Instinctively, we all dived into the furrows between the ripening wheat. A split second later the deafening roar of the engine pounded against our backs. Having spied us a split second too late, the pilot scattered a burst from his guns into the neighboring sweet potato field as he passed over our heads. I immediately looked up, not out of some thrill-seeking curiosity but in a deliberate act of will, as if it were my duty to ascertain exactly who the attacker was, and I followed the plane with my eyes as it flew on by. The plane banked into a steep climb, showing a brightly colored cartoon figure of some kind painted on its fuselage.

I still remember the powerful impression that flashy cartoon figure made on me. To someone whose country had been fighting in isolation from the rest of the world for so long, it symbolized the sheer foreignness of the culture that was now bearing down on us so relentlessly.

I could sense the pilot's vexation at having missed such easy prey. What if he came back for a second volley? He wasn't likely to miss again. We had no time to lose. Summoning up our courage, everyone sprinted across the field toward the cover of a pine grove three hundred meters away. But we still had fifty meters to go when the roar of the plane was upon us again. Perhaps because we were in such a panic, the noise failed to register until it was much closer than before. And this time we were in the flat, open sweet potato field.

Even so, we threw ourselves down into the potato furrows, no more than twenty centimeters deep, shrinking in anticipation of the enemy bullets that we knew would riddle our bodies. But for some reason, the spray of bullets never came.

We'd been saved, I realized. I timidly raised my head to see why, and watched a plane that looked nothing like the first pull up over the tops of the pine trees. And as it banked into a turn, I saw a red sun fringed in white painted on its dull brown wings and fuselage.

I cannot forget—nor adequately describe—the triumphant emotion of that moment. It was an overpowering explosion of love that made me want to cry and throw my arms around somebody, anybody, for sheer joy. In that moment, I first truly understood the life-and-death struggle that was being waged, each side utterly bent on protecting its own. And I also understood that I was inalienably bound to the nation of my birth.

Closer still to the end of the war, my middle school class was mobilized as student labor to dig trenches around the air force base at Atsugi. The job did not last long, but in the space of barely a week, we had to take cover in four air raid alerts. The fourth time, they'd detected a large squadron of bombers approaching, and every working fighter plane on base was scrambled to meet the attack. Even to our youthful eyes, it was clear that the afternoon's battle in the skies could be a fateful turning point.

The showdown apparently took place not over Tokyo, as had been the pattern, but over water far to the south. This made us all the more impatient to learn the outcome, and the wait was nerve-racking. There was virtually no way anyone could actually know anything, but plausible-sounding rumors began to circulate through the shelter where we'd taken cover.

The day's air battle had been fought more fiercely than ever, but in the end our forces sent two aircraft carriers—no, three—to their watery graves in a tremendous victory for Japan. So went the initial story. But this was quickly followed by whispered denials saying that our side had in fact suffered heavy losses; virtually every Japanese plane sent to meet the bombers had been shot down by an endless swarm of enemy aircraft that met them over the ocean and attacked them from every direction.

Someone had data on the maximum flight times of the planes that had gone out, and when the time remaining dwindled to less than an hour, even though the all clear had not yet sounded, most of us in the student labor corps crawled out of the shelter to join the men in uniform anxiously watching the sky.

Before long, first one plane, then another, then another appeared in different parts of the sky, and converged on us. The widely divergent headings from which they came told us just how vast and fierce the battle beyond the horizon must have been.

As further evidence, every one of the returning planes limped back severely damaged and run-down. The third plane came flying in low to the ground and belching smoke, barely making the airstrip. The fourth had damaged landing gear and was forced to touch down on one wheel; it skidded off the runway and snapped a wing.

We'd heard of this sort of thing, we'd even seen it in films, but here it was all taking place before our very eyes. As we watched the events unfold, suspense soon turned to stunned horror, and horror to a gallant desire to somehow participate in the drama.

As the planes came in one after another, ground crews rushed to pull the pilots covered in blood and sweat and motor oil from their cockpits. Soon even us students were called on to assist in rescue operations. We couldn't do much more than hold up the end of a stretcher or serve as runners for the medics, but even so I felt inexorably part of the war effort, immersed in the very vortex of the fighting. For the first time, I knew the thick smell of blood and sweat and motor oil that is the very odor of war—heavy, oppressive, suffocating—and the heart-wrenching sadness that goes with it. Within that unforgiving smell smoldered the fates, not only of those individuals caught up in the totality of war, but of the nation itself.

When a pilot defeated in a dogfight plunged toward the sea, this was what he breathed in the closeness of his cockpit during those last seconds before death. I now knew that smell for myself, not in the abstract, but in its stifling reality.

A number of men continued to stand and watch the sky without lending a hand in the rescue efforts. No one rebuked them for their inaction. We students quickly realized they were ground crewmen for planes not yet returned. With dwindling hopes, they anxiously scanned the sky for any dark speck that could be their plane.

Finally one of them pointed in an unlikely direction and shouted, "There he comes!"

169

A moment later the man standing next to him shouted back, as if wresting something from his grasp, "No! It's mine! It's mine!"

How anyone could have recognized a plane from such a distance I'll never know, but as the speck drew nearer it indeed proved to be the second man's plane. The plane's wheels were barely on the ground before he sprinted after it like a madman, screaming the pilot's name with tears in his voice.

Out of seventeen fighters that took off, nine never made it home. Although we students had no watches, the sun's descent beneath the horizon told us the point of no return had been passed. Every one of us was silently counting the number of dead.

Even after the sun had gone, several men still stood gazing at the sky with their backs to the crimson glow in the west. No one had the heart to suggest they do otherwise.

Today still—or perhaps I should say today more than ever—you hear certain people singing the old air corps song that includes the lines:

> As the sun sets in the west,
> I scan the southern sky,
> Still searching for any sign
> Of the lead plane's return.

On such occasions, I sometimes find myself fighting the urge to shout, "I actually know what those lines are talking about, you know. I lived through that very scene myself. What could you know about it?"

I want to shout this not only for the sake of the men who failed to return that evening, but for those who continued to hope beyond hope until who knows what hour, standing in the light of the crimson sunset, standing through the long lingering afterglow, standing through the gathering twilight, and then when they noticed the stars beginning to flicker overhead, sitting down to wait still longer for their comrades' return.

BROKEN BONES

Just the thought of breaking a bone is enough to send a shudder through me, but it's amazing how easily it can happen. I know from experience—though the bone belonged to someone else the first time around.

One winter, many years ago, a community soccer team I was on played another squad at the Zushi High School field. Afterwards I suggested we challenge our opponents to an informal game of rugby with the ball I'd brought along.

It was one of those freezing days when you can't seem to get warm no matter how long you run around. I soon regretted my enthusiasm, even though I was the one who had first suggested the game.

We all knew well enough how to handle ourselves in soccer matches, but rugby involved scrums and mauls and other formations where you could easily get hurt. I decided my best bet was to avoid getting too carried away with the game. Even when things got exciting and the other players were really fired up, I made a point of passing the ball as quickly as I could whenever it came my way.

I don't know how long we'd been playing, but the game was close. One more score would put our team ahead. A teammate found me in the open, and passed me the ball, whereupon our opponents came after me with bloody murder in their eyes. I thought at first I could outrun them, but I was also wary of getting trapped in a maul, so when I saw the ever-hustling Rick Suzuki—a member of my yacht crew—come up alongside me, I quickly passed to him.

Which of course meant Rick got caught. Other teammates raced to his aid, and joined in a large maul with Rick still holding the ball, getting thrown this way and that, when suddenly something like ten players all collapsed in a heap. I myself managed to avoid the pile-up, but I saw it all happen from close by.

As the maul collapsed under the force of all those straining bodies, I heard a loud snap. I knew right away someone had broken a bone.

The whistle sounded, and the players released their holds. As I watched one player after another peel himself from the heap unhurt, I started to think I was wrong, and the sharp report I'd heard came from a rip in someone's heavy canvas shorts instead. But then they got down to the last couple of men, with Rick still hugging the ball on the very bottom.

"I don't believe it," he cried. "I busted my leg."

The last man on top of Rick rose to one knee, then got to his feet and stepped away. Rick lay on the ground with his right leg twisted in a sickeningly unnatural position, looking like it didn't belong to his body at all.

As if to hastily correct a terrible mistake, someone tried to straighten the leg, but Rick let out an ear-piercing shriek. There could be no doubt about what had happened to him.

The sun was out, but the temperature remained extremely cold. We didn't think Rick should be left lying on the frozen ground. Someone found a board to wedge under him for the time being, but every tiny movement brought another agonized shriek. The force of all those people piling on top of him had shattered the bone into five pieces.

"You certainly did a bang-up job of breaking it," quipped the surgeon, the head of the local hospital, whom I knew from before.

Later, Rick had a second operation to remove the metal rod inserted to hold the healing bone fragments together. Even after that, it took a good three years before he could walk normally again. In fact, considering that Rick subsequently gave up on all participatory sports that require running, you'd have to say he was injured for life.

Only a few minutes after Rick arrived in the emergency room, two victims of a traffic accident were brought in. A light truck drove up with its side flaps and tailgate hanging down; the two men lay on the flatbed like a couple of big game fish someone had hauled in, their faces and arms and legs covered with blood. A gruesome sight. They were still breathing, but I distinctly remember thinking they probably weren't going to make it.

When I went back to visit Rick in the hospital three days later, though, I was surprised to see the accident victims walk in with bandages around their heads and arms, but no need for crutches or canes. It just goes to show how easily blood can fool us. Only the person actually affected can say which is worse—breaking a bone or shedding blood.

I also have my own story about how breaking a bone can injure you for life.

A number of years ago, what with one thing and another, I'd been too busy all summer long to get in any scuba diving, so as the season was coming to a close I took my second son Yoshizumi with me on a trip to Hachijojima. I knew a typhoon was making its way up from the south, but it looked like we still had a one-day window of opportunity, so I contacted a fisherman I knew and chartered his boat for an outing.

Starting around noon, we made two dives. By the time we came up from the second, the sea had changed dramatically from only a short forty or fifty minutes earlier. Choppy waves and a strong wind foretold something big and ominous approaching.

At times like that, no matter how seasoned you are, your first instinct is to get out of the water as quickly as you possibly can. Having my son with me redoubled that impulse. But along with this urgency came the satisfaction that our little gamble under iffy conditions had paid off: we'd had our fun while dodging the fearsome storm, if only barely.

The change that had come over the sea in less than an hour was truly astounding, though. The tension on the skipper's face as he brought the boat about to pick us up told us just how close a call it was.

I sent Yoshizumi up the ladder first. Once the boat stopped, the violent rolling on the waves confirmed the power of the approaching tempest.

A diver's time underwater is remarkably free of apprehensions; it's when he makes his way back to the surface that anxiety kicks in. Will the boat be in easy reach? Have the seas turned heavy? Even people who don't get seasick in boats can easily turn woozy from being bounced on the waves while waiting to be picked up. The hazards of diving don't end until you're safely back in the boat.

In this particular case, even after Yoshizumi was aboard, I was still on edge and in a great hurry to follow. The rolling of the boat was quickly growing worse. Once a vessel stops making way, she absorbs the full brunt of the waves hitting her side, causing her every motion to be magnified. From the perspective of the man in the water, it looks like the wind is gaining even more force, the seas rising even higher. So in spite of all my experience at sea, I was just a little too eager to be back in the boat with my son, and I got careless.

I was so taken aback by the surface conditions that I'd already neglected my usual safety checks when I hurriedly sent Yoshizumi up the ladder. Normally these checks were second nature to me, but in my hurry to get on board that day I impulsively grabbed the ladder attached to the side of the boat and started to pull myself up. Just as I put my foot on the first rung, a surging wave rocked the boat in the opposite direction, and the ladder that had been suspended out from the side of the boat crashed against the hull. The rung clamped down on my fingers as the roll of the hull levered the ladder out of the water. At the very same instant, my own weight, together with the weight of my tank, weight belt, and waterlogged wet suit, all came down on the ladder as well. Which is to say, my left middle finger was caught in a vise between the hard wooden hull and a thin metal pipe, with the fingertip bearing the full force of the rolling boat's momentum and all that weight.

The pipe crushed my finger flat as if it were nothing at all. Something I could only assume was bone felt like it had been pulverized inside my fingertip. I automatically dropped back into the water and looked at my hand, but all I could tell through the cotton glove I had on was that it had started to bleed. Someone quickly wedged a spar behind the ladder to hold it away from the hull, and this time I got into the boat without incident. When I pulled off my glove, the nail was in pieces and the fingertip itself was completely deformed. Anyone could tell the bone had been destroyed.

At the clinic back in port, the x-ray showed that the bone in my fingertip had broken into three small pieces—which is to say, it was shattered.

The island's young doctor said he thought it would require pulling the nail and operating on the fingertip, but the facilities on site seemed none too reassuring. The doctor offered to refer me to the hospital at his university in Tokyo, but I decided to call a surgeon I knew and arranged an appointment for late that afternoon.

The finger itself had gone numb by this time, and no longer gave me much pain. Yoshizumi and I showered and changed at the fisherman's house, and since we still had some time to kill before our flight we broke out some beer. The fisherman apologized repeatedly for his young deckhand having neglected orders to put a spacer between the ladder and the hull, but at this point I couldn't even get worked up about it.

The surgery back in Tokyo proved to be extremely painful. Before it was over, I understood all too well why the nurse removing the temporary dressing had taken one look at the finger and gasped, "Oh my, this must really hurt!"

As he was preparing to inject the local anesthetic directly into the fingertip— one of the most sensitive spots on the human body—even the doctor had said, "This is going to hurt, so feel free to cry." The pain was beyond unbearable.

Once, on the way to the Tokara Islands with some friends, we stopped at Tosa Shimizu in Shikoku and went diving nearby. As the first one to descend, I had to wait for the others in a strong underwater current, and when I shifted my hold on a rock, I inadvertently grabbed a long-spined sea urchin. One of the sea urchin's needles went right through my cotton glove, stabbing me sharply under the nail of my index finger. It felt as if I'd touched a live high-voltage wire, the jolt traveling up my arm all the way to my shoulder. Instinctively I screamed, right into the water, and with my regulator still dangling loose, made a mad dash for the surface twenty meters above. It was certainly no textbook example of a free ascent.

The sea urchin's needle had gone in quite deep and I couldn't get it out. Someone said I needed to dissolve it by soaking it in vinegar, so for the next two days I carried around a cup of vinegar with my finger immersed in it. The continual throbbing was enough to drive away the nagging stomach pains I had from drinking too much—which merely reminded me that stomach pain was basically a matter of nerves.

Still, a syringe needle is on an entirely different plane from a sea urchin spine. And to make matters worse, because there are so few blood vessels in the tip of the finger, the doctor had to jab me a second and third time to make sure the anesthetic got spread around properly. Though I managed not to cry, I couldn't help gasping loudly at the pain of each new jab.

Thanks to the anesthetic, the surgery itself did not hurt. But my suffering

175

during the next two days was considerable—very much as the doctor had warned.

On the second day after surgery, I was scheduled to fly to Naha in Okinawa for the first workshop of the newly organized Nakagawa political faction. I hardly felt like traveling such a long distance in my condition, but as chief secretary of the group I had little choice. I rang up our leader Ichiro Nakagawa and told him that I was under doctor's orders to remain at home and rest after surgery. But if he promised to publicly announce his intentions to do what I'd been urging him to do, then I'd accompany him to the gathering. On the other hand, if this meeting was going to be nothing but an empty formality like those held by the party's other factions, then I would ask to be excused.

An election to choose a new president for the Liberal Democratic Party was scheduled for later that fall, and I'd urged him to throw his hat into the ring. I didn't know yet whether he could get the fifty endorsements he needed to be nominated, but I thought he should declare his candidacy anyway, as a way of shaking up the status quo and injecting some much-needed life into a party overcome by inertia. As the LDP's newest and smallest faction, the only way we could begin to expand our influence within the party was through bold actions of this kind, and I'd been trying to get him to take the initiative for quite some time. Being in charge of political strategy for the faction, I'd also promised my colleagues to put Nakagawa in the spotlight, and this gentle blackmail was the only means I could think of to get him up in front of the gilded screen.

I presented my demand to him first over the phone, then made a special trip to his office to reiterate it. I was calculating that the sight of my arm in a sling with blood seeping through the bandage would add persuasive leverage to my blackmail.

"I hear what you're saying," he said. "I assure you I've been giving the matter a great deal of thought, and I do not intend to disappoint you."

"I'm not letting you get away with that kind of mealy-mouthed bureaucrat-speak," I replied. "Are you going to run or not? If you're going to squander a perfect opportunity like this to do battle, what's the point of having started up your own organization? If that's the way it's going to be, I'll tender my notice and be on my way."

"No, really. I chose to become a politician, and I intend to make every effort to take things as far as I possibly can."

"Effort isn't good enough. What we need is a decision."

"And I believe I've made my decision. But there's still the question of timing."

"Look, I know you're a little shy about these things, so if you're uncomfortable broaching the subject yourself, I'll simply get one of the reporters I know to ask you a question. Then all you have to do is drop a vague hint somehow that you're interested."

"Fine. I'll leave it to you."

Having won this assurance, I flew to Okinawa the next day, still not entirely convinced he would come through. Shiro Hasegawa, the most senior member of our faction, also decided to make the trip in spite of a recent illness. I told him what had transpired and asked him to exercise his own powers of persuasion on Nakagawa in the plane on the way down, to make sure he didn't waver.

"I'm glad you did that," Hasegawa said. "That's just the sort of thing we have to do if we want to make a man out of Nakagawa."

Hasegawa huddled with Nakagawa during the flight and, sure enough, Nakagawa remained true to his word.

I have no idea what may have inspired him, but Nakagawa did not wait to be prompted by my reporter friend. Quite to my surprise, he abruptly and unequivocally announced right in the middle of his address to faction members that he would be a candidate for party president in the upcoming election.

As it turned out, Nakagawa's announcement triggered the resignation of then Prime Minister Zenko Suzuki. The intra-party election became a contest among four candidates, and it culminated in the formation of a new government.

Much as I'd anticipated, Nakagawa brought up the rear in the balloting. This was only to be expected. But Nakagawa himself seemed extremely disappointed, and when I told him he should try to be a good loser he didn't want to hear it.

During the campaign, we often drank together after the last of the day's campaign stops. Nakagawa was rather quick to get inebriated, and it loosened his tongue. "Since teaming up with you, I've let you rope me into all kinds of things," he grumbled, "and damned if it hasn't cost me an awful lot of friends."

"Who do you mean?"

"Well, Kakuei Tanaka, for one. You keep shouting, 'No money politics! No money politics!' So I chime in, 'Hear, hear!' But the truth is, I kind of like Kakuei. Then there's good old Shintaro Abe. This whole thing could put a serious rift in our friendship."

One time when he was carrying on like this, it began to make me mad—or I suppose more sad than mad—so I gave him a good slap on the face.

He immediately pulled himself together and sat up. "Sorry," he said. "I'm with you, come what may, even if this boat carries us both down to the very depths of hell."

But then he went and killed himself.

"If you hadn't egged him on to run for the party presidency," someone once told me, "he'd probably still be with us."

Maybe so. From my own point of view, I wonder whether I would have pressured him the way I did if I hadn't broken my finger.

At any rate, it's no trivial matter to break a bone. Not only can it injure you yourself for life, if you're not careful it might even affect someone else for life.

The tip of my left middle finger has remained slightly numb ever since. Each time I touch it, it reminds me of the good friend I lost.

THE MAN WHO RETURNED
FROM EVERY BATTLE

I have something of an allergy regarding gay men. Not only have I no interest in that lifestyle, but quite frankly I can't bring myself to feel much sympathy for those who do. I find it disturbing to learn that someone I'd always thought was straight is in fact gay.

A good many years ago, the late Ranpo Edogawa, pioneer of modern mystery writing in Japan, first took me to an establishment frequented by such people: a gay bar called Blanc Chic in Akasaka, a place of considerable renown at the time. I was at a complete loss about what to do with myself. My skin crawled every time someone sat down beside me, and I could hardly remain in my seat. I couldn't very well scream, of course, so I vented my discomfort by laughing instead. Endlessly, with a silly, nervous giggle.

For his part, even though he brought his wife along, Mr. Edogawa had his favorite pretty boy sitting on his lap. Between bouts of rubbing cheeks with the boy and kissing, he turned to me and said, "So I gather you don't go in for this sort of thing, Ishihara."

The "proprietress" of the bar was sitting next to him. "Yes, so it seems," she said. "Another hopeless one." She continued eyeing me with a smile.

When I asked her what she meant, she explained that for twenty percent of the people in the world, male or female, any kind of homosexual behavior was simply out of the question. A similar percentage was in fact homosexual, whether they knew it or not, and the rest were capable of going either way.

Most men were shocked at the suggestion and insisted they had absolutely no such inclinations. Yet often, if by chance they happened to be offered even a tiny taste of the forbidden fruit, it was as if a secret panel had opened; they became quite captivated by what lay beyond.

So I had been declared one of the glorious few exceptions to the rule. Even after having this explained to me, I've never felt the slightest curiosity about the gay lifestyle.

A number of years later, the "proprietress" of a gay bar in Paris told me the same thing. This time the man who took me there was a Frenchman I'd originally met when he was a cultural attaché to Japan, and he had always been perfectly open about his sexual predilections. I was none too happy when he told me he wanted to take me to his favorite gay hangout, but having come to France as director of the Nissei Theater in order to scout out shows to bring to Japan, I was in the position of supplicant, so I reluctantly went along. When the person running it noticed me shaking in my shoes, she came out with the same assessment given me by the proprietress of Blanc Chic in Japan.

Since two different authorities on the subject came to the same conclusion independently, I suppose they must be right. The term the Parisian madame used for me was *l'homme impossible*.

At the time I thought it highly presumptuous of her to go around labeling people "impossible," but I've come to recognize that this was merely her ironical way of expressing the hurt that gays carry deep inside them.

Sometime after that, I was watching a television feature about gays in America in which a Hollywood star of yesteryear, an actor quite well known for his numerous supporting roles, publicly revealed for the first time that he was a homosexual.

"I don't know any gays who're *happy* they're gay," he said. "I mean, there's no getting around the fact that it's not natural, and how can you expect God to give his blessing to people who can't follow His laws? I dearly hope that in my next life I come back as a man who's capable of loving women."

I could sympathize with every word.

"But you'd be surprised how many of the people around you are in fact gay," he added. "As their neighbor, you need to understand their unhappiness and have compassion for them."

There's really no telling where you might run into someone who is gay, or who it might be.

———————

In the late seventies, I went bar hopping with a friend in Kobe one night, and ended up in a gay bar again. As before, I felt uncomfortable, so I chose to keep to myself at the counter, biding my time until my friend was ready to move on to another venue. I gravitated to the counter partly because the bartender working there was the only man among the bar's employees who was dressed as a man, wearing a bow tie and cummerbund. He was probably a little past middle age.

One of the young "hostesses" was being addressed as "Mama" in the absence of the owner, who apparently was at the bar's main branch in a different location, but the bartender appeared to be the person in charge. The hostesses joked and carried on amongst themselves in the manner of young women, but in spite of the way they were dressed, when they came up to the counter to get something for one of their customers, they instantly reverted to masculine speech and mannerisms. If the bartender gently chided or admonished them about something, they would sometimes snap back petulantly, but on the whole they did as he said.

After I'd been sitting there observing these goings-on for a time, there came a little lull, and the bartender struck up a conversation with me.

"You dislike places like this?" he asked.

"Yes, I'm afraid they make me feel rather awkward," I said.

"Can't say it's exactly normal," he nodded, as if to distance himself from the proceedings as well.

"They certainly seem to be enjoying themselves, though," I said. "I suppose it's a case of their personal tastes also serving their profit motives."

Instead of responding, the bartender slowly surveyed the room with his eyes.

"You know, if you stop to think about it, you really have to feel sorry for people like this," he finally said. "They can't find anything better to get excited about."

"So you're saying there's something else that lights your fire?"

He squinted his eyes a little as he turned to look at me again.

"When I was their age, or actually a bit younger, I threw myself heart and soul into something, and I didn't care one whit if I died in the process."

"Oh? What was that?"

"I learned to be a pilot when I was only sixteen." He threw his chest out a little as he said it. "I was the youngest pilot in the attack on Pearl Harbor."

"What were you flying?"

"A Type 97 carrier bomber."

"The ones that swapped bombs for torpedoes at the last minute?"

"You know about that?" He turned to face me head on and leaned forward a little as he spoke.

"They had to modify the torpedoes for the shallow waters in Pearl Harbor," I said. "And testing the modifications ran late, so you didn't get the thumbs up until after you'd sailed from Hitokappu Bay."

He slowly nodded his head up and down. I felt as if he'd finally acknowledged me as being worth talking to.

"In our training runs over Kagoshima Bay, we had to practice with both bombs and torpedoes—five, six hours a day. We were so dead set on getting it right, we'd forget to eat. At that point, we were the only ones in all of Japan who knew we were going to hit Pearl Harbor."

"When you took off for the attack, I heard the weather in the North Pacific was so bad they'd have canceled the whole thing if it had only been a training run."

"That's right. But only two planes failed to make it into the air. People have a way of rising to the occasion, you know," he said with pride in his voice and a far-off look in his eye. "That was the moment we'd been training so hard for, not caring if we died."

"That's what you meant about throwing yourself heart and soul into something?"

"Uh-huh. For a teenager who'd barely even discovered women, it just didn't get any better than that."

His eyes suddenly opened wide again, but they took on a dreamy look.

"When we joined the others in the sky and the formation headed south, I felt more alive than I'd ever felt before. I also knew for certain I was going to die. I was so happy I could hardly stand it.

"It never entered my mind that we could fail. When we were finally getting close, and I got my first glimpse of Oahu through a break in the clouds and then identified Pearl Harbor, I thought it had to be the most beautiful place in the world. Kagoshima Bay had been pretty, too, but the color of the water just couldn't compare. I really don't know how to describe the feeling. Maybe it was like finally laying eyes on a priceless jewel hidden in the farthest, deepest corners of a castle somewhere. And another thing, I remember being surprised that the harbor was so exactly like the models and pictures they'd shown us in training.

"As the third plane in our attack formation, we were supposed to hit the third battleship from the right, the *West Virginia*. I pointed the aircraft straight at the target, thinking, *She's ours. No one can take her away from us now.* We weren't drawing any fire at all, and I thought, *Man, this is easier than our training runs.* I wasn't the least bit nervous. If nothing else, I knew we could just hang on to the torpedo and fly right into the side of the ship if we had to.

"I dropped down close to the water and got into position for our torpedo run, everything smooth as can be, much smoother than in training, flying straight and true. I called out to my bombardier and we let the torpedo go like we were one mind and body. I wasn't paying any attention to what the two planes ahead of us in the formation were doing. All I cared about was that our torpedo hit its target. Then I could die happy.

"As I pulled the plane up, barely clearing the ship's mast, I was trying like crazy to keep one eye on the wake of the torpedo we'd just released. *It can't miss,* I told myself. *There's no way it can miss.* But things I'd never contemplated before started flashing through my mind, like, *What if it's a dud?* Then, just as I completed my turn, the torpedo struck home and a huge column of water geysered skyward. I really don't know how to describe the thrill of that moment. Like finally making it with the girl of your dreams and reaching the most incredible climax ever—except I don't think even that comes close. It didn't occur to me till later, but in a sense my life ended once, right then and there. I really think it did."

Then, as if putting away a cup full of precious memories, the bartender set down the glass he'd been polishing and pushed it aside.

"After Pearl Harbor, call me lucky or unlucky, I wound up in basically every

183

big showdown of the war—Midway, Bougainville, Leyte, Okinawa. But for some reason I never felt the least bit afraid. To begin with, not one time did I think I would die. Probably because of Pearl Harbor. Because I'd already died there once, you see."

Looking out from behind the counter at that tiny crowded bar, his eyes momentarily drifted far away, as if gazing back over the endless expanse of sea he'd flown. He was looking far beyond the young men crowding the bar, beyond any disdain or pity for the gay lifestyle in which they were indulging at the same age he had been all those years ago. For a brief moment, he seemed to be seeing something only he could see, something he hadn't revisited in a long, long time.

"Uh-huh," I said, nodding. I realized I was in the presence of a man who could genuinely be called chosen, and who perceived himself that way as well.

"So, what brings you to a place like this?" I couldn't help asking, though I knew the question might rub him the wrong way.

"This bar belongs to the guy who kept my plane running all those years. He's at the other place, so I look after things for him here."

"I see. So the mama-san used to be your grease monkey."

It struck me as a most satisfying conclusion to the story. A former mechanic who had made good running a gay bar, and the pilot who had flown the plane; the grease monkey who must have stayed up to all hours tuning the machine, and the flyboy who by some miracle returned safely from every battle. It was not my kind of bar, and I had gone there reluctantly, but within its walls I'd had the pleasure of hearing a truly marvelous story.

———

There's just one question I kicked myself later for neglecting to ask: had the pilot who survived Pearl Harbor ultimately opened that secret panel to be united with his former mechanic, the owner of the bar?

But as a man who'd been declared "impossible" by other denizens of that world, I somehow couldn't help feeling that asking the question might have been a kind of sacrilege.

MINAMIJIMA

One of the experiences all divers cherish is a chance encounter with some truly enormous creature in the water—though when one of those eagerly sought meetings actually occurs, it's not necessarily all thrills. If you want to see orcas or other large sea mammals, you often have a pretty good idea where you can go to find them, but when it comes to meeting large species of fish, it's generally a matter of luck. Which makes such encounters that much more dramatic.

I once saw on television a young Japanese diver on a whale-watching trip to Hawaii. It having been her lifelong dream to see the majestic animals up close in the water, she was so overcome by the experience that she started crying as soon as she got back in the boat. I think I know exactly how she felt. The two guides with the group were friends of mine, who say that the excitement and wonder of seeing a whale in the water never fades, no matter how many times you experience it.

Whales are shy but inquisitive animals. If you try to approach them, they will swim away, but if you remain still and wait patiently, they'll soon succumb to their curiosity and come to investigate. To be in relatively clear water and see a distant shadow loom closer and closer until all of a sudden it takes shape as a whale must be a truly breathtaking thrill.

Although not quite the same thing, I experienced a similar encounter during a diving trip to the Kerama Islands in Okinawa with a group that included a couple of friends new to the sport. We started out at some novice sites frequented by tourists, but this quickly lost its appeal, so we decided to head for a large pointed rock east of Zamami Island known as Otoko-iwa, or "Male Rock," where giant trevally were sometimes to be seen.

First into the water was an Osaka dentist named Tamaoki, a veteran diver who specialized in free diving. Wearing a hooded five-millimeter wet suit even though it was the height of summer, he strapped a compass to his wrist and tied a line with a thirty-centimeter plastic float on the end to his spear gun in case he caught something big. His practice was to fish from the surface while free diving, letting the current take him where it would, until his boat came to pick him up. I suppose he had full faith in his companions, but even so it always seemed pretty gutsy to me.

Carried by the current, he immediately drifted off to the right of the rock, but apparently wasn't finding anything worth diving for, since we never saw him go under. After making sure he was all right, the rest of us—myself, my two novice friends, and Shiroma, my own original diving instructor—swam off in the opposite direction. As we moved around to the left of the rock and started our descent, we almost immediately spotted three giant trevally of very considerable size—one dark male accompanied by two lighter-colored females.

For some reason, all I had with me was a puny single-band spear gun. I suppose I figured I couldn't do any serious fishing anyway with two novices along. In fact, probably the only reason I had any kind of spear gun at all was to momentarily deter any inquisitive shark we might encounter. But as soon as I laid eyes on these prize specimens, I was of an entirely different mind; I pulled the band back full, set the spear, and swam straight for the three fish.

Although the water around this rock is usually crystal clear, visibility was quite poor on that particular day, and I had difficulty gauging the distance. I could see well enough to know the fish were big, but I didn't want to get too close and scare them off, so I aimed at the male and shot before I had a clear fix on exactly how far away he was.

The spear flew straight and true, right to where I'd aimed, a little behind the fish's eye. But the amount of line playing out before it hit told me that my target was in fact much farther away than I'd gauged. The spear did strike behind the fish's eye but fell limply away. Embarrassed in the presence of my two novice friends, I quickly began to pull the spear in; and just as quickly the fish turned to look at me as if someone had poked him with a finger and he wanted to know who the joker was. I expected him to turn and dart away once he saw me, but instead he coolly started swimming toward me with his two female companions in tow. I could almost hear him say, "Yeah? Whaddya want?"

Only then, as they came closer, did I realize how truly big the three fish were—nearly two meters long. The giant trevally swam slowly on by, eyeing us sideways as if wondering who these strange creatures were to interrupt their leisurely stroll through the water.

I was awestruck, but the sheer astonishment on my friends' faces was priceless. Their regulators nearly fell out of their mouths as they gaped at the fish, and the three of us remained frozen in place as we watched them go past. In the spot where my spear had struck, behind the male's left eye, I could see a faint white scratch that looked like an eyebrow drawn in with a pencil.

Sensing something behind me, I turned to find Shiroma laughing in the water.

Back on the boat, I asked him, "What if I'd been closer, and my spear had really sunk in? What would have happened then?"

"Probably nothing much, not with that spear," he said blithely. "Besides, you wouldn't have cared about losing a cheap spear like that. You'd have let go as soon as he started dragging you away. Otherwise, you'd be drowned by now, somewhere in the deep."

That sounded about right.

"But I imagine our beginners learned a little something," he added.

More likely it had been a bit more than the two of them had bargained for at this stage, before they'd even held a spear gun in their hands.

"I figured you'd get taken first, because you were in front," one of the novices said to me. "But with three of them coming at us, I thought we'd all wind up as fish bait."

I suppose one lesson even a beginner could learn from such an experience is that you never know what you'll encounter in the water. As for me, what I learned twenty meters below was how it felt to go chest to chest with a giant fish and feel the wash of its powerful fins as it moved past. I can still remember exactly how the movement of the water felt.

When sailing off Manazuru in Sagami Bay one time, I came within touching distance of a lost, ailing whale. But apart from that, the largest marine animal I ever encountered was a huge rock cod I saw under a reef off the southern tip of Minamijima in the Ogasawaras.

To my mind, Minamijima is an island that offers the greatest concentration of spectacular vistas on earth—a place of truly mystical beauty. The first time I visited, I remember being struck—or perhaps I should say bewitched—by the feeling that I'd been transported to an entirely different planet. The island is long and narrow from north to south. Almost the entire coastline rises in sheer cliffs inhospitable to human access, and strong currents surround the island, swiftly pushing aside any boats attempting to let passengers ashore. Indeed, the only practicable means of getting ashore is by way of the so-called "Shark Pond," an inlet reminiscent of an ancient volcanic crater at the south end of the island.

But even this has its challenges, for the mouth is very narrow, admitting only boats the size of a small runabout, while the channel between Minamijima and the larger Chichijima is always extremely rough due to tidal movements, making it a forbidding crossing for such small watercraft.

Our chartered fishing boat dropped anchor near the inlet, and we dived in to snorkel toward the Shark Pond. Just as we were about to enter the narrow channel, I saw a large, blanket-like object undulating toward me from inside. I realized with a start that it was a spotted stingray measuring nearly two meters across. Even with my wet suit on, I cringed to think of being raked across the creature's broad back, but luckily the ray dived lower as if to comply with the standard rules of the road and slipped by just beneath our bellies. As it glided past, I saw grouper and parrotfish measuring maybe forty centimeters eye to tail, and barracuda nearly a meter long circling about below.

The water outside had been clear, but once we passed through the narrow channel it grew cloudy. The inlet was home to large numbers of sharks—white tip reef sharks, to be exact—so I couldn't help feeling a little nervous, even if they rarely attacked humans.

As we swam on apprehensively—the visibility was no more than four or five meters—a large shark suddenly emerged from the murk. The creature was apparently as startled as we were, for it did an immediate about-face and disappeared back into the gloom.

"He was just checking us out because of the noise we were making. He won't bother us again," our guide Yamada assured us. Fine, but what about the scores more lurking in the inlet?

Leery as we were, we screwed up our courage and swam on to the landing point at the far end. Sure enough, beneath the rocks nearby we saw more of these sharks lying motionless in the water, too many to count, the bigger ones some two meters long. People have nicknamed the members of this lethargic species "sleepy sharks" because they spend whole days resting on the bottom. Here, they lay in mounds, one on top of the other. A shark specialist told me later that such a sight is rarely seen anywhere else in the world.

Once everybody climbed ashore, we heard a sudden disturbance in the water behind us, a sort of barking or growling coming from out in the middle of the inlet. We turned to see what it was, and spied two green sea turtles that had come to the surface to catch their breath while mating.

We started up the steep slope from the inlet, amazed to find our path strewn with rock fragments as thin and sharp as razor blades—certainly not the sort of place you'd want to go with bare feet. Stone Age axes and blades assiduously honed to a fine edge could not compare with the natural sharpness of these rocks. Stumble and put out a hand to catch your fall, and you'd come away with gashes on your palm. I've heard that the only other place on earth with rocks like these is Crete.

Thick clumps of flowering grass with unusual pale purple blossoms grew from between the larger rocks along our path. The leaves underfoot released a wonderful minty fragrance that refreshed us as we continued our climb up the arduous slope. When we came over the divide, we found ourselves gazing out across an expanse of pure white sand. The western edge of this desert descended gently to meet another small inlet, this one filled with dazzlingly clear blue water. Over the entrance to the inlet, as if to hide it from the outside world, rose a low, dome-like rock arch, at the base of which waves from the sea beyond came crashing through a narrow channel.

As we walked across the sand, the white shells of spiral univalves long since extinct, now practically fossils, were scattered everywhere at our feet. In stark contrast to the crystal blue water of the inlet at the western edge of the desert, a short distance to the north lay a cloudy green freshwater pond on a table of land elevated perhaps twenty meters above sea level. It bristled with an unusual reed-like water grass we'd never seen before; waterfowl, also of a species we'd never encountered, called to one another and flitted about.

It was truly a scene from another world. Were it not for the sign standing in the middle of the sandy desert prohibiting visitors from taking any of the shells away with them, a person dropped here unawares might think he'd been transported to another planet. Though undeniably on this earth, the landscapes of Minamijima belong to an entirely different dimension of tranquil mystery and beauty.

This is why I make a point of visiting Minamijima whenever I'm in the Ogasawaras. And each time I go, I'm moved by the island's beauty even more than before. It's something akin to a religious experience. I can think of no other place on earth where I feel so distinctly that I'm standing on sacred ground.

When I encountered the enormous rock cod under a reef off the southern end of the island, it served to further reinforce the sense that Minamijima is a sacred place.

I had come to the islands for the 1979 Ogasawara race, and I decided to leave various maintenance and outfitting chores to the younger members of the crew while I paid a visit to Minamijima with my bosun Ishikawa and crew leader Akioka, both of whom were divers. Once again our guide was Yamada, the professional diver I'd known from earlier trips.

We decided to get a dive in first, before going ashore. Yamada said he had a secret spot he wanted to take us to: a nameless bit of rocky reef located about one kilometer off the southwestern tip of Minamijima. He had recently discovered a T-shaped underwater tunnel about twenty-five meters down in the base of the reef, where he'd seen some very big fish hiding in the shadows.

We dropped over the side of the boat and descended easily to the bottom. The water was magnificently clear. The reef rose out of the white sand on the ocean floor like a supernatural monolith. Countless species of tropical fish swam about in exactly the kind of underwater tableau people came to the Ogasawaras to see.

With Yamada in the lead, we swam around the base of the reef toward the tunnel he'd described as being bent in the middle but going all the way through to the other side. We had our first encounter just as we came to the entrance: a large rock cod measuring about a meter and a half was resting on the seabed in front of the mouth of the tunnel. The fish failed to notice us until we were almost right on top of it, and when it finally did, it leapt into motion in a cloud of sand and disappeared into the tunnel.

The four of us swam through the sand cloud into the tunnel, some two to three meters high by about two meters wide at the entrance. In the dimness just inside, Yamada spied a large painted spiny lobster on the ceiling, over fifty centimeters long in body alone, and at least twice that if its antennae were included. Grabbing it easily with his hand, he handed it to me, and I passed it on to Akioka behind me. With any kind of spiny lobster, once they reach a certain size the spines on the carapace can hurt your bare hands, but with one reaching a meter in overall size you aren't so much grabbing it with your hands as grappling it in your arms. In any case, I could see Akioka's eyes widen with astonishment inside his facemask as I handed him the specimen. Obviously it was on an entirely different scale from any he'd ever seen before. By the time I turned back again, Yamada had already nabbed another one, this one slightly smaller. As we proceeded deeper into the tunnel, I felt a little like we were stealing into the treasure-filled magic cave of the *Arabian Nights*.

The entire tunnel was only about twenty meters long, so some light reached the middle from both ends, allowing us to see well enough to go without the help of dive lamps. As we came to the middle, Yamada pointed to a branch tunnel leading off to the left at a right angle. Just then, a large rock cod that had been keeping still along the wall near us—most likely the one we'd startled at the entrance a few moments before—fled toward the far end of the main tunnel, kicking up another cloud of sand. What these two little flurries of excitement were a prelude to, we were soon to find out.

We followed the beckoning Yamada into the spur that branched off to the left. In this direction, the tunnel dead-ended after about thirteen meters, but maybe five meters before that, Yamada suddenly signaled for us to stop by spreading his arms and legs as if to physically block our advance. After making sure we'd all

191

come to a full stop, he very slowly raised his arm and pointed into the dimness ahead.

For several seconds, I didn't see anything at all. But as I squinted and strained to make out whatever might be there, I suddenly realized we were practically face to face with an unbelievably enormous fish.

At first, it almost looked like something painted on the far wall. But what initially suggested the bold strokes and sepia shadings of an ink brush painting proved to be the wide, mottled stripes of a gigantic living fish pressed flat over the entire wall. I could see it breathing: this was no painting.

A chill went down my spine. With that telepathy shared by all animals, I sensed distinctly that the fish had become aware of our presence and was pondering the implications of our intrusion. It was studying us with nearly imperceptible twitches of its wide-angle eyes, and bracing for whatever might come.

To say that the fish was large hardly does it justice; it was a truly monumental creature. Seeing this fish, I could now believe the legendary story of the monster rock cod that had supposedly swallowed a diver whole in the Arafura Sea. I thought I must be dreaming, yet I knew from the near-paralyzing fear surging through me that this was all too real.

The fish had no doubt sensed the panic of the smaller rock cod we'd sent scurrying near the opening of the branch tunnel. But this one was much too big to dart away anywhere: it must have been nearly three meters long and weighed at least a ton. We froze at alert, scarcely able to breathe. Quite obviously, if the fish were to take fright and decide to flee, its only route of escape would be to plow through the four of us. It would be like getting run over by a truck twenty-five meters under the sea, for even very large fish can sometimes move with surprising speed. In that case, we could count on being slammed against the wall and seriously injured. Or worse, we could be knocked unconscious, lose our regulators, and drown.

I'd brought along my spear gun in case of sharks, and on a nervous impulse I now pointed it at the fish. Behind me, Yamada raised a cry of alarm—though a somewhat muffled one, since he didn't want to startle the fish—apparently thinking I really intended to shoot the monster with my puny little spear. He grabbed me from behind and tried to wrest the weapon from my hands, grunting with the effort.

For my part, I grew alarmed that the fish might react to two tussling humans by suddenly deciding to move, so while still struggling with Yamada over the spear gun, I began to ease us both back toward the entrance of the tunnel. Satisfied that I'd gotten the message, Yamada gestured for the other two to do likewise. The four of us backed very slowly down the narrow passageway together, never taking our eyes off the monster fish.

The farther away we got from the behemoth, the more otherworldly it seemed. Like the mystical landscapes of Minamijima, the fish loomed like a creature that had stolen into the cave from an entirely different world and dimension.

As we continued our cautious retreat, I felt something hit me on the back of the head. Instinctively, I ducked, then looked up to see the two painted spiny lobsters I'd given to Akioka drifting above me. He had apparently dropped them in a moment of panic. Wasting no time, I let go of my spear gun and recaptured the two lobsters. Yamada then retrieved my gun, and the four of us finally emerged from the tunnel.

Our dive boat was waiting directly over the tunnel entrance, having followed the air bubbles from our regulators. We climbed aboard without delay, and just sat there for a while staring mutely at the two large lobsters I'd tossed onto the deck.

"So what did you think? Was that thrilling enough for you?" Yamada finally broke the silence. "I only knew about the one at the entrance. I saw that one before. I guess the tunnel got a prince of a new tenant since the last time I came."

"What would've happened if that monster had panicked and tried to make tracks?"

"We'd have all gotten killed down there," Yamada said without hesitating.

No doubt he was right. Ishikawa looked like he wanted to say something but couldn't find the words. Akioka stared off into space, his mouth agape.

Our plan had been to bide our time until we could dive again by going ashore on Minamijima, so we had the boat return to the entrance of the southern inlet. It had been a while since my own last visit. On our way out from Tokyo to the Ogasawaras, I'd told Akioka all about the Shark Pond and the breathtaking island it served as the gateway to. But now that the time had come to go ashore, Akioka shook his head.

"I've had enough excitement for one day," he said. "I'll wait on the boat."

"What are you talking about?" I said. "You can't come all this way and not see the island!"

"No, really. I've had enough for today."

I took Akioka's arm, trying to urge him to reconsider, but he pulled free and leaned back against the boat's railing, shaking his head adamantly from side to side.

"Forget it," Ishikawa said. "We can go without him."

Reluctantly, we jumped into the water, leaving Akioka behind on the boat.

───────

After the Shark Pond and the steep climb up to the top of the divide, the vista that opened out beyond was every bit as stunning as it had been on my previous visits. In fact, it struck me as even more dazzlingly beautiful than I remembered.

From on top of the ridge I turned to look at our boat waiting a short distance beyond the channel into the Shark Pond, and I could see Akioka sitting on the coaming near the starboard bow, right where we had left him.

"What an idiot," I said. "The son of a bitch is still sitting in that same spot."

"No, I think he'd really had enough," said Ishikawa, taking Akioka's side.

Ishikawa had served as bosun on my yacht for many years, and Akioka had been a no-nonsense crew leader. The three of us had come through many a life-or-death situation together under horrendous race conditions, so I was sorely disappointed that he'd missed this chance to see Minamijima. But Ishikawa seemed to see things differently.

"Think about it," he said. "How many people in the whole world have ever experienced anything like what we did today? For Akioka, that was really more than enough. It outdid by several magnitudes anything you'd see diving off Hayama. And besides, his wife just had a new kid."

"What's that got to do with anything?"

"Look, for a minute even I thought you'd lost your mind down there. I really thought you wanted to go after that monster with your spear gun. I was quaking in my flippers."

"Just a second. I don't think I've ever asked you guys to do anything *that* crazy in the races we've been through together."

"Well, what about the time the mammoth oil tanker was bearing down on us, and you had us hold our course, insisting you'd rather crash than take down our spinnaker?"

"The rules of the road said we had the right-of-way."

"Well, lucky for us they managed to turn at the last minute, but they didn't miss us by more than thirty meters." Ishikawa sounded as though he still resented being put through that nail-biter.

"So if we actually had to get out of that sucker's way a while ago, how many centimeters of clearance do you suppose we had?"

"Be serious! Hell, I could tell you were about ready to piss in your pants, too."

"He didn't seem to think so," I said, nodding toward Yamada.

"I can never be sure what fool thing you might do," Yamada said.

"Actually, he's a very level-headed skipper," Ishikawa said in my defense, then added, "That fish is a perfect match for this island. Even Akioka's gonna be glad for the experience once we're back home. It was the sort of miraculous encounter you could only have at a place like this."

I couldn't have agreed more.

THE CHILEAN BROTHEL

No matter who you are or where you're going or when it may be, traveling to a place you've never been before will make your heart race. All the more so if the time was the late fifties and the destination overseas.

In those days, largely due to Japan's limited foreign exchange holdings, travel abroad was severely restricted by the government. Anyone wishing to make such a trip had to apply to the appropriate government agency to get approval. The amount of foreign currency you could take with you was limited as well, and the rate was frozen at a punishing 360 yen to the dollar.

The purpose of my journey overseas was a road trip across South America. The plan was to start from Chile, cross into Argentina, and proceed on to Brazil, traveling with a group of four college students and a young doctor in a convoy of scooters and a support truck.

This was back when the Pan-American Highway was still being built, and we had little information about the actual road conditions we'd face. But we didn't imagine there could be any great dangers.

A well-known scooter manufacturer was sponsoring the trip. A year earlier, the same company had sent a group of students from the Tokyo Institute of Technology on a similar trip across Europe with the late essayist, critic, and professor of metallurgy Shigeo Oketani as their leader. In an era of limited entertainment options and very little information from overseas, Professor Oketani's account of the trip had created a sensation. The company decided to recruit a new team of adventurers for an even more attention-getting plan, and since this was shortly after I had made my first big splash in the literary world, they apparently thought I would make a good leader.

Both for the students and for myself, being asked to join the team was like a gift from heaven. The route, which was off the beaten track, was our own choice, though to be honest none of us had the slightest idea what we would encounter. In any case, it wasn't often that chances like this fell into one's lap. Because our costs were viewed as "advertising expenses" for a major corporation, we were permitted to take a considerable sum of foreign exchange currency with us. And in fact the yen was quite solid by then, and the countries we passed through proved to be less developed than we'd imagined, so our journey became a veritable royal progress.

Thinking back on it now, I realize what an extraordinary journey it was—one that lingers in my mind as a symbol of my entire youth. Today I've become a man of means, and even grown accustomed to certain extravagances, but there's no sum of money that would allow me to experience a trip of that kind again. Two of the students on the team were utterly changed by their experiences, and when they graduated into the working world the following year, they disappointed their parents by shunning the mainstream job market and pursuing independent careers without any safety nets.

The students and vehicles left Japan by boat ahead of me, and I followed by plane after completing some other work. In those days this meant a four-engine turboprop. I made a stopover in Hawaii, another in Los Angeles, then touched down again in Panama for a midnight change of planes before reaching my final destination of Santiago. En route, both Hawaii and Los Angeles were firsts for me, and I was naturally curious to look around, but I was too eager to get to Chile to feel like doing any serious sightseeing.

When I finally arrived in Santiago after something like fifty hours in the air, I was surprised to find a large contingent of resident Japanese at the airport to greet me. The sponsoring scooter company had asked the Chilean branch managers of a Japanese trading company and Japanese steamship company, both graduates of my own alma mater, to look after me in Santiago. The two men seemed as surprised as I was by the size of the turnout. They did tell me, though, that the expatriate community regarded our planned trip as something of a heroic endeavor in their name as well.

"Remember," Hayashi of the trading company urged me with a straight face, "we're all counting on you. So that means you're going to have to be on your best behavior."

I took care of some paperwork at the airport and checked into my hotel, and even then a sizable retinue of well-wishers still crowded the hall outside my room. Hayashi winked at Yamazaki of the steamship company, and called for everyone's attention.

"Since I'm sure Mr. Ishihara must be exhausted from his long trip, and the ambassador will be holding a reception for him tomorrow, we'd like to ask everyone to go on home for today so he can get some rest."

The crowd quickly dispersed, and the three of us finally sat down to some quiet.

"Well, then," Hayashi said, "perhaps we can celebrate your safe arrival with a drink or two. You're a young fellow. I don't suppose you're actually all that tired."

We went downstairs to the bar and ordered a round of drinks. When our glasses were empty, Hayashi glanced at his watch, and leaned over for a hushed consultation with Yamazaki.

"We were thinking," he finally said, straightening up. "It seems a shame to keep you cooped up here on your first night in Santiago. How about a little cultural adventure? When you decide you're too tired, just let us know, and we'll bring you back here."

"Don't worry about me. I feel quite all right," I said.

We headed out of the hotel.

"¿A dónde?" the driver said.

"A la Embajada Americana," Hayashi said.

Even with my limited Spanish I knew this meant the American Embassy. I was still wondering why they wanted to take me there when the cab pulled up to a large mansion that indeed looked the part. But as the driver was preparing to pull into the circular driveway, Yamazaki told him to stop.

"We'll get out here," he said.

My two companions then proceeded to lead me a block away to an imposing white three-story building on the same side of the street as the embassy, and walked up to it with a well-accustomed air. The gold-plated plaque on the building read 4567, four numbers in sequence.

Yamazaki rapped the door-knocker. A small window in the upper half of the door opened and the face of an elderly woman peered out.

"*Soy japonés,*" Yamazaki said.

The woman nodded and opened the door, and I instantly realized what kind of house it must be. We were shown into a large hall on the first floor with a great many young women seated about the room. There were only four or five other customers there before us. Three girls joined us at our table as soon as we sat down.

"If you're too worn out today, this can be just a dry run," Hayashi said, and went on to explain: "You should know that the Chileans are pretty easy-going about these things. These girls aren't professionals; they're moonlighting. Apparently it's not uncommon for a working girl to run into her boss from the office."

And so the party began, but unfortunately, in spite of being surrounded by beautiful women, I found myself struggling with the language. I had to keep asking my two hosts how to say this or that, then wound up endlessly repeating the same thing.

Hayashi was talking me up to the girls, telling them what a famous writer I was in Japan; I was rich and was financing a scooter expedition across South America out of my own pocket. Meanwhile, I could only stammer out clumsy half-phrases.

"*¿Usted . . . nombre?*"

"*Alda.*"

"*¡Ay, qué bonito nombre!*"

But once I'd gone through this same exchange with the other two and learned that their names were Gloria and Sophia, I was at a loss what to say next.

"So, which girl do you like?" Hayashi said. "It's about time we picked."

"Actually, I think maybe I'm more worn out than I realized," I found myself saying prudishly. "Perhaps another day, sometime soon."

"Can't say I blame you. Jet lag really starts to hit right about now."

Fortunately, Hayashi accepted my decision without any fuss, and we all got up to go. The madam seemed a little puzzled by our abrupt departure. My two hosts saw me back to the hotel in a cab, and we said good night.

After they were gone, I took a shower and poured myself a nightcap, but when I looked at the clock I discovered it was still only ten o'clock. Back in Japan where I typically worked until dawn, that was like the middle of my afternoon. I suddenly started to regret my foolish reserve earlier.

Lying on the bed with a towel wrapped around my waist, I stared at the ceiling for a time. I simply wasn't in the mood for sleep. Here I'd come to Santiago for the first time in my life, and what had I seen of the city? The whitewashed colonial buildings held an exotic allure; I was eager to go out somewhere. But I was alone now, and I didn't know my way around. I kicked myself for timidly retreating from that white mansion after having been so graciously shown through its doors.

"This is ridiculous!" I finally decided.

I quickly threw my clothes back on and headed downstairs. As we had done the first time, I got into a waiting cab and told the driver, *Embajada Americana.*

The driver looked like the same fellow to me, but in any case the cab soon deposited me back in front of the American Embassy. After that it was a simple matter of walking one block to the white building with the unforgettable 4567 plaque. I knocked, the small window opened as before, and the same old lady peered out.

"Soy japonés," I said, easily remembering that much, and once again the door opened for me without delay.

Inside, I found Hayashi and Yamazaki sitting at the same table with the same three girls, except that this time each of them had one of the girls on his lap.

"Good grief, Ishihara. Were you trying to look like a goody-goody or something?"

"It's not that," I said. "I just couldn't get to sleep. I suppose it has something to do with the time difference."

"Of course, of course," my alumni brother said amiably, then added, "Now, which of these girls was it that you liked? This one? That one?"

Needless to say, my Chilean sojourn was filled with many very fond memories, not the least of which can be credited to my second escape from the hotel that evening.

BELIEVE IT OR NOT

In recent times, it has become impossible to think of manufacturing without the help of robots. Japan in particular has gained a reputation for using robots in factories more effectively than any other nation. Not only are we good at building them, but we know how to get the most out of them.

I thought I'd discovered why this is so when someone told me that young factory workers at major manufacturers like Nissan and Toyota often nickname their robots after favorite actresses and singers. They even hang pictures of these celebrities on the robots, and before switching them on in the morning give them a gentle pat or a kiss, saying, "Time to start another day, sweetheart. Show us your stuff."

Treated this way, even robots are motivated to work harder, which naturally leads to increased productivity. That's the secret of the superior quality control that Japanese manufacturing is known for. . . . At least this claim is always good for a laugh in speeches.

Once, however, I made the same remark to an eminent robotics engineer, who to my surprise took me quite seriously. "You're absolutely right," he told me.

The truth is, I more than half believe it myself.

You've got to be kidding! some might say. *In this day and age?* Yet there are many things like this in life that ultimately come down to whether you believe them or don't.

Meanwhile, as the flip side to robots responding to the human touch, there are plenty of cases where machines—of whatever kind—are shown to be no match for the power of the human spirit.

I live near a major motorway loop around Tokyo that for many years lacked one short connecting section where construction had halted. It was a source of endless frustration for drivers, but the problem was that the planners drew the future route of the road straight through a Buddhist graveyard. Given my position as a member of the Diet at the time, a steady stream of people asked me to use my influence to break the impasse, but I made a point of not getting involved in the dispute. Because it was essentially a question of belief.

My weekend home in Zushi was built by a fairly well-known construction company. The president of the company was a rational, no-nonsense young businessman who'd brought impressive growth to the firm during his tenure.

While the house was still in the planning stages, an acquaintance of mine who seems to have clairvoyant powers—a psychic of sorts—told me, without ever having been there, that a stream running through the property had once been used by mountain ascetics for their spiritual disciplines. If I didn't believe him, he said, I should take some photos of the site. He was quite sure I'd find glowing, halation-like auras in the resulting prints.

The property did indeed straddle a small stream, so the remark got under my skin enough to make me mention it to the construction company boss. To my surprise, he also urged me to do as my psychic friend said. With this additional push from him, I dug out a camera and took dozens of shots all around the site. And sure enough, a number of them showed white haloes of light—which I was quickly told couldn't actually be what was normally called halation.

I didn't really understand what this meant, but before he would start building, the head of the company insisted that I have elaborate rituals performed to purify the site. Not that I had any objections. I can't say exactly why, but the ritual services brought peace of mind for me as well.

When I told him so after the services were over, he replied gravely, "I'm a bit younger than you, but because of the nature of the work I do, I've learned to take things like this very seriously. I didn't at first, even though my general manager

203

kept insisting that I should. But I suppose experience is your best teacher. If it hadn't been for what happened on a job we did some seven or eight years ago now, I might still be skeptical."

The company was redeveloping a site in Akasaka where a Buddhist temple once stood. Since the place obviously had profound connections with the past, priests were summoned to perform elaborate prayers for the repose of souls. The entire graveyard area was carefully dug up by hand to a depth of five meters, and all of the human remains found there were reburied with additional prayers for their repose. Only then did they break ground for the new construction itself.

In laying the foundation, they had to drive concrete pilings into the ground. All the others went in easily to the prescribed twenty-meter depth, but then one got stuck at about twelve or thirteen meters and refused to go in any further.

Since their pile driver was an old model, the foreman thought maybe they needed more horsepower. So they brought in brand-new equipment, but still the piling wouldn't budge. They kept pounding on it full force, trying to ram the piling through whatever was blocking it, until suddenly the pile driver started shaking and toppled over on its side, nearly pinning the foreman under its massive weight.

It made no sense that there'd be impenetrable bedrock in just that one place. The foreman decided they would have to dig by hand straight down along the pile to check.

The digging took two days. On the evening of the second day, the workers finally reached the depth where the piling had stopped some twelve or thirteen meters down. There they found a human skull, battered and stained.

After summoning his boss to the site, the seasoned foreman, without any further explanation, solemnly handed him the skull.

On the crown of the otherwise blackened skull was a single faint white mark, made by the tip of the concrete piling. The pressure exerted by that tip had to have been on the order of several thousand tons, and yet a single tiny spot at the very top of the skull had somehow withstood that massive force and sent it bouncing right back up the shaft.

"I never imagined we'd still find something like this way down there," said the foreman, who had barely escaped with his life when the pile driver fell over. The rest of the workers stood in silence; no one so much as cleared his throat.

All of a sudden, the skull in the boss's hands began to crumble around the edges—even though he was exerting no pressure on it. Everyone stood watching the disintegrating bits of bone sift through his fingers as if it were an unspoken, long-lost message from an unknown soul in the distant past.

I accepted the company president's account without the slightest twinge of doubt. What he experienced at that moment must surely have been a deep sense of connection with a fellow human being that transcended the vast abyss of time.

THE MAN-EATING SHARK OF NIIJIMA

Niijima in the Izu Islands has long been famous for a brined and dried fish product called *kusaya*, sometimes made with shark meat.

One autumn in the eighties, I went longline fishing on a friend's boat out near Zenisu. This is reputed to be one of the best fishing spots in all the Izu Islands, but we failed to catch a single decent fish. What we did haul in were three tiger sharks, each weighing more than three hundred kilos. Apart from being amazed by their size, I was surprised—shocked even—to discover that such an aggressive species of shark still frequented the waters around Zenisu. I'd gone scuba diving in the area many times.

Taken together, the three sharks weighed a full ton—enough for the stern of the twenty-meter boat to ride noticeably lower in the water and list to one side. Since it was not the sort of catch you can simply take home with you, someone suggested we haul them to Niijima and sell them to a kusaya maker.

I'd never heard of kusaya made of shark meat before. With something as big as a shark, I could easily guess that they didn't brine and dry the animal whole, as with smaller fish. So I asked about it and learned that they cut the meat into long rectangular filets two or three centimeters thick. When I expressed doubt that even the strong, foul-smelling kusaya brine could neutralize the ammonia stench so characteristic of shark meat, I was told that to those who liked it this cocktail of pungent aromas was its very appeal.

We radioed ahead to the island, and a man from the processing plant was waiting for us at the dock. Once we'd dragged the three massive carcasses off the boat, he forklifted them onto his truck and drove off.

I never heard how much the man paid the owner of the boat. I doubt it could have been much, since he was hauling away what was useless waste to us. But as a bonus he brought us some shark-meat kusaya to sample from a previous batch they'd made.

It was really something. You barely had to touch it and the odor instantly assaulted your nose. Roasting it made no difference. And when you raised it to your mouth to take a bite, the ammonia fumes made your eyes water.

In the end, I threw most of mine away, but I could see how people who go for strange foods might consider it a delicacy. The human appetite is willing to send almost anything down the gullet, it seems—even shark meat.

From this perspective, the legendary appetite of sharks themselves should surprise no one.

At any rate, the Niijima islanders were still making shark-meat kusaya, so it could only mean that the waters around the islands continued to be infested with the key ingredient.

I've heard that in the past, sharks sometimes showed up at international surfing competitions held off the white sand beach stretching along the eastern shore of Niijima. Our own Japanese surfers were apparently little concerned, but contestants from overseas made a beeline for the shore any time a fin appeared among the waves—I suppose because they'd witnessed shark attacks elsewhere.

On at least one occasion, competition organizers went to great lengths to keep the news media in the dark about why an event was canceled—which begins to sound reminiscent of a certain famous Hollywood blockbuster featuring a great white shark. But that wasn't a very recent thing, so I'd assumed sharks were no longer a problem. It was decidedly unnerving to haul in three big tiger sharks at Zenisu, such a short distance away.

Divers will tell you that sharks rarely attack humans. Even when they do, they're really only after the dead fish the person is carrying with him. But it also depends on the species and the size of the shark. Tiger sharks, like the ones we hauled in at Zenisu, are known to attack humans quite indiscriminately. Other species, especially the larger ones, will attack as well, so long as the human-shaped fish they see in the water doesn't seem big enough to present a threat. All the more so if the person is on the surface. To a shark, a man or woman splashing about on top of the water apparently looks like a fish that's crippled or in distress.

A year or two before my Zenisu outing, a middle school girl on vacation in Kyushu's Goto Islands was attacked by a shark while swimming with an inner tube tethered to the stern of her family's yacht anchored in the offing. The shark bit off half the girl's torso and she died instantly.

I have in fact seen with my own eyes how frightening—and how horrifyingly swift—the attack of a large shark can be. The attack I witnessed was so one-sided and unreal, like some macabre daydream, I still sometimes wonder if it really happened. To call it cold-blooded would be a gross understatement.

It was in fact the first time I ever saw a shark in the flesh. In the years since, I've come upon many others while diving. Though my memory of that first incident did not make me particularly scared of them, every subsequent meeting has seemed anti-climactic by comparison.

One summer in the early sixties, not long after I first learned to scuba dive, I went diving with some friends near the mouth of Kanbiki Bay at Shikinejima, a tiny island to the southwest of Niijima. A fishing boat had caught its net on some underwater rocks while trawling for horse mackerel, so we dived down to free it for them. There was really nothing to it, but for the fishermen it meant we'd saved them the trouble of calling in professional divers all the way from Miyakejima, and they thanked us profusely.

We became quick friends, and they asked us if we'd be willing to help them out again if they got into trouble the next day. Having just received a large bucket of horse mackerel from them, we readily agreed.

Due to tidal conditions the following afternoon, the fish had moved away from the island, so the three boats had to go in search of them out on the open sea between Niijima and Kozushima, where they would drive-fish instead of trawl.

I was curious about drive-fishing, a practice still quite common around the Izu Islands in those days, so I decided to ride with them and watch the action from on board one of their boats.

Drive-fishing is a decidedly low-tech method for netting fish. The fishermen look for signs of schooling fish on the surface, then drop swimmers into the water on one side and circle their boats around to spread a net on the other. If the fish are near the surface, the swimmers beat the water with sticks to frighten the fish into the nets; when they're down deeper, they dive below and chase them underwater. That day, the horse mackerel were teeming just under the surface, so they sent in six swimmers to start whacking the water with sticks.

The three boats lined up behind the large net they'd dropped in an arc, and I watched as the net filled to near bursting with fish fleeing from the beaters; it was obviously going to be a much larger haul than the day before. The frantic, thrashing mass of silvery bodies changed the color of the sea. Although impossible, I even imagined I could hear the sound of their panicked breathing. This was the moment, the thrill for which so many men go to sea at risk to life and limb. Nothing quickens the fisherman's heart quite so much as an immeasurable quarry that's still struggling valiantly to escape.

It was at that very moment, when all hands on deck were reaching for the ropes to haul in the seething mass of fish, that one of the men raised a cry and pointed across the water.

Off to starboard, still at a considerable distance, a dark blade-like object broke the surface. Supremely ominous, it immediately began heading in our direction. You could just see everybody aboard mentally calculating the distance between the advancing blade and the boats. It looked huge for how far away it was.

"Shark! Shark! Everybody out of the water!"

A clamor of voices erupted all at once, alerting the beaters to the danger.

What followed was like one of those nightmares we've all had: you strain desperately to flee, but your every movement turns sluggish as sludge, while your pursuer gains on you with graceful, sinister swiftness, certain of triumph. The swimmers scrambled frantically toward the boats. How excruciatingly slow their arms must have felt as they churned through the water! The scene still replays itself vividly in my mind, like flickering frames in a slow motion film.

The shark, for its part, showed remarkable acumen. It apparently had taken full measure of the situation, and instead of pursuing its quarry into the net, it circled outside the arc, heading for the swimmer who was about to be first out of the water.

The boat I was on lay at the right end of the net, with her stern pointing outward, and the young swimmer had almost reached us. Men knelt at the stern with outstretched arms, ready to pull him aboard. But the very instant the swimmer reached up for those arms, his pursuer struck.

With a pitiful whimper more like the cry of a small animal than of a human voice, a sound so weak it barely reached our ears, the swimmer disappeared beneath the waves. The power of the creature was shocking; the man was dragged under literally in the blink of an eye.

Then, as if to make sure we knew what was what, the man-eater returned to the surface with the human prey still in its jaws. What we could see of the shark's head alone suggested a monster nearly as long as the fishing boat on which we stood.

The image etched vividly in my mind is of the young man held sideways in the beast's massive jaws, his eyes wide open but his face an utter blank. I have no memory of the shark's own face, nor of its color or anything else.

To our horror, the shark proceeded to swim lazily about with the young man clamped in its mouth just beneath the surface next to the boat, almost within arm's reach. The light skin of the lifeless human figure marked the shark's position like a float being dragged through the water. And as if to show us even more clearly where it was, the shark rose to display its tall dorsal fin from time to time.

I heard a wild shriek from the middle boat. Two men were struggling to restrain a third, who was brandishing a harpoon: one tried to work him into an arm lock from behind, while the other attempted to wrest the harpoon from his hand. When the shrieking man refused to give up, two others jumped in to grab his legs out from under him, and the four men together finally wrestled him to the deck. I later learned that the man so determined to dive into the water with his harpoon was the father of the young fisherman wedged between the shark's teeth.

How long did that giant shark carry the young man about in its jaws, and where in the deep, vast sea did it ultimately go to tear the body apart and devour it?

Several days later, some passengers arrived from Tokyo clamoring about a gigantic shark they'd seen from the deck of the ferry. They described it as the size of a yacht. Publicly, the locals scoffed at the report, saying it was probably a whale, or possibly a harmless whale shark. But the island's fishermen could hardly rest easy with a shark like that roaming their fishing grounds. They tried everything to hunt the man-eater down, to no avail. They set out a large hook baited with the head of a pig and attached it to a wire that was in turn attached to a thick rope. When they went back to check, although no one could be sure it was the same shark, the pig's head and wire were gone and only the rope remained.

Whether due in part to that tragic shark attack, or merely to the depletion of fish stocks in the area, the Izu fishermen no longer practice drive-fishing today. You don't hear of any surface sightings of sharks in recent times either.

Years later, when I directed a documentary film on the Tokara Islands, I made a side trip to Amami Oshima and shot some underwater footage of drive-fishing there. The haul was a far cry from the huge catch I'd seen off Niijima, but afterwards, on returning to the head fisherman's house, I saw the razor-toothed jaws of a colossal tiger shark hanging on his wall. He told me it had wandered into the inlet four or five years before, weak enough to be captured with a net. The picture he brought out showed a beast over ten meters long. It immediately brought back memories of what I'd witnessed at Niijima.

I asked the fisherman about the contents of the shark's stomach, but he said they found it almost empty. The shark had apparently been too weak to do much hunting by the time it neared their inlet.

Could the Amami Oshima shark have been the same one that made off with the young Niijima fisherman? There's no way of knowing. It occurred to me that I might borrow the photo to show the victim's father, the man who tried to jump into the water with his harpoon, but I decided against it.

Would the picture have brought him some small measure of comfort that his son's death had been avenged? Perhaps. But time lets us forget most things, and, indeed, we must forget in order to go on living. This holds all the more for those who live and die by the sea and its unfathomable whims.

SOUTH PACIFIC

Over the years I've dived in many places around the world, but nowhere is the sea so lovely or so replete with surprises as Palau. The uniquely sculpted islands that dot Palauan waters have no rival among the myriad other islands in the South Pacific—or anywhere in the world for that matter.

The Maldives and the Seychelles also lie at a distant remove in the middle of the ocean, but neither can match Palau for its astonishing variety of underwater scenery or the sheer diversity of its islands. The marine life you encounter can vary dramatically according to time and place, of course, but I remember one dive on the seaward side of Peleliu when a massive school of fish took nearly half an hour to swim by. It was a truly magnificent spectacle.

Each of Palau's countless islands has its own character, so no matter where you dive there's plenty to enjoy. At one island, divers can swim under a small arch and through a subterranean channel into a landlocked pool that is a marvelous garden of soft coral. At another island you paddle flat along the shallows where dozens of giant clams remain curiously unattached to any rock; keep swimming over a sharp drop-off, and without diving anywhere near the bottom you find schools of large napoleonfish roving about at shallow depths.

There are far too many islands for even the local guides to know all the dive sites. And with the only big hotel located at the south end of the main island, the waters to the north remain pristine and free from tourists. I've long wanted to make a trip up north, for I'm sure there must be many marvels to see there, but since I never get to visit Palau very long, I always find myself limited to the more accessible southern waters.

One year I flew to Palau at the very end of December with my wife and two older sons, Nobuteru and Yoshizumi. By our second day there, which was New Year's Eve, even hard-to-impress Yoshizumi was wowed.

"You were right about this place, Dad," he said. "It's really awesome. There can't be many places like this in the world."

On the third day, after toasting the New Year with beer at breakfast, we headed out for another day of diving. Our boat had been a little cramped on the previous two days, so I'd asked our guide to get us something bigger. Unfortunately, all his other boats were taken, so he arranged for us to charter one belonging to a member of the Palauan parliament he happened to know. Despite being a national legislator, the owner himself brought the boat around, with his two sons along as deckhands; it made a nice family outing for them, I suppose, even with company aboard.

We completed one dive in the morning, and made another after lunch and a brief nap. Then we killed time cruising among some of the more strange-shaped, uninhabited islands while waiting for the tide to let us visit a half-submerged Zero that sits on a shallow strand next to one of the islands. I'd seen it before, but I wanted to show it to the boys.

Whatever the pilot's reasons for setting down there, the aircraft rests virtually intact in water shallow enough for low tide to expose the upper half of the fuselage. Rust has taken its toll over the years, but the basic shell of the World War II fighter plane retains its original form. No doubt the pilot chose to ditch in that particular spot after seeing the terrain on shore.

Another Zero submerged in a shallow channel at Kohamajima in Okinawa is missing a wing and obviously met a tragic end, but this Zero in Palau has every appearance of a successfully executed emergency landing. One can just picture the pilot extracting himself from the cockpit and wading across the shallow flat to shore.

We brought the boat up to the sandy beach and waded across those same shallows to the half-sunken aircraft.

The more I looked at the plane, the more I marveled at how small it was: the fuselage measured less than a meter across. Obviously, the men who flew these machines must have been chosen not only for their piloting skills, but also for their small build to fit the very tight cockpit. Yoshizumi, the tallest among us, had trouble with his knees when he squeezed into the pilot's seat.

"Man, it must have gotten real lonely flying in one of these things all by yourself for hours on end," he said.

Indeed, a former Zero pilot I know, who miraculously survived the war in spite of being downed three times, told me how sick he got of being cooped up in the tiny little plane and having to do everything by himself: looping the loop, firing the guns, navigating, manning the radio. Sitting in that cockpit in Palau brought his words to life, giving us a hands-on feel for what it must have been like. Especially if you'd been wounded in a dogfight, it would have been sheer hell.

"I sure wouldn't want to go anywhere in a thing like this," said Nobuteru.

Of course, in wartime, "want to" was not a consideration.

When we were done there, we still had time for one more dive. Since this was my sons' first trip to Palau, to top it all off I suggested we find a spot where we could see some migratory fish, maybe even a shark or two. Both boys immediately objected to the sharks, but I assured them we had nothing to worry about so long as we were only observing. I told our guide what we had in mind, and he pointed across the lagoon from the Zero where, he said, fish and sharks often came in from the open sea through a break in the barrier reef.

We sped across the water and dropped anchor about half a mile from the break he'd mentioned. Before jumping in, I asked about the set of the tide. The guide said it was going out, but to my surprise the owner of the boat immediately contradicted him.

"I used to make my living as a fisherman, and I fished around here a lot," he said. "I know this area better than you. The tide is still coming in."

The two men proceeded to argue right in front of us. I quickly lost patience and broke in.

"Look, we'll just plan to swim straight out to the side and straight back, all right? If the tide seems too strong, we'll come back right away and call it a day."

My wife begged off, saying she was tired, so she stayed on the boat while the boys and I made the dive, together with the owner of the boat and our guide.

The break in the reef nearby made the site everything I'd hoped for. Schools of rainbow runners and giant trevally came swimming by, and before long several sharks as well. Although we hadn't been able to tell on the surface, the tide was moving very slightly out to sea.

The boys were obviously none too enthusiastic about seeing the sharks. I motioned for them to swim in for a closer look, but they'd have none of it. Since my prodding-father routine wasn't working, I decided to show them myself how perfectly safe it was, but the startled sharks turned and swam away as soon as I approached. Then a pack of larger sharks, easily over three meters long, emerged from deeper down—and I decided that was enough of that.

With so many more eye-catching things to see than at any of our previous dive spots, we stayed down enjoying the sights until nearly all our air was gone. By the time we finally turned around, the tide had picked up speed and carried us quite a way out from the rock we'd chosen as a marker to lead us back. If we ascended right there, I guessed we'd have to swim at least a hundred meters to reach the boat, so I took a stab at where I thought the boat was anchored, and we all headed in that direction. But when we surfaced, the boat was nowhere in sight. Flabbergasted, I pushed high out of the water to look around and saw the boat waiting for us way off in the opposite direction, at least five or six hundred meters away.

"What the hell happened?" I yelled at the boat owner. "We told them to wait for us right where we went in."

"Sorry," he said. "I misjudged the tide. I was sure it was still flowing into the lagoon, so to save us swimming so far I told the boys to take the boat a little closer to shore."

"Are you crazy? Why the hell couldn't they just do as I said?" I was furious, but of course the deed was done.

The wind was whipping up a surface current that ran even faster than what we'd had below, quickly washing us back toward the opening in the reef. By this time, the sun was dropping low in the sky. The closer the current carried us to the reef, the larger the waves grew, and whenever we sank to the bottom of a trough we found ourselves in twilight gloom. Each time we rose on a crest, we frantically blew the whistles attached to our buoyancy compensators, which also served as life vests at times like this. But the roar of the waves pounding against the reef not far away drowned us out; there was no way the people on the boat could have heard.

I realized we were in real trouble, and we needed to start thinking of survival strategies. The first thing I did was drop the five kilos of weights strapped to my waist. Nobuteru was nearest to me, so I called him over and helped him remove his weights, too.

I'd dived with my sons many times, but never had we needed to jettison our weight belts before. When I told Nobuteru to do precisely that, we both understood implicitly that this was no longer an ordinary diving situation.

Yoshizumi came swimming after us, and Nobuteru yelled at him, "Your weights! Your weights!"—parroting what I'd said only a few seconds before. But over the roar of waves in the background, Yoshizumi only heard "Wait! Wait!" and responded, "Don't worry. I'm not going anywhere." Then as he swam closer he added, "The waves are getting bigger, so I figured we three should stay together."

Obviously he, too, understood how serious our situation had become.

A numbing heartache spread through me. I didn't care about myself, but my boys were still in the prime of their lives. How could I let them die here, in a foolish accident so far from home? I was beside myself with remorse and anger.

Suppose we got swept farther and farther from the boat, on out past the barrier reef? What kind of rescue effort could we expect in a remote island nation like this? I doubted the islanders could organize any sort of timely search for a missing tourist or two. My wife would return to the hotel and make a fuss to get the staff to contact the police, but it would probably be noon tomorrow before they could get a rescue team ready. Would the five of us, or even just me and my two boys, be able to stay together until then? Would the sharks leave us alone as we drifted helplessly on the surface?

I quickly gained new respect for the power of waves. Even with seas at only one to two meters, all it took was one good bounce to pull our locked arms apart. As a stopgap, we tied our life vest cords together, but I wondered how much good this would do if conditions got worse.

We were in the tropics, so luckily the water was warm. Still, how many hours could we hold out like this? I'd heard countless stories of divers getting washed out to sea, but it was one of those things you never thought could happen to you.

I was already distraught at having dragged my two boys into this predicament, but what if I really started to panic? What if these flimsy life vest cords gave out during the night, and I drifted apart from my sons? Would I come completely unglued? What if one of those sharks were to attack? I'd assured my boys that people generally had nothing to fear from sharks so long as they did nothing to aggravate them, but "generally" aside, would it be the case with us? What if they attacked one of my sons right in front of me? However willing I might be to die in his place, no shark would read my mind.

I wanted to scream, but not wishing to alarm the others I fought back the urge, only to feel like throwing up instead.

Somehow, I held this second urge in check as well. It was vital that I keep my wits about me. But whatever sense of calm I managed to convey was only an empty front. My mind leapt from one dire thought to another, going around and around in useless circles. I could see this, but was helpless to stop it. I needed to pull myself together, calmly assess our situation, and come up with a plan, but as the tide carried us out to sea, my stomach churned and my body grew numb with mounting panic.

At each large wave, I'd rise up as high as possible on its crest to look across the water toward the boat, and I could feel the rays of the setting sun on my cheek. This could be the last time I saw the sun, the last time I squinted in its bright glare. I needed to say something to my boys while it was still light. But what? The phrases refused to line up coherently in my head.

Although I'd visualized situations like this before, it had always been as someone else's predicament. Now it was my own—and, worse, my two sons' as well. It was a nightmare. To distract my thoughts from the worst, I tried to focus on how to survive. What if we continued to drift like this for three whole days? How could we stave off starvation? How much seawater could we safely drink?

Even though it was obviously no use, the boat owner kept shouting and waving his spear gun. Now he suddenly thrust the gun into our guide's hands and began swimming madly toward the boat. With the wind and waves and tide against him, I didn't think he'd make much headway, but by some stroke of luck his course took him a little closer to the reef, where he picked up a reverse flow from the waves crashing in over the barrier. Slowly but surely he made progress toward the boat. Then he must have run out of breath: after about a hundred meters, he stopped swimming and started jumping up and down on the waves again.

I could see him waving his arms frantically in the air, but I could no longer see the boat; from where the current had carried us, she was now hidden by the waves crashing over the reef. I had no way of telling whether his waving and shouting might get anyone's attention.

The next thing I knew, he dropped his arms and started swimming back in our direction, pausing to wave at us. I was still wondering what to make of this, when our guide shouted, "The boat's coming!"

We all looked in the direction he was pointing. Still half-hidden by the waves, the boat had weighed anchor and was moving toward us.

Swimming back with the current, the owner reached us in no time at all, well before the boat arrived. Exhausted by the effort, he grabbed my shoulder to keep from going under; gasping for air and unable to speak, he just kept nodding over and over.

The boat took her time reaching us. When she finally did, the owner impatiently shouted up at his boys, but they just gave blank, puzzled stares. I suppose from their point of view they'd merely done what their father told them to.

My wife didn't appear the least bit concerned, either. "Why'd you swim way over here?" she wanted to know.

"The tide was flowing this way," I said. "We blew our whistles and shouted our lungs out. Didn't you hear?"

"Not a thing. The kids here said you should be coming up over there, so I was looking the other way the whole time. You'd been gone long enough, we were beginning to wonder. We were just talking about going to look for you."

I wanted to scream at her, but I knew it wouldn't accomplish anything, so I held my tongue.

"But then the younger one said, 'You know, it's actually possible they went the other way. Maybe we should go take a look up by the break.' So I turned to look this way, and I saw their father waving at us."

"You didn't hear him shouting?"

"No, I didn't hear a thing. I just happened to look."

"We could have died, you know."

"Goodness. What makes you say that?" She looked dubious.

"Forget it," said Yoshizumi. "Just let it go."

I realized he was right. Only moments before, we'd been facing a different reality entirely, and it was still much too soon for us to try to convey what we'd been through to anyone who hadn't been there.

As the boat started up, I turned for one last look at the island of Peleliu in the distance—a lingering shadow floating in the twilight after sundown.

How long would it have taken them to find us if we'd been swept all the way down there, I wondered, but quickly pushed the thought from my mind.

I knew the owner was itching to say something more to his boys, but he remained silent all the way home. My sons and I fell quiet, too.

After a while, I popped open a beer and took a swig.

"Could you toss me one?" asked Nobuteru. I glanced toward Yoshizumi as well, but he just shook his head.

As the first flush of alcohol spread through my body, loosening something inside me, I felt my normal perceptions returning. It finally began to sink in that we'd escaped from the brink of disaster, and regained something infinitely precious in doing so.

Soon Nobuteru and I began recapping the experience together, making silly jokes and laughing. It was our little way of affirming our deliverance.

Nobuteru recalled how Yoshizumi had confused "weights" with "wait" and yelled back that he wasn't going anywhere. For some reason, it now seemed hilarious, and we laughed on and on.

"Stop it!" spat out Yoshizumi. "Enough already!"

Taken aback by this sudden outburst, we looked at him.

"What's so funny? How can anyone laugh at that?" he stormed, his whole body trembling. I doubt his anger was really directed at us, but we took the brunt of it all the same.

We understood what he was feeling only too well. Yet even so, we couldn't stop laughing. We were drunk on being alive.

"It's getting kind of late," my wife said. "What did you want to do about dinner? At home we'd have a whole New Year's spread, but I don't suppose we'll find anything like that here."

As if struck by something else hilarious, Nobuteru and I burst out laughing again.

———

By the time the boat dropped us on the dock at the hotel, the sky was completely dark. Diners crowded the tables on the restaurant terrace, which I could see from where I rinsed off my gear. I experienced a twinge of apprehension that the gods might not be too pleased about the immodest sense of contentment I felt washing over me. And yet, at that moment, nothing could have changed my profound satisfaction with absolutely everything, including even the pangs of hunger gnawing at my stomach.

ON THE RAILS

The overcrowded trains of the period immediately after the war seem almost a fond memory now, but we took our lives into our hands every time we got on—or more accurately, every time we *tried* to get on.

As we stood waiting on the platform gazing down the tracks, the approaching train's silhouette would tell us just how crowded it was. Instead of a square box, we often saw a rounded bulk, bulging on both sides from passengers overflowing out the doors. Having verified what we were about to go up against, we'd steel ourselves for battle as we waited for the train to pull in. In many cases, no amount of pushing or clawing could get us onto the train, and we'd have to wait for the next.

At first I resisted boarding through the windows, but when I finally did it was a little bit like losing one's virginity: I felt I'd cast off my inhibitions, and it emboldened me in other things as well. In my childish way, I wondered if this was what it meant to grow up.

The times being what they were, there was no telling what kind of human dramas you might witness when traveling by train.

It was at a train station that I learned how easily a human limb could be separated from its host.

One day on my way home from school, I had caught the train from Fujisawa as usual, but when I got off one station up the line at Ofuna, the police were inspecting people's bags for black market goods. Seeing what was going on, a man fled out the door opposite the platform and jumped down onto the tracks, only to be run over by a passing freight train. The freight train sped on by without even noticing, but it had cut off the man's left leg at about the knee. When I saw the man after our train pulled out, he was screaming something unintelligible at the top of his lungs as he held his severed limb in his right hand and tried to walk using his left arm and right leg.

Everybody on the platform stared in horror at the man hobbling along just one track away. He paid no attention to us; he merely kept screaming as he awkwardly made his way along the rails. When quiet returned after the train had gone, I finally could make out what he was screaming: "Help! Stationmaster! Help!" Everybody stood in stunned silence, listening to his cries.

A station attendant and a policeman jumped down onto the tracks to offer help, but as soon as he saw the policeman the injured black marketeer fled—or tried to flee—in the opposite direction.

I had another train to catch, but my feet felt glued to the spot. Only with immense effort did I finally manage to peel them loose and drag myself toward the pedestrian overpass leading to the other platform. On the way, I threw up on the stairs.

This was the first time I'd ever seen a body part wholly severed from a person. I'd witnessed some shocking things during the war, too, but nothing put life and death in quite such stark relief as that scene at Ofuna Station after peace had returned.

A short time later, on that same rail line, I watched a close acquaintance of mine thrown to his death right before my eyes.

After school one day, as I was waiting for the train at Fujisawa Station, the silhouette of the train coming down the track told me it was already packed to overflowing. I quickly ran to the end of the platform, and as soon as the train came to a halt I jumped down onto the tracks behind it, ran along the other side, and climbed up into the doorway of the second car from the rear. At first

I was just barely hanging on, but then the shifting crowd loosened up some space inside, so I asked people to please squeeze in a little further. I managed to swing around to face outward with a grip on both handrails and my feet firmly on the step. From that position, I pushed back hard against the passengers behind me, trying to wedge my way as far inside as I could.

The train was about to start moving when a boy named Sonoda, who commuted to our school from Kamakura, came dashing along the tracks to my doorway. From my point of view, it was always safer to have someone else on the outside, so I let him up. He stood facing me in the doorway, hanging onto both handrails.

Sonoda had always been something of a clown. Once the train started moving, he leaned out with both arms as far as he could. As we gained speed and the wind got stronger, his cap almost flew off, so he grabbed it with one hand and handed it to me. "Hold this, will you?" he said, still leaning out with one arm.

Just then the train tilted into a curve, closing the gap between the train and a steel gantry post beside the tracks. His head smashed against the support.

Sonoda was ripped away from the train like he was nothing at all, his body flipping several times end over end in the air before landing alongside the tracks. He then bounced and rolled several more times before finally coming to rest, his eyes closed and face buried in the rocky rail bed. The entire sequence seemed to unfold in slow motion. I knew instantly that I was witnessing the devices of death.

I clung to my perch in a daze. The strength drained from me, as if something at the very core of my being had suddenly withered. My body no longer felt like my own. I hung on for dear life, gripping the handrail over the cap given me moments before by my now-dead friend. It was all I could do to keep from being shaken off the speeding train.

As soon as we pulled into Ofuna, I raced up to the first station attendant I could find and told him what had happened. The young attendant looked bewildered as he fingered the cap I'd thrust at him.

After reporting the accident, I quickly fled toward my connecting train. I couldn't bear the thought of being dragged back to the scene of the accident. I knew I'd fall apart if I had to face my schoolmate's lifeless body lying beside the tracks.

The man I'd seen crawling about on one leg as he held the severed other was, at least at that moment, still alive. Sonoda's eyes, however, had already closed by the time I saw him on the tracks. His face was curiously tranquil, yet I knew it could only be the face of death.

I did not throw up this time, as I had when I saw the man without a leg, but the dazed, withered feeling within me refused to go away for quite some time afterwards. When I noticed several days later that I was now constantly on edge, I told myself it was an entirely understandable reaction to what I'd seen.

This was the first time I'd come face to face with the physical extinction of another human being. Yet it didn't really sink in that what I'd seen could happen to me. I suppose I was too young. Throwing up after the earlier incident was no doubt a way of purging that event of any relevance to me as well.

As a footnote, I should add that Sonoda miraculously survived his apparent death. After a long absence, he returned to school one day with his head in a big bandage. Then not long after that, he transferred to another school. Rumor had it that the effects of his head injury left him unable to keep up with his studies at Shonan.

Still later, soccer teams from two other schools came to use our field for a preliminary game in the prefectural tournament. Among the visiting players I spied Sonoda.

I watched as he got reprimanded by the referee for fighting over the ball with an opposing player after it had crossed the touchline. When the referee finally gave him the ball, he shouted something to his teammates and threw the ball in, then raced back onto the field to join the attack.

Another student standing near me had recognized him, too. "Hey! That's Sonoda!" he said. "Since when is he still alive?"

His words came from typical adolescent irreverence, nothing more, but they rang quite differently in my ears. I knew very well, of course, that Sonoda had survived the accident. Yet somehow the boy I now saw on the field was not the boy I'd seen tossed end over end through the air and dashed facedown on the rail bed; he was a completely different boy.

And if this was how a mere witness felt, then what must the incident that remained so horribly vivid in my memory mean to the boy himself?

I turned the question over and over in my mind as I stood gazing through the shimmering midday heat at the field, all but convinced I was watching a ghostly apparition.

THE DAY MY FATHER DIED

Because my father worked for a steamship company and we moved around a lot, we almost never had any relations living nearby. As a result, I went through childhood without ever experiencing firsthand the death of close kin.

During the war, my grandmother fell seriously ill, and Father somehow got time off to make the long trip home to Yawatahama on Shikoku Island. When he came back, I heard him say to my mother that he doubted Grandma would ever leave her bed again. I'd met my grandmother only once that I could recall, when the whole family visited Shikoku during summer vacation one year. I remembered a woman of quiet demeanor patting me and my younger brother on the head by turns. She was already very advanced in years at the time.

Finally a telegram arrived saying her condition was critical. The telegraph office was shorthanded due to the war, so two girls on student labor detail from the local girls' school delivered the message. They found me playing with some friends outside my house.

"We've brought a telegram for your dad," said one of them, holding out the envelope. "It's bad news. You should open it."

Naturally, with nothing else to do along the way, they'd peeked at the message.

I unfolded the paper addressed to my father, and read the standard message for such occasions: *Mother critical. Come immediately.*

I remember how nervous and bewildered I felt reading this in front of my friends.

I took the telegram inside and gave it to my mother, but for some reason she handed it back and told me to give it to Father myself when he got home from work. I did as I was told, and took it to him as he was changing out of his work clothes that evening.

"It says Grandma's critical," I told him.

He accepted it without a word, then finished tying the sash of his kimono before slowly unfolding the message. He studied it for a few moments and gently nodded his head. That was all.

Young as I was, I understood enough about my father's job to know he wouldn't be able to get away again so soon to go to his mother's bedside. A few minutes later Father sat down to dinner with us as if nothing were amiss, looking as calm and relaxed as ever. Knowing how he must be feeling, I kept quiet and made my little brother do the same.

Noticing our silence, Father spoke up. "I already said my good-byes to your grandmother when I went to visit her," he explained. It sounded almost as if he were trying to persuade himself.

"What did you say to her?" Yujiro asked.

"I told her to keep her spirits up. Grandma knew she probably wouldn't get to see you kids again, so she asked me to remember her to you. I could tell she really wished she could see you."

"I bet you really wish you could see her, too," Yujiro said.

Father smiled without saying anything. It was the most tranquil smile I'd ever seen on his face.

My first direct experience of the death of a loved one was when he died himself. Twice before, he had been seriously ill with high blood pressure, but each time he'd recovered after a lengthy convalescence and returned to work without any apparent aftereffects. This was after most of his company's top management were forced out for their involvement in a shipbuilding kickback scandal, and at the age of barely fifty my father had been promoted to a top level executive position where numerous heavy responsibilities fell on his shoulders. It was obvious to the entire family that his long hours were increasingly taking their toll. The proprietress of an exclusive restaurant in Yanagibashi where my father held many of his business dinners visited her vacation home next to our house in Zushi on weekends, and she related to us with both admiration and concern the tremendous effort he put into his business dealings at her restaurant.

To the rest of us, his continued good health was paramount. My mother pleaded with him to stop pushing himself so hard, and even to resign. If nothing else, we could all become farmers, she said. But no matter how insistent she was, my father merely responded that nothing would suit him better than to die on the job. I think he probably felt more alive then than at any other time in his life.

I remember a walk I took with him in the hills near our home. The path was not especially steep, but the effort to keep up with me was apparently a strain. He suddenly said he felt lightheaded, and lowered himself onto a large rock to rest. Afraid that some kind of an attack might be coming on, I watched nervously as he sat with his fingers pressed to his temples waiting for the dizziness to pass.

Because of his long commute into Tokyo, Father always rose before the rest of us, and I'd hear him reciting sutra verses in front of the Buddhist altar in the next room. Some days he would chant haltingly, other days more smoothly; I listened from my bed, trying to tell from his voice how he might be feeling. Today we have all kinds of anti-hypertension drugs he could have used, but they weren't available in those days, so my father tried a variety of other treatments like moxibustion and compresses of foul-smelling medicinal herbs, none to any noticeable effect. He'd drink at business dinners to keep from being a wet blanket, knowing full well that the alcohol was killing him. Then when he got home, he'd sleep fitfully. We all cringed at the sound of his strained, high-pitched snoring in case it might attract the attention of the grim reaper.

It was quite plain both to Father and to us that death was gaining ground, but no one could predict when it might finally claim him.

On the fateful day, I remained after classes for an editorial meeting to plan the next issue of our school journal, then stayed to work on an article I was writing.

So it was very late in the afternoon before I left school. I'd walked about halfway home from Zushi Station, when I saw our maid hurrying toward me, all out of breath.

She told me with tears in her eyes that my father had been taken ill while visiting a client that afternoon. Having no time to wait for me, my mother had immediately set out for Tokyo with my brother. She'd called the school as soon as she got there to tell me to come straight to my father's office, but I'd already left, so then she'd called home hoping the maid could catch me at the station.

I threw my bag into the maid's arms and raced back to the station. On the train, as her words played over in my mind, I knew with suffocating certainty that the decisive moment had arrived.

It was the evening rush hour, so trains heading into the city were not very crowded. I had a four-seat box all to myself. I began reciting a sutra and a Shinto prayer I'd learned by listening to my father's daily devotions. I arbitrarily vowed to recite each of them one hundred times before I reached Tokyo.

Passengers came aboard at stops along the way and the boxes around me began to fill up, but the sight of a teenager staring into space and mumbling something under his breath must have given people pause. I got strange looks, and no one sat with me all the way into Tokyo.

Though fully aware of the inquisitorial eyes around me, I had neither the words nor the strength to explain. I was learning for the first time how bereft a person feels when faced with the loss of a loved one—a profound sense of emptiness wrapped in a swirl of grief and fear. I doubt even the dying person himself could feel quite so dispossessed.

By the time I reached my father's office building, it was well after closing time and the workers were gone. One of my father's direct subordinates, a man I'd met before, was waiting for me at the otherwise deserted entrance.

He shook his head when he saw me. "I'm so sorry, Shin," he said.

I cursed myself for the foolish hope that reciting a hundred sutras on the train might save my father's life. It was what I'd expected to hear, yet the unequivocal confirmation of his death made me want to lash out at someone.

My father was lying in the middle of the floor of a large conference room. I suppose they couldn't find a couch long enough for him; instead they'd brought in a single tatami mat from somewhere and covered it with a sheet.

Though my mother and brother had arrived long before me, I don't recall whether they were in the room when I first entered, nor do I have any memory of who else was present. So far as I was concerned, I was entirely alone with my father.

I drew back the white cloth covering his face. He looked a little paler than usual. I touched his cheek, and nearly jumped at the lifeless chill of his skin. I could feel the stubble his thick beard had produced since morning, and wondered for a moment if the beard had continued to grow even after he suffered his stroke.

His cold skin drove home the fact with unmistakable finality: yes, he was gone. This was indeed the event we'd all been dreading. I gazed on and on at his face to let it sink in.

Then all at once, out of the blue, it struck me: the relationship I had with my father, the ties that bound us together, did not come to an end just because he'd died. What it meant for us to be part of each other's life, *the very fact of our being part of the other's life*, would never change. The realization came, not just as a feeling, but as a powerful conviction that even I cannot explain. It was then that my tears began to flow.

I subsequently became a professional writer, and in the course of my writings I've had occasion to ponder life and death and human existence from many different angles. Whenever I turn to these subjects, I always feel I owe more to the insight gained on touching my father's icy cheek than I can begin to express.

Then again, after I reached adulthood and got married and my own first child was born, I realized anew that the connection I felt with my father when he died was but one link in a larger chain that invisibly connected my father to me, and me to my newborn son.

***

Later, I heard a marvelous story about my father's death that seemed to reaffirm what I had so inexplicably felt in those moments at his side. At the very hour of his death, he apparently visited the home in western Japan of the elderly couple who had served as go-betweens at his wedding.

My father slipped away while in a meeting at another firm, but the others in the room thought he had merely nodded off in his chair. Knowing how exhausted he must be from the grueling schedule he'd been keeping, they decided to let him sleep, and it was apparently this delay that erased any lingering chance there might have been to revive him.

I can only guess that it was during this time, when he appeared to be dozing peacefully in his chair, that my father suddenly showed up at Mrs. Kono's tearoom half a country away and sat down on the edge of the veranda, laying his felt hat down at his side. Surprised by his unexpected visit, Mrs. Kono went to get a cushion for him to sit on, but by the time she came back he was gone. When she asked, no one in the house had seen anyone come to the gate or circle around through the garden to the tearoom. She realized then that he must have died.

I believed every word of this story. It gave me a tremendous reassurance about what I'd felt at my father's side after his death.

A WORLD OF DARKNESS

To be born with a physical disability is one thing, but a disability acquired later in life, especially one that involves our sense of perception, brings heartache and suffering beyond the ability of anyone but the afflicted person to comprehend.

I once called for a massage at a hotel in Okayama. The masseuse was a pretty young woman of about thirty who had lost her eyesight. She told me both her eyes began to dim shortly before she turned twenty, and soon they went completely dark. Her impeccably groomed looks made me feel her tragedy all the more keenly.

She'd decided she would rather be dead, and twice tried to kill herself, but on both occasions her mother saved her against her will. The tears welled in her eyes as she told me this, and I regretted having asked about something so painful to her. I suppose her misfortune was still too near in the past for her to put it behind her.

I wonder what it's like for tears to well in unseeing eyes.

Feeling sorry for her, I made a show of kindness by telling her about a self-massage technique I sometimes used myself that was supposed to be good for the eyes. She immediately asked me to teach it to her after she finished my massage. A person in her situation is apt to grasp at any straws offered.

Unfortunately, I'd taken a sleeping pill before she arrived, and was quite exhausted to begin with, so by the time she finished I was sound asleep. I awoke to find her invoice next to my pillow, but she was gone. I felt as if I'd done something horribly unkind.

With recent advances in medicine, many people who lose their eyesight can be brought back into the world of light. But the apprehensions and fears they must experience before returning from darkness, I imagine, go well beyond ordinary terror.

Many years ago, a friend of mine named Mitsuo Hakama underwent surgery for detached retinas. I received word that everything had gone well during the operation, but he still had to remain hospitalized for nearly a month with bandages over both eyes.

When I visited him, he was lying in bed listening to the radio. I watched from the doorway in silence as he reached for his cigarettes and lighter on the nightstand and lit up with practiced dexterity. If one discounted the thick pads of gauze taped over his eyes, he didn't present a particularly sorry sight.

I decided to keep quiet and observe him for a while, but within a very short time he started twitching his nose and turned to look right at me—even though he couldn't possibly have seen me.

"Is someone there?" he asked.

"It's me, Ishihara," I said, approaching his bed.

"Hey there. Good of you to come," he said. "Oh. You brought flowers, did you? Sorry, but I have to pass on the flowers. You can just take them home with you."

"Why's that?"

"Well, with my eyes out of commission, my nose has turned super sensitive, and anything with a fragrance to it bothers me. Smelling flowers when you can see them is fine, but it's kind of annoying when you can't, and all you get is the smell. Everybody brings me flowers, but it's really not such a good idea for a sightless patient. It's like being bombarded with a whole bunch of strong perfumes at once."

Once he explained it, I had to admit it made sense.

"Let me tell you, when you spend day in and day out confined to a bed without being able to see, you start noticing all sorts of things you never noticed before. People who go blind must live in a special world. At any rate, one of the things I've learned is just how sharp an instrument my ears are.

"You remember that big earthquake we had the other day? Well, when it hit, the whole hospital went crazy. I could hear people crying and screaming in every direction. But this entire opthalmology wing stayed completely quiet. For one thing, there wasn't a thing we could do unless someone came to rescue us, so we all just resigned ourselves to whatever might happen—except we did prick up our ears. I suddenly realized that if the building came crashing down on top of me, I would die without having seen a single blessed thing since my operation. I actually thought about ripping off these bandages so I could have one last look at the world, but I decided I'd better not."

"Come to think of it, you got your start as a writer for radio, didn't you?"

"Forget that. That experience hasn't helped at all. I mean, I nearly went nuts that first week. I kept telling myself I wasn't going crazy, but then being all alone in here with no one else around, I started feeling like this big heavy slab of a ceiling I couldn't even see was pressing down on top of me. When they brought me in here, at first it felt roomy enough. But then the walls and ceiling started to close in on me. Pretty soon I could've sworn the ceiling was right at the tip of my nose. Like lying awake in a closed coffin."

"So how big does the room feel to you now?"

"I don't know, maybe something like a four and a half mat tatami room."

The room was actually closer to eight mats in size.

That summer, a short while after he got out of the hospital, Hakama and I went golfing at Lake Yamanaka, where we both have cabins. We sat down for a drink afterwards.

"So, did your vision get any better?" I asked.

"I think it's exactly the same."

"Which means the operation was a success."

"I guess."

"You seem pretty blasé about it. By now does it feel like it happened to someone else?"

"Not really. I still dream about it."

"What's it like to dream about going blind?"

"Not about going blind. About when the bandages finally came off."

Nearly a month after the operation, the doctor told Hakama the bandages could come off the next day.

"And I'll be able to see normally, right?"

"You should be fine. Unless you've been up to no good behind our backs," he said, as if to hedge his bets.

Hakama found this less than reassuring. "But Doctor," he said, "I swear I haven't done anything. I stayed right here in bed all along, just like you told me."

"Then you should have nothing to worry about," he said. "But this is one of those things nobody can know for sure until the bandages actually come off."

That night, Hakama couldn't sleep. His mind spun with imaginings of what might happen when the bandages were removed the next day. The more he thought about it, the more he was convinced that his chances were no better than fifty-fifty—an odd-or-even roll of the dice. What if the results were no good? Just thinking about it made him thirsty, and he kept sipping water from the spout feeder next to his pillow. Finally, despite weeks of experience, he inadvertently knocked the bottle onto the floor, where it shattered—which seemed an ill omen, and got him even more wound up.

He soon realized that even if he'd kept his wits about him this far, he could still go out of his mind that very night if he wasn't careful. He felt the hands of his bedside clock to see what time it was, and reasoning that it was now only a matter of hours until the next morning's rounds, he decided he'd test his eyes on the sly right then and there.

"I was praying pretty damn hard, let me tell you."

He knew a sudden burst of bright light could be dangerous, so he groped for the bedside lamp and turned it off. Then he pulled the sheet up over his head and slowly removed the gauze pads from his eyes. Raising his eyelids, he cautiously peered out from under the sheet to see light from the window reflecting on the ceiling. He let out a shout of joy, but couldn't remember what he actually said.

After sticking the bandages back in place, Hakama was so exhausted he fell asleep without even offering a prayer of thanks. Then he slept straight through until the nurse woke him in the morning. It was the soundest night of sleep he'd had since coming to the hospital.

A short while later, the doctor came and removed the bandages.

"Okay, now, try opening your eyes," he said.

As instructed, Hakama opened his eyes fully all at once. He saw the doctor looking straight back at him from close at hand. He could see much more clearly than during his sneak peek in the middle of the night.

"So what's the verdict? All bright and clear, right?" the doctor said.

He said it with such complete assurance that Hakama couldn't resist quipping, "Yes, but everything's upside down."

"Then you can go home tomorrow," said the doctor without even cracking a smile.

"You asked if it felt like it happened to someone else by now. Not by a long shot. I still feel like I've come back from a hundred safaris in the jungles of Africa."

Hakama had a way of turning everything into a punch line, but I didn't laugh. He wasn't smiling, either.

THE HOUSE ON THE HILLSIDE

Just once, I broke into a strange house.

Near the end of the war, many of the houses in my neighborhood stood empty after the naval officers living in them received their orders and had their families evacuated to the countryside. The yards of these deserted homes made inviting playgrounds for my buddies and me. At first, letting ourselves into them without permission brought twinges of guilt, but we soon got used to never being challenged.

In time, our curiosity turned toward the houses themselves. Now and again we took time off from our games to peer through cracks in the storm shutters or curtains. It wouldn't have been difficult to open the shutters and force our way inside, but we hesitated to go that far.

Even to a child's eyes, it had become apparent that the war was going badly for Japan. The very fabric of society was being ripped apart, and the effects began to spill over onto us kids as well. For example, when the all clear sounded after an air raid warning, we were supposed to return to school, but one time when we knew we'd only get sent right back home after roll call—an obvious waste of everybody's time—I decided, as leader of the local boys' association, that we should skip school and regroup in the yard of a nearby villa to play sumo. How easily I persuaded the others to join me reflected a cocky confidence that the grown-ups were no longer in any position to punish us.

Around this time, the son of a local landlord who owned a lot of properties in the area told me and two other friends about a vacant house perched on the hillside at the head of our valley. He didn't say whether it belonged to his family, but he knew that it had been empty for quite a while and that the occupants wouldn't be back any time soon.

I don't recall whose idea it was, but before long we made up our minds to break in.

"The place is haunted, you know," one of the guys said, but obviously he was only trying to add a little thrill to our adventure. It was a neatly painted two-story wooden structure, nicely appointed for its day, and in no way did it look like a lair for ghosts.

The house stood on a precipitous slope with a bamboo grove rising behind it. Concrete stairs zigzagged up from below, at the top of which we entered the front yard—a minuscule patch of level ground owing to its hillside location. From there we were in full view of the houses on the other side of the street below, which told even first-time housebreakers like us that we'd better go around to the back. There, we found the door secured with large nails in place of a padlock. We pried out the nails and walked right in.

The downstairs had four rooms with a few pieces of furniture untidily left behind. One cupboard held an assortment of kitchen utensils; a closet revealed a disorderly stack of cushions. With the storm doors along the veranda drawn shut, the rooms were dark, but enough light came in through the small transom windows for us to see our way around. Once inside, the place had none of the spookiness we'd anticipated, nor anything to satisfy the curiosity that had brought us there.

Finally, the last set of doors I opened revealed a heap of thick magazines, heavily fingered and dog-eared. Picking one up and flipping through it, a pen-and-ink drawing caught my eye. It was an illustration to a short story. At a time when we were starved for reading matter, these were definitely of interest.

"You think I'll get in trouble if I take some of these?" I asked no one in particular.

"Just say you borrowed them," the landlord's son said smugly.

I knew I was crossing a line and could be considered a thief, but my curiosity won out. Egged on by my friend's remark, I picked out two magazines and followed the others upstairs.

The second floor had two rooms, with a short hallway between them. The curtains were drawn but the windows had no shutters, so it was much brighter than downstairs. In the room on the right, the sliding doors to the closet had been removed and set against the wall, showing us instantly that there was nothing there.

We turned next to the smaller room on the left, the last room in the house. By this time our curiosity was fading; we strode right into the middle of the room and looked around. Once again, nothing. The only thing left to check was the closet at the far end, which the landlord's son pulled open. Empty, just as expected.

Or so we thought at first glance. But then, all at once, everybody saw. There in the shadowy depths of that meter-square closet, large enough to hide two or three small children among the clothes that had probably been hanging there, a pair of human eyes stared back at us. As if they'd been waiting there just for us, the eyes—and I really do mean only eyes—hovered in midair at roughly our own height.

The same questions flashed through all our minds simultaneously: What could they be? How could two human eyes float all by themselves in an empty clothes closet?

For several moments the four of us stood frozen in a trance, uncomprehending, gazing dumbly back at the eyes. It was clear we were indeed looking at human eyes, not some ornament or child's toy.

"What the hell is it?" one of the guys muttered, reaching out for the floating eyes. With an annoyed blink, the eyes withdrew deeper into the darkness and suddenly began to glow brighter. Then almost as quickly, the now-glaring eyes thrust forward again, exactly the same distance they had pulled back.

We nearly jumped out of our skins, screaming and tumbling over each other to get down the stairs and out the door. Without once looking back, we raced right on down the street, stopping only when we reached the safety of our own homes.

For some time after that, we kept our little adventure to ourselves. Finally, after a month or so, we told our closest friends about what we'd seen. Naturally, no

239

one took us seriously. I told my mother as well, but she didn't believe me either. For once in my life, I truly regretted having told my parents so many obvious fibs over the years.

I don't know how much later it was, but one day the landlord's son told me the house on the hillside had been torn down.

"Then what do you suppose happened to those eyes, or whatever the hell those glowing balls were?" I said, lowering my voice.

"They probably just moved to the bamboo grove behind the house," he said, also in hushed tones.

That seemed about as satisfying a guess as any. But did this mean that if we went to the bamboo grove above the house, we'd find those eyes still glowing, still hovering in midair, somewhere in the deepest recesses of the thicket?

Long after I reached adulthood and moved away, I revisited my childhood haunts and walked up to the head of the valley where that house had stood. Not only was the house gone, but the bamboo grove behind it had been cut down as well, and the entire area had been bulldozed to make room for a row of new houses. Steps led up to them from the street below, just like before, but I wasn't curious enough to want to repeat the climb.

Over the years I've sometimes wondered who those eyes could have belonged to, or if they weren't in fact eyes, then what else they could have been. But wonder as I might, the answer continues to elude me.

ON A GLACIER LAKE

The scooter and truck expedition across South America that I headed up the year I turned twenty-six was, for the most part, a glorious progress. Night after night, we were welcomed with open arms in every town we visited, and the assortment of nylon scarves we'd brought with us from Japan were our ticket to hours of after-dark amusement in the company of lovely *señoritas*. But there was one time we faced genuine peril.

Our route took us from Santiago in Chile south to Patagonia, where we turned eastward over the Andes and crossed the pampas to Buenos Aires. En route, we sometimes covered as much as five hundred kilometers a day on unpaved roads. A scooter rider keeled over with heat exhaustion from time to time, but only once did danger strike our entire party. We were crossing a lake called Lago Frío on the border between Chile and Argentina in the Patagonian Andes.

Everybody we met in Chile had been *muy simpático* and *muy curioso*, but they'd warned us that we would find things quite different in Argentina: the people there would not be so friendly, the roads would be much worse, and the climate would not be as pleasant either. *Cuidado*, we'd need to be very careful. As if to bear these warnings out, our crisis came the very instant we crossed the border into Argentina.

True to its name, the waters of Lago Frío come from a nearby glacier, making it icy cold even in midsummer. No roads go around the lake, so we had no choice but to cross by a small ferry that operated only during the summer months.

Checking ahead, we knew the ferry could carry a maximum weight of fifteen tons, just enough to haul all of our vehicles and gear across in a single trip. To be safe, we'd arranged to charter the entire ferry for that particular crossing.

The docking facilities were in good order, and we loaded the vehicles without a hitch. This was a welcome change from the previous lake we'd crossed, where drought had lowered the water level so far that the ferry deck came in well below the pier, and a makeshift ramp had to be improvised with boards. Everybody watched with bated breath as our multi-ton truck inched across the sagging ramp.

By the time you reach Patagonia the Andes no longer rise so high, and with the many lakes nestled among the peaks, the landscape begins to look more like Japan. I was also feeling a little more relaxed now that we'd completed our trek through one country and were entering a new stage of our journey. While we were still loading, a local policeman and his young son rushed up saying they had urgent business on the other side, so we agreed to let them come with us.

Taking the opportunity to brush up my Spanish, I was talking to the two of them on deck, when suddenly someone in the cabin below started shouting in a high-pitched voice. I ignored it and went on talking, but almost right away the policeman got to his feet with a panic-stricken look on his face. He yelled back and forth to someone below, then turned to me and gestured that the boat was sinking.

I had to be misunderstanding something. I asked our interpreter from Santiago—a Japanese-Chilean we all called Yotchan—to find out what was going on. He soon returned after talking with the captain, who'd been the one shouting below, and explained that the ferry's hull had dried out during the off season, opening seams between the boards. Now with the boat so much lower in the water due to the heavy load, water was seeping in through the cracks and flooding the area below.

I hurried downstairs to find the passenger cabin already knee-deep in water.

The frightened captain knew I was the leader of the group. "It's all your fault!" he cried as soon as he saw me. "You overloaded the boat! We'll be going down any minute now, so you might as well jump and swim for your lives!"

242

The policeman picked up a similar refrain. "How could you do this to us?" he clamored. "My son and I, we don't know how to swim!"

I was dismayed to learn the ferry had no lifeboats, but I also knew if I let myself fall apart like the others, the situation would spin completely out of control.

"Is the engine still safe?" I asked, putting on my most unruffled face.

The water had not reached the engine room yet, but it was obviously only a matter of time unless we did something to stem the flooding. We didn't have a second to lose. The boat was in the very middle of the lake, and although our hotel for the night was now in sight, it remained quite some distance away.

I considered our options. Should we head for the nearest shore and beach the boat? Or should we tie up to a rock somewhere while we figured out what to do? But having been carved out of the mountains by a glacier, the lake had no beaches so far as I could see. And even if we were to find a suitable rock to tie up to, glacial lakes typically drop off so sharply from the shoreline that our waterlogged boat would quickly break its moorings and disappear into the depths.

I could just picture the scene: a ferry boat laden with four scooters and a truck slowly sinking beneath the surface of a sublimely beautiful Patagonian lake. (Stupidly, I remember wondering if we'd have to hike across the pampas on foot.)

Even in the few brief moments these images were chasing each other through my mind, I could see the water level inching up slowly inside the cabin. Our situation was obviously dire, yet for some reason I felt remarkably calm. Somehow I couldn't believe the ship would go down.

"Maybe we should push the truck overboard to lighten the load," said one of the students frantically.

"That'd leave some of us without any wheels," said another. "It's the scooters we should dump."

To put a quick end to this argument, I turned to the policeman shaking in terror beside me. I didn't know whether the sound would carry, but I told him to go up on deck and fire his pistol as a distress signal.

"I've never fired this thing in my life," the big man protested, his voice breaking.

"Then give it to me," snapped our stouthearted Yotchan.

He grabbed the gun from the policeman and dashed up on deck. Seconds later, the crack of the gun reverberated through the air as the rest of us hastily gathered up whatever towels and rags we could find and stuffed them between the boards of the wall separating the cabin from the engine room in a desperate attempt to keep the motor from swamping. Then we smashed the cabin windows, and everybody—the policeman and his son, captain and crew included—lined up in two bucket brigades and started bailing water with our motorcycle helmets.

"Keep your cool. Bail as steady as you can," I called out. "This much water isn't going to sink us. So long as we keep pace and don't let the cabin fill any higher, the water will swell the wood and the leaks will stop."

We continued bailing. I told the helmsman to keep the boat moving as slowly as possible toward our destination. The water could not really seep in all that fast through the cracks between the hull planks, and we'd started our bucket brigade in time. The water level in the cabin soon stopped rising.

Exactly as I predicted, the parched boards swelled as they soaked up water, and after a while the leaks stopped altogether. Once we were sure the flooding was over, I told the helmsman to step up our speed, but suddenly a shout rose from the lake behind the boat. Our scooter team leader Narumiya was swimming frantically to catch up with us.

"What the hell are you doing in the water?" I yelled.

"I was going to swim to the hotel for help, but even from here I could tell things were going to be all right."

"Likely story, you son of a bitch!" said his fellow team member Kobayashi. "You were just goofing off while the rest of us slaved to save the ship!"

Then Narumiya got out of the water, and everyone could see how blue his lips were. No one repeated the accusation after that.

"I'd bet 100,000 pesos you couldn't make it even halfway to the hotel in that water," I said.

"You're right about it being cold," Narumiya agreed. "So long as I stayed on the surface, I could sort of stand it. But try to tread water, and my legs went numb."

"Look," I said. "We can't afford to lose you any more than we can afford to lose the truck. So from now on, don't do anything I haven't told you to do. Understand?"

"Yes, sir," he nodded obediently, still shaking all over.

That evening we raised our glasses to celebrate our first night in Argentina.

"I have to say, you were amazingly cool through the whole thing," said Kobayashi.

"That bucket brigade was a real stroke of genius," the team doctor chimed in. "I guess that's the war generation for you. You saved us with that."

I, too, was feeling quite pleased with myself and the way I'd taken charge of the situation, but I didn't really think of what I'd done as saving lives until a young man named Niimura, who came from Buenos Aires to meet up with us, said he'd overheard the policeman carrying on about the episode in the hotel kitchen and saying, "My son and I owe our lives to those Japanese fellows."

As it happened, this slightly harebrained youth also touched off a bit of a stir when he notified Buenos Aires of our arrival, and carelessly used the word "disaster" to describe our close call on Lago Frío. The error was then relayed to Japan, where it was reported that we'd gone to the bottom of an Argentine lake.

When we eventually learned of this mix-up after reaching Buenos Aires, it struck me as a rather fitting conclusion to the events on the lake. At any rate, we all found it immensely funny by then, and had ourselves a good laugh about it.

We encountered still further difficulties crossing the vast seas of pampas grass toward Buenos Aires. One of our scooters gave out, and the truck that somehow managed to cough and wheeze its way across the plains broke down just as we pulled up to our hotel in the Argentine capital and refused to go one step further. Meanwhile, Narumiya continued to nurse his own personal memento of Patagonia: the cold he caught from taking a dip in that icy lake.

RAINBOW

When my brother Yujiro spoke of an overwhelming sense of fatigue that made him feel "worse than death," I thought I understood what he meant. The fact was, though, I really didn't have a clue.

Looking on from his bedside, I could tell he was in intense discomfort. But since the living can never truly know what dying involves, being told something felt worse than death didn't tell me very much. Rather, from the perspective of those trying desperately to snatch him back from death's door, anything had to be better than death.

From what I knew of my brother, I thought we should tell him the true nature of his illness, but the others wouldn't hear of it. So at least when they were in the room, out of respect for their feelings, I had to be a team player and join in with the usual platitudes of encouragement. But in some ways you could probably say I was playing my own separate game under a different set of rules.

No matter when I went to visit, I invariably found Yujiro dozing fitfully, drifting in and out of consciousness. It seemed he was sleeping constantly, yet never getting any real rest, an aggravation I could well understand. His nights and days had become reversed, and the doctors continually urged him to try to get back on a normal schedule, but he couldn't seem to do it. He had come to dread the approach of each night, which I could appreciate as well. Meanwhile, talking with members of his production staff who took turns keeping vigil around the clock at his bedside, I learned that what sleep he got was painfully irregular, so whenever he did drift off they let him sleep as long as he could, no matter what the hour. Which is to say, his illness was calling the shots.

Probably only the patient himself can know the toll a grave illness can take. But Yujiro's close colleagues seemed to intuit what he was going through, and looked after his needs as if he were their own flesh and blood.

"What time is it?" Yujiro would ask in a low voice, drifting back into consciousness. "Evening already? The dreaded night approaches. I never thought I'd get to be this age and shrink in terror of approaching darkness, all because I can't sleep. What a miserable drag."

"I think that's mostly in your mind. You were sound asleep when I came in last night, so I decided to just go on home without bothering you," I lied.

As I made my way home after saying good night, I tried to imagine what the fatigue he'd described as "worse than death" might be like. Yujiro had always been tough—capable of enduring anything. Yet he spat out those words like a bitter curse. I doubted I myself could have held up under such extraordinary torment.

One time, when he seemed to be in better spirits than usual, I asked him point blank what the worse-than-death sensation was like.

He flashed a faint smile. "I'm not exaggerating, you know. It really is torture. Even though I'm lying here flat on my back, it's like I can't keep afloat, I just keep sinking and sinking, and no matter how hard I try, I can't stop it. It's pure agony. I think I'd rather have someone chop off my arm than have to go through this all the time.

"It's as if something inside me is quietly chewing, chewing, chewing me up. Pretty soon it'll have devoured my whole body, and spit out nothing but garbage."

"Now you're really letting your imagination run away with you," I said, though he'd described what the hateful cancer was doing more accurately than the doctors themselves had.

Anticipating the possibility that Yujiro might experience excruciating pain, I'd asked his doctors to administer whatever constant dosage of narcotics was necessary to ease his suffering, even if it also meant hastening his death. But what awaited my brother instead was this feeling of utter enervation that he'd gladly have exchanged for pain. Had it been pain, I, too, could have pretended to know what he was up against, but I had no idea how to help him fight an enemy that struck as an unbearable fatigue.

When my brother was awake, I tried to engage him in conversation as much as I could. The members of his staff keeping vigil were always glad to have someone else there for him to talk to. They'd coax him awake from his fitful dozing whenever I came in. The less he slept during the day, they said, the more likely he was to sleep at night—which was of course what the doctors had said, too. But I knew that dozing endlessly was the only means his illness left him with for fending off that torturous sense of fatigue or his terror of the night. So when I was there, I often asked his staff to leave us alone, then urged Yujiro to go back to sleep.

"Go ahead and sleep some more if you want. I'll be right here."

Sometimes he'd drift off, but then he'd soon be awake again, and we would go back to our usual exchange of useless patter that hardly even amounted to a conversation. When he reemerged after a mere five or ten minutes into the weariness that bore down on him so unforgivingly, it was almost as if he'd been shaken awake by the cruel hand of some unseen figure; he would come to with a start and a shudder. I so wished he could simply be left undisturbed instead to sleep forever.

Yet when he was awake, we soon ran out of things to talk about—or rather, there really weren't that many things we *could* talk about under the circumstances. Our conversations usually turned to such "safe" topics as the ocean and sailing. And even on these themes, I doubt it was with any real enthusiasm that he engaged in the conversation. My impression was that he forced himself to talk about these things in the hope that their power of suggestion might somehow help induce a return to better health.

According to the members of his staff, the only times he responded with relative vigor, often looking ready to sit right up, were when they talked of work or I talked of sailing. If the conversation turned to anything else, he drifted back to sleep.

Of course, my yacht talk differed considerably from their shop talk. He had always been the man in charge at work, whereas the sailing stories I told involved no responsibilities for him and centered on my own racing exploits. I couldn't help wondering what made him respond so eagerly to these anecdotes, nodding his head over and over with attentive interest.

It brought to mind how, all those years before, in our poorer childhood days, we would lie in bed talking in minute detail about a movie one or the other of us had seen. This was in the days before television, and sharing stories this way was how we both got to enjoy the film for the price of one.

Now I was recounting details of a yacht race I'd taken part in over the previous two days, but unlike in those earlier times when my brother and I took turns exchanging movie stories, his turn to race in my place would never come again. I knew this beyond any doubt, and I suspect he knew it as well.

One thing led to another, and the conversation turned to our wonderful mutual friend and one-time racing crew member, Toshio Tanaka, who had risen to become president of the Hawaiian Regent Hotel. While on a recent visit to Japan, he'd developed some disturbing symptoms and immediately went under the knife, but all for naught. After returning to Hawaii, he learned the truth from his own doctor there: he had inoperable cancer. It was a severe blow, of course, but he was determined to live out the rest of his life to the full. My brother remembered a visit Tanaka had paid to his vacation home, when he somberly shared with him his thoughts on life.

"I feel so sorry for him," he said. "At his age, and just when he's reaching the top of his game, he gets blindsided by cancer. I guess I have to consider myself lucky. At least I don't have to deal with the dreaded C."

I realized I was gaping at him and hastily looked away.

As with Yujiro, the intensity of Tanaka's suffering was truly painful to behold, but he ultimately outlived my brother, prolonging the distress of all those loved ones who had to witness his torment.

At our private services for Yujiro, Tanaka's wife came up to me and said, "Maybe my husband will finally be able to let go, now that Yujiro will be there to greet him."

Tanaka died exactly one week after my brother.

I can't help wondering what was going through Yujiro's mind when he made that remark about cancer. He was an astute person; he had to have doubts about his illness. But the question remains: just how much did he know, or at least sense, about its true nature?

Everybody who came into contact with Yujiro had made a pact to give him no hint of the truth, ever. I had argued otherwise: it was more like my brother to want to know, and then be able to say he'd fought the good fight. But he was a married man with a family of his own, and also the head of a sizable business enterprise. Even if he was my one and only brother, he belonged to others more than he belonged to me.

Yujiro had come through many trials before: a very nasty broken leg; miliary tuberculosis as a result of trying to power his way through a bout of pneumonia; cancer of the tongue; and major surgery to repair a dissecting aortic aneurysm, from which only seven percent of patients recover. His survival after the last of these was declared a miracle. But then—what more could his creator want of him?—during a follow-up examination, the doctors discovered primary cancer of the liver.

I wanted his doctors to tell him the truth, but the others—people who, when I stopped to consider, had spent a great deal more time with him than I had—insisted he was in a much more delicate state than I realized.

I could offer no response. I knew if I were the one being handed the terrible news, I might well choose a quick death. I was hardly in a position to assert that my brother could endure such a devastating death sentence—or that he should have to.

And so his close associates searched for information they could use to deceive him—particularly Masahiko Kobayashi, the man Yujiro trusted as his right-hand man. Gathering information even the doctors didn't have, he brought out an arsenal of technical terms fit to shame a specialist, explaining each time the question came up why my brother's affliction could not possibly be cancer. At least at first, Yujiro seemed fully persuaded by Kobayashi's reassurances.

When he went into his final decline, the doctor summoned me for an update on his status, and told me to remain at his bedside as much as possible. I swiftly distilled what the doctor said down to its hard essentials. "In other words, you're saying it's time to accept the inevitable."

The doctor seemed momentarily at a loss for words, but then collected himself to respond with a grave nod.

"There's nothing more you can do?" I said. "Nothing that will do any good?"

"No," the doctor quickly objected, "we will continue to do everything we can to ease his suffering."

That was all I could ask.

"What Kobayashi's been telling me is all a bunch of crap. None of it makes any sense," Yujiro said one day between labored breaths as he endured his harrowing fatigue.

I gazed back at him in silence, trying to gauge what kind of response he hoped to provoke by saying this. I still wonder today what I would have done at that moment if he'd added, in so many words, "Look, I know you know what's really wrong with me, so give it to me straight."

Was that actually what I wanted him to do? Or was it what I dearly hoped to avoid? It could have been a rare chance for the two of us to connect as we hadn't done in a very long while, yet I know I feared it.

In any case, Yujiro said no more. I held his gaze, feeling exposed and vulnerable. We studied each other for several more moments—exactly how long, I can't say, but long enough to begin to feel awkward.

His eyes looked anxious. Was he afraid I might take it on myself as his only brother to reveal that his condition was incurable?

"Look," I finally said, breaking the silence. "When something is this intractable, you can't expect a layman like Kobayashi to get it right. For one thing, he wants to believe the best, so he's always looking for the silver lining when he talks with the doctors, and the doctors try to oblige his hopes. The fact is, a self-infected liver that's started to fail isn't suddenly going to turn around and get better overnight. Not so long ago it would have killed you, simple as that. You survived the operation for the aneurysm, but that sapped most of your strength and compromised your immune system. So no wonder this infection gained such a good foothold. You've got to be patient."

I was faithfully repeating the story we'd all agreed upon. Yujiro nodded slowly as he listened. After a while, he drifted off, but as I was getting ready to leave I saw his eyes crack open. Thinking maybe he wanted me to stay, I paused on the edge of my seat. He nodded ever so slightly to let me know I could go, then looked away.

"Tell me what you will, Bro," he said as his eyes fell shut again, "I say it's gotta be cancer."

I had no idea what kind of answer he hoped to get from me. I simply pretended I didn't want to hamper his sleep, and quietly slipped out of the room.

Yujiro had recently moved to a newly built house, and he longed to pay a brief visit home, but the doctors rejected the idea for fear of what might happen away from the hospital. As if to bear out their concern, his condition continued to decline day by day.

Soon even I could tell he was too weak to care any more about making a trip home. Unable to fight off that unbearable weariness, he simply lay there stoically drawing labored breaths. I watched him breathe, wondering exactly how much time he had left—or rather, how much time *we* had left to share with *him*.

Time could no longer have had any normal significance for him. He was not delirious; rather, his agonizing weariness had reduced him to a witless silence. Still, every so often, he'd ask the person sitting with him to lift him, and as he spent a few brief moments sitting part way up in bed, he'd ask, "What time is it?" What could checking the time have meant to him by then? Was the passage of time for him measured in eternities, or in instants?

We kept the shades drawn because bright light bothered him. Outside, the rainy season was lifting, and summer was just around the corner. Each time the rain let up and sunshine poured through breaks in the clouds, young people flocked to the swimming pool directly across the way. I mentioned this to Yujiro once when he awoke, but the season that had always meant so much to the two of us now belonged to a world beyond his reach.

The poet Jun Takami wrote of riding the train to the hospital on the morning he was to undergo surgery for cancer of the esophagus, describing how he watched out the window as healthy young laborers headed off to work, seeing in them his own former youth. Although it was my brother, not I, who faced death, I could identify with Takami's sentiments as I stood there looking at Yujiro. Even as the hospital room filled with imminent death, the swimming pool practically within arm's reach outside the window overflowed with young people in the prime of their lives—kids who neither contemplated nor believed in death.

Curiously, this invoked no sense of bitterness or injustice. I simply watched the crowds frolicking in the pool, and sighed to myself, "But my brother is going to die."

Three times the doctors announced my brother was breathing his last, but each time he rallied, and each time new tubes joined those already hooked up to his body.

Then one morning, the doctors agreed beyond any doubt that he wouldn't last out the day. I stayed with him about two hours that morning, then left to attend a meeting that required my presence. I informed my colleagues before the proceedings began that I might have to excuse myself at any moment.

Apart from insects or fish, I'd never witnessed the moment of any animal's death, let alone that of a human being. Even in my hunting days, I'd never warmed to the task of delivering the coup de grace to a downed animal, and managed to avoid it. Not that I was afraid of looking the creature in the eye as it crossed the border between life and death; it simply seemed like an act of hubris.

This time, however, I wanted to be present at the moment of my brother's passing. I felt it vital that I be there, not only for my own sake, but for his. I suppose partly it was just that I'd reached a certain age. But more importantly, this was going to bring to a close the precious ties that bound us during our time together in this world, and I wanted to witness that last moment with my own eyes. I wanted to be there to take in whatever wisdom my brother might have to offer at my first experience of the instant of death.

Around two in the afternoon, Yujiro's breathing grew more labored. Only by straining and convulsing his entire enfeebled body could he seem to find the strength for each breath. Several new medical devices had been wheeled in around my brother's bed that day; now the doctors called for one more, and prepared to stick yet another tube into his body.

"Just let him go, Doctor!" Kobayashi cried. "Just let him die in peace!"

While the prizefighter was taking a merciless drubbing, his second had urged him with cruel resolve to fight on, but now the boxer's standby was finally throwing in the towel.

Everybody in the room, even the doctors, seemed to breathe a sigh of relief at Kobayashi's outburst. The doctor with the tube stepped back, and Yujiro's wife fell on his chest.

"It's me, Yu! Can you hear me, Yu?" she cried, shaking him by the shoulders.

To my amazement, I saw my brother distinctly nod to his beloved wife, even as he was straining desperately to draw his next breath. The champion was still fighting, even after his team had given up.

The movements accompanying his breaths began to grow smaller now. We could tell he was near the end of his strength. The doctors no longer watched his face; they watched the instruments to which he was connected. These inanimate machines would make the final pronouncement.

As his convulsive gasping diminished, he appeared to be in greater distress than ever. I was witnessing for the first time what I'd long heard called the "throes of death."

A person is capable of hoping for absolutely anything according to the time and circumstance. At that moment, as much for me as for my brother, my only wish was that death should come swiftly. Clearly, that was his only salvation.

"It's okay," I said to him. "It's okay to let go. It's really okay."

For some time after that, the doctors kept their eyes glued to the instruments rather than watch Yujiro himself. Finally, the senior physician looked in our direction and nodded gravely, then just to be sure held his stethoscope to my brother's chest before declaring, "He's gone."

But as the doctors' eyes were moving away from the instruments, I glanced toward them for a final look. At the very instant my eyes fell on the heart monitor, Yujiro's heart suddenly pulsed back to life and set the needle in motion again.

"His heart's beating, Doctor," I said. Only a short time before I'd been hoping for exactly the opposite.

The physicians looked at one another in surprise. Twice more during the next hour, Yujiro's heart stopped beating and resumed, then stopped beating and resumed. The doctors looked on in blank amazement as their instruments told them that their patient had died and come back to life, then died and come back to life again.

I decided I needed to be the one who announced the moment of my brother's death to the doctors. Keeping one eye on the heart monitor, I nudged my sister-in-law aside and leaned forward over Yujiro until our faces almost touched.

For all the vastness of the sea, when you've spent much of your life coursing its surface or exploring its depths, you can sometimes read the precise instant when the tide ends its rise and begins to recede. In the same way, I recognized the precise instant when my brother's life expired.

It was like a flame that wavers and flickers until suddenly one moment it's gone, sucked into the darkness. As the gasping, wheezing struggle that seemed to last forever came to an end, the tension on his face began to ease; then at one distinct moment, an utterly changed, unbelievably tranquil look spread across his face. Finally, suddenly, at long, long last, he had reached a perfect repose.

I let out a sigh of relief. *Ah, you're finally free*, I said in my heart.

I looked up at the doctor and nodded. He glanced at the instruments one last time and said, "Yes, he's gone."

As the others in the room crowded close to say their final farewells, I moved to the window and opened the venetian blinds. Outside, the sun was shining brighter than ever. As if to herald the coming season, a strong gust of wind blew through the trees, stirring the lush branches. The rain-moistened leaves glistened in the sun.

Immediately I knew: Yujiro had left not at night but at the height of a bright, sunny day just to catch that gust of wind. And as if to bear this out, when I emerged from the hospital a short while later, a glorious rainbow arched high in the sky overhead.

（英文版）わが人生の時の時
Undercurrents

2005年12月20日　第1刷発行

著　者　石原慎太郎
訳　者　ウェイン・ラマーズ
発行者　富田　充
発行所　講談社インターナショナル株式会社
　　　　〒112-8652　東京都文京区音羽1-17-14
　　　　電話　03-3944-6493（編集部）
　　　　　　　03-3944-6492（マーケティング部・業務部）
　　　　ホームページ　www.kodansha-intl.com

印刷・製本所　大日本印刷株式会社

落丁本・乱丁本は購入書店名を明記のうえ、小社業務部宛にお送りください。送料小社負担にてお取替えします。なお、この本についてのお問い合わせは、編集部宛にお願いいたします。本書の無断複写（コピー）、転載は著作権法の例外を除き、禁じられています。

定価はカバーに表示してあります。

Printed in Japan
ISBN 4-7700-3007-X